OXI: An Act of Resistance

OXI: An Act of Resistance

The Screenplay and Commentary

Ken McMullen and Martin McQuillan

ROWMAN &
LITTLEFIELD
───────INTERNATIONAL
Lanham • New York

Published by Rowman & Littlefield International Ltd.
Unit A, Whitacre Mews, 26-34 Stannary Street, London SE11 4AB
www.rowmaninternational.com

Rowman & Littlefield International Ltd. is an affiliate of Rowman & Littlefield
4501 Forbes Boulevard, Suite 200, Lanham, Maryland 20706, USA
With additional offices in Boulder, New York, Toronto (Canada), and Plymouth (UK)
www.rowman.com

Copyright © 2015 by Ken McMullen and Martin McQuillan

All rights reserved. No part of this book may be reproduced in any form or by any electronic or mechanical means, including information storage and retrieval systems, without written permission from the publisher, except by a reviewer who may quote passages in a review.

British Library Cataloguing in Publication Data
A catalogue record for this book is available from the British Library

ISBN: HB 978-1-78348-268-9
PB 978-1-78348-269-6

Library of Congress Cataloging-in-Publication Data

McMullen, Ken, 1948-
  Oxi : an act of resistance: the screenplay and commentary / Ken McMullen and Martin McQuillan.
      pages cm
  Includes bibliographical references and index.
  ISBN 978-1-78348-268-9 (Cloth : alk. paper) — ISBN 978-1-78348-269-6 (pbk.) — ISBN 978-1-78348-270-2 (electronic) 1. Oxi, an act of resistance (Motion picture) 2. Global Financial Crisis, 2008-2009—Greece. 3. Financial crises—Greece—History—21st century. 4. Greece—Economic conditions—21st century. 5. Greece—Politics and government—21st century. I. McQuillan, Martin. II. Oxi, an act of resistance (Motion picture) III. Title.
  PN1997.2.O97 2015
  791.43'72—dc23
                                                                              2015017281

∞™ The paper used in this publication meets the minimum requirements of American National Standard for Information Sciences—Permanence of Paper for Printed Library Materials, ANSI/NISO Z39.48-1992.

Printed in the United States of America

It will be enough if my words are judged useful by those who desire insight into the past. Into events which—human nature being what it is—will inevitably be repeated in the future.

Thucydides 460–400 BC

Contents

List of Illustrations	ix
Acknowledgements	xi
Preface	xiii
The State of the Debt, Martin McQuillan	1
OXI: An Act of Resistance: Screenplay, Ken McMullen	23
Credits	87
Memories, Dreams, Ghosts and Friends: Free Associations on the Making of a Feature Film, Ken McMullen	93
Spartan Helotry, Martin McQuillan	133
Post-Structuralist Politics, Martin McQuillan	141
False Economy, Martin McQuillan	145
The Godfather, Martin McQuillan	163
Interviews	187
I Étienne Balibar: 'Thinking things through differently: in fact the right way 'round'	189

II *Hélène Cixous*: 'To out Ajax Ajax'   201
III *Antonio Negri*: 'An example of a very bad example'   211
IV *Manolis Glezos*: 'I don't need Tiresias. I just need
    my comrades'   217
V   *Theodoros Terzopoulos*: 'Today God does not exist. In God's
    place we see the bank'   225
VI *Kostas Vaxevanis*: 'Europe is neither the dream of
    Mrs Merkel, nor the dream of the Bundesbank'   233

Whatever Still Remains, *Richard Wilson*   241

Filmography   257

Index   261

Notes on Contributors   265

List of Illustrations

1   Athens Demonstration
2   Gabriella Wright as The Sphinx
3   Eleni Kallia as Jocasta
4   Dominique Pinon as Investigator
5   Della Saba as Ismene
6   Lex Shrapnel as Oedipus
7   John Shrapnel as Creon
8   Julia Faure as Antigone
9   Dominique Pinon, investigator in Athens
10 Don Mousseau as Tiresias
11 Ithaca (Themisstoklis Michalacos and Eleni Kallia)
12 Oedipus and Tiresias
13 Ismene
14 The Sphinx
15 Étienne Balibar, philosopher
16 Hélène Cixous, writer
17 Antonio Negri, social scientist
18 Manolis Glezos, resistant
19 Theodoros Terzopoulos, theatre director
20 Kostas Vaxevanis, journalist

Acknowledgements

'Spartan Helotry' first appeared in *Times Higher Education* 3 January 2013 and 'Post-Structuralist Politics' first appeared in *Times Higher Education* 26 March 2015. A version of 'False Economy' first appeared in the edition of *Postmodern Culture* listed as 23(3) May 2013, although it was published in 2014. Martin McQuillan is grateful to the editors of these journals for permission to republish here.

We would like to thank our friends and colleagues at The London Graduate School and Kingston University for their support in the production of the film *OXI* and this book. We are grateful to the actors, crew and post-production of *OXI* for their contribution to this philosophical adventure. We would like to acknowledge and thank the Greek Film Archive for their support in the production and distribution of *OXI*. We would also like to thank the staff of Rowman & Littlefield International for their attention to detail in the production of this book, especially Oliver Gadsby, Martina O'Sullivan, Sinéad Murphy, Meaghan White and our editor Sarah Campbell.

Preface

OXI: An Act of Resistance is an international cinematic response to the current economic crisis imposed on Greece. The film seamlessly weaves a web of fiction and documentary. It is a vital international feature film for today, which draws on the great classical dramas of Sophocles (Antigone/Oedipus Rex), Aristophanes (The Frogs), and the poetry of C. P. Cavafy. It underpins these with the contemporary philosophical and political insights of Étienne Balibar, Hélène Cixous and Antonio Negri. The film holds a mirror to the ever-present abuse of state power by those who act out their roles on the political stage.

The film is a direct response to the current crisis being imposed on European countries under the name 'austerity'. It also addresses many of the misperceptions of Greek culture and history that are promoted as part of a program of destructive propaganda against the country and its people. Though the film is deadly serious in intent, it contains flashes of comedy, offered by Dominique Pinon in the role of a mysterious 'Investigator' as he confronts a modern day 'Sphinx' (Gabriella Wright), whom he accuses of stealing and profiting from the rewriting of Greek classics. On his quest to find the truth in present-day Athens, we are introduced to leading contemporary figures in Greek culture: Manolis Glezos (politician/Resistance fighter, World War II), Antigone Lyberaki (politician/economist), Theodoros Terzopoulos (theatre director) and Kostas Vaxevanis (journalist). But, is the Investigator's search just another myth being created by the Sphinx as she manipulates the characters in Sophocles plays?

By looking to the past, *OXI: An Act of Resistance* builds on a transhistorical theme investigating the nature of power and the fragility of the human condition, not just relevant to Greece today, but in all places that are vulnerable to blind unthinking economic forces.

The situation in Greece is fast moving; as this book goes to print, in the week of correcting proofs, Greece has defaulted on a payment to the IMF, held a referendum rejecting the demands of its creditors, then signed up to an even more stringent austerity package that has been condemned as unworkable by the IMF. The texts and interviews in this book do not make a pretense to full-spectrum coverage of the Greek crisis; rather, each one is specific in time to the moment it was written or recorded, responding in turn, step-by-step, as these events unfold. They are a record of an artistic and philosophical endeavour, not a textbook on economics. They document an intellectual journey and process of inquiry that speaks to a specific historical moment in the life of the people of Greece. Their truth is the truth that we find in film, literature and philosophy, for this crisis is a crisis of and for European culture. The questions that determine it are cultural and political as much as fiscal and economic. *OXI* and the films of Ken McMullen have their place in a European cinema of ideas, an artistic practice that unites film and philosophy as an idiom of cultural research. This present project utilizes the resources of that European tradition as leverage for an understanding of this most European of crises, finding tools in our cultural heritage to explain our economic present.

This book combines the screenplay of the feature film *OXI: An Act of Resistance* with critical commentary by the director Ken McMullen and the executive producer Martin McQuillan. It also includes full transcripts of interviews with the philosophers, politicians, economists and journalists who contributed to the film. It concludes with an appreciation of the film by the critic Richard Wilson.

Martin McQuillan and Ken McMullen
Athens-London-Lisbon
July 2015

The State of the Debt

Martin McQuillan

When we first set out to make a film about the crisis in Greece, the idea of a radical government in the form of the Syriza election victory of 2015 was still a distant prospect. It was not until the film had been completed and screened at the Moscow International Film Festival and the London Film Festival that the administration of Alexis Tsipras was formed. The worldwide phenomenon of the Syriza government and its subsequent encounter with the so-called Troika of Greece's creditors (the European Central Bank, the International Monetary Fund and the European Commission) has now given the film and this book a certain currency, but it was never part of our original motivation. Rather, the film is about the debts that global culture owes Greece and what we might learn about the nature of money from Greece yesterday and today. Philosophy (φιλοσοφία), economy (οἰκονόμος) and cinema (κίνημα) are all part of that same Hellenic inheritance.

The situation in Greece is at once unique to that country and of the greatest significance to what we now call the 'global economy'. On the one hand, the Greek crisis is a symptom of a wider global conjunction that began with the subprime mortgage crisis in the United States (which has its origins in the Clinton years) and runs to the threat to the continuation of the Euro currency zone today. On the other hand, it is a singular concentration of all of the questions that arise from that conjunction, demonstrating in a precise way the failings and challenges of our present world system of capital. It is also, as every economic crisis is, a story of intense personal difficulty for individuals and families. As Émile Durkheim observed in his seminal sociological work, rates of suicide always grow during times of economic downturn. The only growth that Greece has seen in the last few years is that of rates of self-harm, mental health issues and mortality among the population. The Greek economic crisis is also a humanitarian crisis and not just because of the cuts to health services in Greece as a result of the regime of austerity. Austerity has human consequences and this is what makes it the proper subject of film and literature alongside economics. Perhaps, film and literature is better placed than economics to highlight the effects of austerity. Economists are, in the words of the Medea of Euripides, 'novices in grief'. It takes an artist to capture the wounds of a society, and as W. H. Auden put it, 'about suffering they were never wrong, the old masters'.

*

In 2000, Greece was accepted as the twelfth member of the European monetary union. The country was due to host the Olympic Games in four years time and had committed to sizeable infrastructure projects as a consequence. For much of the previous decade, Greece had recorded significant deficits often running above 10 per cent of GDP. In the years leading up to entry into the Euro, the deficits reported to the European Union (EU) were surprisingly much lower. With a reported deficit of less than 3 per cent of GDP, it was thought that the Greek economy had met the convergence criteria for entry into the eurozone. We now know that these figures had little to do with the performance of the Greek economy and much to do with potentially fraudulent reporting. In 2002 the European Union refused to validate the annual audit of Greece's accounts, insisting that a reported surplus be written down as a deficit. In 2004, the European Commission again declined to accept the audited figures presented by the Greek government. A newly elected conservative administration agreed to investigate the previous returns, only to conclude that the misunderstanding was the result of changes to accountancy conventions within the EU rather than an attempt to mislead the Commission. The question of Greece's entry into the Euro may have been contentious, but it now pales in comparison to some of the practices that followed, including a currency swap arranged by Goldman Sachs that allowed the Greek government to disguise 2.8 billion euros of debt in 2001 in the year after entry into monetary union. Irregularities were also found in the reported deficits of other eurozone members such as Italy and Portugal, while Germany and France at the time simply defied the rules of structural deficits with seeming impunity.

The consequence for Greece of the 2002 and 2004 audits was to have its credit rating downgraded, making it more expensive to service loans with other countries and to sell its own debt on the international bond market. While the conservative New Democracy government and the opposition social democratic PASOK argued over whose audit techniques were the most fraudulent, further trouble was being stored up within the Greek economy. Within weeks of the closing ceremony of the 2004 Olympics, the Greek government flagged to the European Commission that the deficit was now running at 6.1 per cent of GDP (twice the contested eurozone entry rate) and that national debt sat at 110.6 per cent of GDP. The Olympics had cost 9 billion euros to host, the most expensive games ever at the time, while national debt sat at 168 billion euros. The Olympics in themselves had not caused this growing mountain of debt but were perhaps symbolic of wider problems within the Greek economy. Greece became the first country to be placed under fiscal monitoring by the European Union in 2005. Despite this scrutiny, huge fiscal imbalances developed in the years up to the 2009 crisis. Between 2000 and 2007, Greece was one of the fastest growing economies in the eurozone, with an annual growth rate of 4.2 per cent. This growth was based on a flood of foreign capital and easy credit (now that there was no currency exchange barrier with other eurozone members). However, as growth stalled in an uncompetitive economy, public expenditure continued to increase, by 87 per cent over the period, with the tax take only increasing by 31 per cent. Levels of public spending had not seemed such a worry when accompanied by significant economic growth. Large military budgets for the southern flank of NATO were matched by a commitment to a social model that supported public-sector jobs and pensions. However, the European Commission agency Eurostat continued to query the audited returns of the Greek government, resulting in the National Statistics Service of

Greece becoming independent of government in 2010 in an attempt to restore investor confidence and international credibility. To fund the difference between public expenditure commitments and the tax take exacerbated by evasion and corruption, the centre-right government that ruled between 2004 and 2009 borrowed heavily. By 2011 European banks were exposed to 45.8 billion euros of debt in Greece, despite the warning signs in the preceding years that neither the Greek government nor the Greek economy would be good for it.

When the global economic crisis hit in 2009, Greece was in an extremely vulnerable position with high levels of government borrowing and personal debt, and a sharp decline in demand for Greece's two main industries: tourism and shipping. The new PASOK government of George Papandreou, elected in October 2009, admitted that previous reported statistics had been flawed, revising the 2009 deficit from 6 per cent to 12.7 per cent of GDP; Eurostat subsequently revised this upwards to 15.7 per cent. National debt was also recalculated to 130 per cent of GDP, sitting at 299.7 billion euros in 2009. It was no longer credible to put such discrepancies down to contested accountancy conventions in reporting official figures. Until March 2010, the Greek government was still able to sell bonds but with ever-increasing yield requirements that only served to worsen the public deficit. In April 2010, international rating agencies downgraded the Greek economy to junk status, causing an immediate freeze in the private capital market: 70 per cent of Greek bonds were then held by international banks. With no one willing to buy Greek debt anymore, only international bailout loans could prevent a sovereign default on maturing bonds. The European Union and International Monetary Fund accordingly came up with a 110 billion euro bailout in 2010. The bailout has been used to pay off bond yields (i.e., covering the potential loses of the banks that held Greek debt) and to a lesser extent cover the spread in the structural deficit, while the loan came with stringent conditions on deficit and debt reduction, notably in relation to levels of public spending. By September 2011, Greek ten-year bonds were trading at an effective yield rate of 23.6 per cent, making it highly questionable as to whether Greece would ever be able to pay off its debts.

The bailout of May 2010 came with the conditions of massive cuts to Greek public spending and increased taxes. Strikes and social unrest followed, including the deaths of three people in protests in Athens. Rather than allow Greece a planned return to the private capital market, the regime of austerity only compounded the problem, with an EU-IMF audit of national accounts in June 2011 calling for further cuts in public spending and Standard & Poor's revising down the Greek credit rating to CCC, the lowest in the world. A series of austerity measures made their painful way through a divided Greek Parliament, as each new tranche of the bailout package was due to fall between May 2010 and June 2011. Strikes and extreme hardship were now commonplace across Greece. In 2010 and 2011, fiscal cutbacks amounted to 17 per cent of Greek GDP, wages fell back to 1990 levels, 20 per cent of shops in Athens closed, unemployment rose by 500,000, around 20,000 people were made homeless, and the suicide rate rose by 40 per cent. In July 2011, the European Union announced an additional 109 billion euro bailout for Greece, Ireland, and Portugal and an agreement with banks to write off 50 per cent of Greek debt by 2020. By now, Greece was in profound recession, recording −7.1 per cent growth in 2011, and a national unity government had been formed, led by Lucas Papademos. The economy tanked, with youth unemployment recorded at 55 per cent in July 2012. Rapid fiscal consolidation in the Greek economy was causing an unmanageable social crisis, and an exit from the eurozone began to look not only desirable but also a distinct possibility.

In October 2011, in order to avoid a disorderly exit from the Euro with all the risks that this posed to the banking system and the possibility of contagion across other eurozone economies, the EU, IMF and European Central Bank offered an orderly default of loans and a further 130 billion euro bailout. This would make it possible for Greece to remain a member of the Euro, but contingent upon a further austerity package. In February 2012, with the country in flames, the Greek Parliament passed the additional austerity measures with a 199–74 majority. Those PASOK and New Democracy deputies who voted against the package were immediately expelled from their parties. However, the second bailout essentially involved a debt restructure for Greece's creditors with a scheduled debt swap for Greek bond holders, exchanging maturing Greek bonds with high-yield rates for more secure European-backed bonds with lower rates. This would reduce the debt repayment rates of the Greek government but would add nothing to public services for those suffering under the regime of austerity. The second bailout was intended to return Greece to the private-capital markets after the scheduled general election in 2015. It required 11.9 billion euros of spending cuts in 2013–2014 and required Greece to run a current account surplus rising to 3.7 per cent of GDP by 2016. It would be immediately cancelled in the event of these conditions not being met, or of an uncontrolled exit from the Euro.

An election in June 2012 saw Antonis Samaras lead a cabinet of New Democracy and independent deputies; PASOK and the Democratic Left (DIMAR) offered support to the government on a case-by-case basis to enable a functioning parliament as the vote was further fragmented by the emergence of Syriza and other new dichotomous parties, including the neo-Nazi Golden Dawn. DIMAR withdrew from that arrangement in protest at the closure of the state-owned Hellenic Broadcasting Corporation, leaving the coalition with only a slim majority. With austerity measures increasingly difficult to pass through parliament as a result, the Troika changed some of the terms of the latest bailout from cash imbursement to debt swaps. In 2014, Greece made a modest return to the bond markets, while doubt remained as to the country's ability to fulfill the forecasts required by the bailout or compliance with the austerity measures. However, Samaras was confident enough to negotiate with the Troika over an early exit from the programme, swapping the final tranches of the bailout for unused recapitalization funds, held in reserve in the Hellenic Financial Stability Fund, for 2015–2016. In December 2014, Samaras's government fell over the failure to have its candidate for the presidency approved by parliament. The resulting election in January 2015 brought victory to Syriza, which had campaigned on a rejection of austerity measures and a stated desire to renegotiate terms with the Troika. The party had grown in the years of crisis as an alternative to the neoliberal consensus of PASOK and New Democracy, as the Greek social crisis highlighted the complicity and compromise of the ruling political class.

For example, in 2010 Christine Lagarde, Head of the IMF, had passed to the Papandreou government a list of some two thousand names, recovered from HSBC Bank's Geneva branch, of wealthy Greek depositors who may have been evading taxes. A cursory investigation by the Greek tax authorities resulted in no action, and the list went missing. The PASOK finance minister George Papaconstantinou, in charge of austerity measures at the time, was later accused of editing the list to remove names of his relatives and was ultimately dismissed from the party. His successor and, later, leader of PASOK, Evangelos Venizelos, was also drawn into the affair for failing to act on the list while finance minister. Tax evasion in Greece is estimated at 27 billion euros a year, the single biggest drain on the public deficit. However, the political significance of the scandal was that the 'neoliberal', 'pro-Western' reformers who were imposing austerity on public servants and pensioners were seen to be up to their elbows in tax avoidance and corruption. Lagarde had, after all, given the list to Papaconstantinou as a favour to an ally; when he was removed from office in 2011, he received a text from Lagarde that read, 'We miss you!'

In October 2012, a former defence ministry official, Yiannis Sbokos, was arrested in a bribery and money-laundering investigation. The next day, the former deputy interior minister Leonidas Tzanis hung himself in the basement of his own home. Five days later, businessman Vlassis Kambouroglou, a defence contract supplier to the Greek military, was found dead in a Jakarta hotel room. There was speculation as to whether both Tzanis and Kambouroglou appeared on Lagarde's list. However, as this latest scandal was unfolding on 28 October 2012, the journalist Kostas Vaxevanis (who contributes to *OXI*) claimed to have a copy of Lagarde's document and published a list of 2,056 names in his news magazine *HOT DOC*, including New Democracy MPs and officials in the finance ministry. Although others had also published versions of the list, Vaxevanis was immediately arrested for breach of privacy laws and faced up to two years in prison. In a rushed trial three days later, he was acquitted of all charges. Vaxevanis complains in *OXI* that independent journalism in Greece is dead because no newspaper is prepared to print a criticism of the banks during the crisis while those same banks provide the advertising revenue that keeps the media afloat. This is a claim that chimes with Peter Oborne's recent resignation as chief political correspondent at *The Daily Telegraph* in the United Kingdom following that newspaper's refusal to print any story critical of HSBC for fear of losing its advertising account. It was in this atmosphere of accusations of corruption and complicity within the political elite that a radical alternative to the neoliberal consensus gained traction in Greece. Given the scale of Greece's economic problems (a social crisis that became a humanitarian crisis) and the extent of the 'irregularities' in the public accounts, the only thing that is surprising about the election of a decisively left-wing, anti-austerity government is that it took so long.

The construction of the eurozone and its enlargement to include countries such as Greece was fundamentally a political decision and not a fiscal one. In the name of an idea of European integration, expansion of the eurozone was encouraged despite clear warning signals about the state of the economies that were being incorporated into monetary union. This remains the case today with new entrants to the European Union being required to join the currency union simultaneously, despite the obvious difficulties that this presents for both the EU and the new member. The Euro locks weaker national economies into a relationship of permanent competitive disadvantage against the strongest economy in the eurozone, namely Germany. Unable to devalue a currency to reestablish competitiveness or set their own national economic priorities, eurozone members are to a large extent the victims of German intransigence over its own surplus.

Imbalances within the eurozone have as much to do with Germany profiting from its neighbours as it does with Mediterranean countries' failure to control costs. The eurozone is a currency union without political union, in which fiscal sovereignty resides in the rules of the European Commission, but political responsibility sits with national governments that no longer possess any of the tools to correct their economic ills. As the strongest economy in the eurozone, Germany is under no pressure to correct its behavior but rather has a vested interest in maintaining the status quo. In the past, this has taken the form of German banks finding a home for surplus capital through excessive lending to its Latin partners; now it takes the form of protecting the euro by insisting on deficit reductions in the heavily indebted economies of its fellow Europeans. Quite what is in it for any country other than Germany to be part of the eurozone remains open to question. The only conclusions that one can come to is that values and ideals beyond the merely fiscal are what bind the countries of European monetary union and that the Euro is a political project through and through.

This in itself is not necessarily a bad thing. The currency unions of the United Kingdom or the United States are also political and ideological events. However, the tensions in the eurozone arise in the diremption between the political imperative of European union as a democratic idea and the insistence that the Euro is a purely fiscal entity that relies upon rules and criteria that are independent of national democracies. The challenge of the Syriza government to the European Commission is that of a sovereign democratic mandate against the rules of continued eurozone membership. To refuse the request of Syriza for debt flexibility is to refuse the sovereignty of Greek democracy. By insisting that Syriza comply with the terms and conditions entered into by past Greek governments, the Troika is saying that only the nation-state as a credit entity within a currency union matters rather than the nation-state as the expression of a democratic consensus. In other words, there is no sovereignty in a sovereign debt crisis, or at least this sovereign debt crisis demonstrates the extent to which the very idea of sovereignty is always indebted to powerful external mediations that ruin any capacity to act in a sovereign manner. Equally, the German government has had to move reluctantly towards the acceptance of supporting a Eurobond scheme and the purchase of distressed assets in order to prevent a disorderly exit from the Euro by Mediterranean countries. Even the sovereignty of the most sovereign nation (the first among equals) is compromised in a currency union without political merger.

Syriza had promised in opposition to face down the Troika and restore dignity to Greece by refusing the terms of austerity imposed upon it by its creditors. In the early weeks of the new government, a fresh finance minister, Yanis Varoufakis, set out to speak to his fellow European treasury ministers and with the European Commission. With 1.5 billion dollars worth of bond yields due to be paid to the IMF in March 2015, there was a real prospect that Greece would default on those payments or that capital controls would have to be introduced in Greek banks in order to pay the bill (literally the ATMs would be switched off and depositors would be unable to access their money). The alternative would have been a rapid exit from the Euro. With at least political capital in the bank, the new government challenged Greece's creditors over the terms of the previous bailouts and requested a bridging loan rather than the next tranche of the restructure package, while Syriza worked on a new plan to kick-start an economy that had shrunk by 25 per cent in the last five years. Varoufakis's tour of European finance ministries was met with derision, intransigence and suspicion. In part, it was said that a new Greek government could not renegotiate commitments previously entered into by past governments. This position provided a public front for the private fear that should Greece be successful in altering its international debt obligations, then other countries such as Spain, Ireland, Portugal and Italy would also want some form of debt relief. This risk of contagion across Europe posed a threat to the integrity of the Euro rules and so the hegemony of the German economy in Europe. On the other hand, European finance ministers simply did not understand Varoufakis's position; it was as if he was speaking Greek to them, as the Anglo-Saxon idiom runs. They could not understand why any Greek government could not accept a package that would see 50 per cent of Greek debt written off by 2020 and an exit from fiscal controls by 2016. The plight of the Greek population was not the concern of European ministers; their priority was the security of the Euro and the implications for the wider European economy.

It was widely reported that Varoufakis failed in his efforts to persuade Greece's creditors and was forced to accept the ongoing terms of the bailout. On 20 February, a four-month extension of the bailout was agreed to, on the condition that the Greek government provide a list of measures they would take to control public spending. The European creditors said they wanted to rebuild 'trust' with the new left-wing government. Syriza gained the notable victory, however, of at least having the Greek debt crisis discussed openly, shifting the terms of debate, while gaining time to negotiate further and to provide a convincing Plan B. On 20 March, the European Commission president, Jean-Claude Juncker, announced 2 billion euros worth of development funds to address the humanitarian crisis in Greece. It was a gesture that finally recognized the extent of the social problems created by austerity in Greece. However, it was small beer compared to the 6 billion euros worth of debt repayments due to fall in the weeks that followed Juncker's announcement.

As I write this text towards the end of March 2015, a Greek exit from the Euro remains a real possibility. An exit would enable the government to devalue the currency and go some way to restoring competitiveness to the Greek economy. However, it comes with the risks of economic side effects, such as serious inflation and a possible challenge to Greece's status as a member of the European Union. Syriza have always adopted the position that they wish to remain within the Euro; it is only the severe terms of the bailout they wish to reconsider. However, they have the option in the coming months to prepare for an exit from monetary union. It will take time to reintroduce the drachma. One possibility is the introduction of a crypto-currency, an electronic drachma that runs in parallel to the Euro. The government could declare that all taxes must be paid in the e-drachma and so force the purchase of the new currency in order to meet legal obligations. This could be part of a transition towards dropping the Euro as Greeks sold Euros to buy the drachma. The reintroduction of the drachma would also open up the possibility of loan default. Restoring sovereignty to the Greek central bank that controlled its own currency would make it unnecessary to continue to seek the approval of the Troika to access loans in Euros. This would come with the considerable risk that Greece would then be locked out of the private finance market, being deemed to be a sovereign bankruptcy unable to borrow in the future—a situation even more difficult than having the world's worst credit rating. Syriza would have to be sure that the ability to print their own currency also ensured the capacity to provide sufficient resources for the country. Do Syriza really want to make Greece the Cuba of Europe? The risk for the European Union of this scenario is both the losses to European banks and the possibility that longer-term pressure on the Greek economy would push the country into the sphere of influence of Russia and China.

Syriza have to manage a fine balancing act. They will be judged at home on their promises to reduce unemployment and to rehire public service workers. They are wary of making Greece an international pariah. For the moment, Syriza has adopted the pragmatic approach of taking both a pro-NATO and pro-Euro stance, making reassuring noises on their commitments to be good European citizens. However, if they are to deliver to the Greek electorate, they will have to find room within their spending priorities for the sort of social programmes that they promised while in opposition. This will require them to ease the pressure of international debt repayments in the short to medium term. One possible solution is the tapering of the debt obligations over a longer period of time: The worst effects of austerity always come from the speed at which fiscal consolidation is imposed on a country.

There may yet be recognition on the part of the Troika that there is no realistic prospect of Greece ever being able to meet its debt repayments on time, and nothing is gained from presenting them with an impossible task. However, if a renegotiation of payments is not forthcoming, then there will come a point when Syriza will have to make the choice between honouring the debt or dropping out of the Euro. The stakes are extremely high. One scenario would see the Syriza government fail to make progress and a future election result in Greece turning to another anti-austerity option in the form of the extreme right. This might also be a possibility following a botched exit from the Euro that saw runaway inflation and a country unable to trade with the outside world. Syriza would by inclination want to adopt a Keynesian model of investment in public projects and state spending in order to return growth to the Greek economy. This will remain impossible as long as Greece is part of the eurozone and locked into the terms of the bailout. In the absence of a national bank able to facilitate demand-side economics in Greece, the only route for such investment would be European Union development funds. This may yet prove a face-saving alternative for both sides. The choice to be made for Syriza is between fidelity to a progressive social agenda and retaining Greece's place within a community of nations tied together by a commitment to a neoliberal global economy. The skill with which they negotiate this aporia will determine not only the longevity of their government but also the significance of their election for the rest of the world. Syriza have not been elected on a ticket of 'third-way' social democracy; rather, they offer an explicit challenge to the economic status quo. How far they will be pulled in the direction of compromise will be the test of whether a genuine alternative to the neoliberal hegemony is possible.

When Varoufakis was met with incomprehension by European finance ministers, it was because they simply did not get it. Ironically, although the project of European monetary union is every bit political, they could not imagine that the politics of Syriza represented anything other than a regressive 'ideological' threat to the capitalist system. However, if Syriza do not wish, for the moment, to exit from either the

Euro or Greece's international obligations, then what they bring to the free-trade party is a concern with equality. The significance of Syriza is that a democratically elected western government is arguing that the effects of the financial crisis of 2008 should be borne not by the citizens of nation-states but by the banking system and the international institutions that caused it. Regimes of austerity necessarily punish the weakest and poorest members of society by removing public services at the expense of fiscal consolidation. The bottom line for Syriza is that money from Greek taxpayers is flowing to relieve distressed banks rather than into health care and social security. The banks win again, and the poor are with us always. Syriza may discover that it is not possible to continue both to be part of a system of global capital and to oppose that system. It is not possible to participate in the global economy without being contaminated by the values and requirements of that system. An alternative horizon that escapes the ambit of the historic values of global capital may require a break entirely with the forms that embody it. Whether Greece is ready to make that choice, or even should make that choice, is open to question. One possible response would be that at this stage they have nothing to lose in doing so.

However, Syriza and the state of Greece are only one example of what is a wider global phenomenon since 2008. The Greek bailouts do not represent an act of political solidarity with European neighbours. Rather, they have been the systematic transfer of losses from the books of private banks to the citizens of Europe: First, to the Greek population faced with public spending cuts; secondly, to the taxpayers of Germany and the other countries of the European Union who have underwritten these loans and debt swaps. Ninety per cent of the combined 240 billion Euro bailouts has gone to financial institutions across Europe and the rest of the world. The finance ministers of the European Union and the IMF are more concerned with preserving the international banking system upon which capitalism depends than upon assisting the impoverished population of Greece. Massive quantitative easing programmes run by the Federal Reserve, the Bank of England, and the European Central Bank have socialized the failures of banks, leaving western taxpayers on the hook for trillions of dollars, pounds and euros of debt while banks and those who run them have been truly 'bailed out'. From the Greek social crisis to the trebling of university tuition fees in England, from the cap on welfare claims to the recapitalization of banks, the years since the economic collapse of 2008 have seen a remarkable transfer of public assets to private individuals. The response of western governments to economic crisis has not been to invest in the capacity of the state to protect its citizens but has been the enclosure of public wealth for private gain by an elite few in more or less brazen ways. The failure to imagine an alternative to regimes of austerity and the preservation of the rights of bankers is a defining characteristic of the poverty of thought that determines mainstream economics and the rebarbative, seeming political consensus. What has happened is the exact opposite of what a time of economic crisis calls for and which we see in the historic examples of Roosevelt's New Deal, the Marshall Plan, or Britain's post-1945 welfare state. There is not anything surprising or extreme in Syriza's political platform when considered from a historical point of view. What is perhaps most shocking about Syriza is that their distributive politics of social justice are considered extreme by the western political mainstream.

The consequence of the cynical enclosure of the commonwealth and the socialization of private debt will not be long-term growth and development among the western democracies. Rather, it will only serve to create unsustainable levels of inequality in these countries, storing up trouble for the next economic crisis. Western states will not be able to provide the infrastructure to serve their people, whose consent they require to rule. Greece may never be able to pay back its debt, and western interest rates may never be able to return to normative levels for fear of initiating recession through an inability to service sovereign debt. Heavily indebted western governments have few resources to survive another economic crisis so soon after 2008. Triggers for that next crisis may be an overvalued U.S. stock exchange, fuelled by cash from quantitative easing (QE) and awaiting a period of correction, or record levels of household debt: both are the result of the bailout of the banks rather than the public. The continued printing of money to ease distressed private assets at artificially low interests is stymieing real economic growth across the western democracies. They can either limp on in zombie mode on a diet of QE and negative interest rates or accept that bankruptcy, crash and reorganization is inevitable. Alternatively, they can stop living in an eternal present of short-term policy making and recognize that a taper will only be possible over a substantial period of time, in which long-term inflation would erode much of the debt, and begin to plan another world that provides services and infrastructure to their citizens rather than insisting on making a return to the status quo of the private money markets at the earliest opportunity. In this sense, the case of Greece is not the endgame of harsh neoliberal austerity; it is rather the canary in the coal mine for a much bigger crash to come, one that may take down the wider eurozone and the United States. The trauma of the Greek humanitarian crisis may be not that we have experienced shock and that we will recover from it over time, but rather this is trauma without end, that what this experience tells us is that there is worse to come in the future. We may yet look back on the Greek crisis and think of it fondly as the good old days when it was possible for the international community to bail out nation-states or that the alternative to regimes of austerity were well-meaning left-wing governments attempting to balance social justice at home with international obligations.

The alternative to Antigone is Medea, not the one who defies the Law to care for her brother, but the one who takes revenge on the wrongs done to her by destroying everything that is dear to her. The tragic element of Sophocles's play does not lie with Antigone; she is a rebel who makes her choice and receives a rebel's fate. Syriza may yet go down in a blaze of glory like the rebel angels that 'dropt from the Zenith like a falling star / On Lemnos th' Aegean'. The tragedy of the *Antigone* properly belongs to Creon who embodies the Law and who has no choice other than upholding its categorical imperative at the expense of his family and his humanity. It is Creon's choice that he has no choice. There is no alternative. To concede to Antigone would be to ruin the authority of the Law, but it is precisely this failure to flex the universality of the Law that ruins the authority of Creon, who embodies it. The risk for the Troika is that it is turning a crisis into a tragedy by refusing the reasonable requests of Syriza in order to preserve the authority of the regime they represent. After Antigone has exited the stage, the ruin of Creon is still inevitable as a result of conditions of his own making. The Troika's tragedy may yet be, not that of the Creon of Thebes in Sophocles, but the other Creon of Corinth in Euripides's play. So keen is he to establish a dynasty by settling privilege on Jason and his daughter, that he never sees Medea coming. There are fates worse than Antigone's and there are undoubtedly more miles to travel in this global economic crisis. How difficult that road becomes will be to a large part determined by the capacity of western governments to accommodate the demands of democracy over those of capital. *Antigone* tells us that the refusal of justice in the name of the Law leads to the ruin of the sovereign. However, perhaps, it may yet be possible to escape the inevitability of the tragic paradigm. Liberal democracy is nothing if not pragmatic and does not ordinarily set out to realize its own destruction, even if it is quite capable of undermining itself. An accommodation of Syriza's request on the reorganization of the debts of Greece may still provide the opportunity for another heading for Europe. It is a question of taking the time to listen to the seemingly incomprehensible, to open up the structures of international institutions to democratic possibility. If European monetary union does not work in the interests of the people of Greece—the cradle of European civilization—then it does not work for anyone. As the great Greek poet C. P. Cavafy writes in conclusion to 'In a Large Greek Colony, 200 BC':

> Let's not be too hasty: haste is a dangerous thing.
> Untimely measures bring repentance.
> Certainly, and unhappily, many things in the Colony are absurd.
> But is there anything human without some fault?
> And after all, you see, we do go forward.

Athens Demonstration

Gabriella Wright as The Sphinx

Eleni Kallia as Jocasta

Dominique Pinon as Investigator

Della Saba as Ismene

Lex Shrapnel as Oedipus

John Shrapnel as Creon

Julia Faure as Antigone

Dominique Pinon, investigator in Athens

Don Mousseau as Tiresias

Ithaca (Themisstoklis Michalacos and Eleni Kallia)

Oedipus and Tiresias

Ismene

The Sphinx

OXI: AN ACT OF RESISTANCE

Screenplay

Ken McMullen

OXI Screenplay

Cast

In Order of Appearance

JOCASTA	ELENI KALLIA (GR)
INVESTIGATOR	DOMINIQUE PINON (FR)
MAN WITH HAT	BRET ROBERTS (US)
THE SPHINX	GABRIELLA WRIGHT (FR)
OEDIPUS	LEX SHRAPNEL (UK)
TIRESIAS	DON MOUSSEAU (USA)
CREON	JOHN SHRAPNEL (UK)
ANTIGONE	JULIA FAURE (FR)
ISMENE	DELLA SABA (UK)
GREEK CHORUS	THE TRAVELLING PLAYERS

Interviews

In Order of Appearance

MANOLIS GLEZOS	WWII Resistance Hero and Politician
HÉLÈNE CIXOUS	Writer and Philosopher

ANTONIO NEGRI — Political Philosopher and Activist
THEODOROS TERZOPOULOS — Theatre Director
GIORGOS VICHAS — Doctor and Medical Volunteer
ANTIGONE LYBERAKI — Economist and Politician
KOSTAS VAXEVANIS — Political Commentator and Journalist
VALERIE KONTAKOS — Documentarist and Citizen of Athens
CHRISTOS KARAKEPELIS — Film Director and Citizen of Athens
MARTIN McQUILLAN — Cultural Theorist
YANNIS SAKARIDIS — Citizen of Athens
ÉTIENNE BALIBAR — Philosopher
ARTHUR I. MILLER — Physicist
PETROS SEVASTIKOGLOU — Film Director and Citizen of Athens
NIKOS CORNELIOS — Film Director and Citizen of Athens
MARTHA FRANGIADAKI — Medical Volunteer

Opening

Long Ago and Far Away
Time-lapse shot across an ancient seascape with distant islands—
Sunrise—

CAPTIONS

Superimposed on Lower Screen over Time-Lapse Shot

It will be enough if my words are judged useful

by those who desire insight into the past.

Into events which—human nature being what it is—

will inevitably be repeated in the future.

(Thucydides 460–400 BC)

---

1. EXT—AN ANCIENT GREEK VILLAGE—DAY (ANCIENT GREECE)

The Greek Chorus is represented by a group of 'TRAVELLING PLAYERS'. At other times in the film when individuals give political commentary INTERVIEWEES and CITIZENS OF ATHENS become The Chorus. We hear lines from Antigone by Sophocles.

TRAVELLING PLAYERS (VO)
(*Attempting to sooth a violent issue*)
Creon, listen to your son . . . learn from what he says . . .
Haemon, you learn from your father too . . .
You both have spoken wisely.

CREON
(*With increasing irritation*)
So . . . men of my age . . . are supposed to learn from men of his?

HAEMON
You should look at my merits, not to my years.

CREON
Am I to rule by the judgement of others . . . or . . . by my own?

HAEMON
No city belongs to one man.

CREON
(*With incredulity*)
Don't men in power own their cities?

HAEMON
You would make a good monarch . . . of a desert.

CREON
SHAMELESS! . . . An open feud with your father!

HAEMON
I only attack your abuse of power.

CREON
Is respecting my own interests an abuse?

HAEMON
What are you protecting when you defy the Gods?

CREON
(*Furious at his son's words*)
O! . . . DASTARD NATURE! . . . A woman overpowers you.

Adapted from Antigone: Lines 800 to 825

CUT

2. EXT—SEQUENCE OF ANCIENT GREEK LANDSCAPES

The voice of MANOLIS GLEZOS—WWII Resistance Hero and political philosopher.

MANOLIS GLEZOS (VO)
In my opinion they had predicted it already.
Both the Ancient Greek philosophers and the Ancient Greek poets.
Menandros, 2,300 years ago, has stated it clearly and categorically;
Sophocles has said it in 'Antigone';
Other ancient Greeks have said it:
'Loans turn people into slaves'.

3. EXT—SILENT PORTRAIT OF MANOLIS GLEZOS

CUT

4. EXT—ANCIENT WOODS WITH BREEZE MOVING TREES

The voice of HÉLÈNE CIXOUS—*writer and philosopher.*

HÉLÈNE CIXOUS (VO)
Death isn't death. That's what the Greeks teach us . . .
They say that after death, there is life in death.
Great literature is there in order to give the dead the chance to talk and to return.

5. INT—SILENT PORTRAIT OF HÉLÈNE CIXOUS

CUT

6. EXT—CITYSCAPE OF MODERN ATHENS . . . DISTANT THUNDERSTORM

The voice of ANTONIO NEGRI—*political activist and philosopher.*

ANTONIO NEGRI (VO)
The Greek people have always been a people in crisis.
They have always been oppressed . . .
By the Romans . . . By the Venetians . . . By the Turks . . .
By a bourgeoisie or an old aristocracy . . .
Elites which were extremely egotistical along with an aristocracy that was very self-contained.

7. EXT—SILENT PORTRAIT OF ANTONIO NEGRI

CUT

8. INT—A PARIS APARTMENT (PRESENT DAY)

The set is part of a Louis XVI palace which seems at first desolate and deserted.

INVESTIGATOR *breaks in through a back entrance to find a man lying fully dressed in an ornate bathtub wearing a hat and nonchalantly smoking.*

INVESTIGATOR
Bonjour Monsieur.

MAN WITH HAT
Hello.

INVESTIGATOR
Do you speak French?

MAN WITH HAT
Do you speak English?

INVESTIGATOR
I do. What are you doing in this bathtub? . . . Hmm?

MAN WITH HAT
What are you doing here?

INVESTIGATOR
I'm investigating . . . Someone's been stealing letters and words from Greece and I want to know who . . .

MAN WITH HAT
So you're an INVESTIGATOR?

INVESTIGATOR
That's right . . . I'm an INVESTIGATOR . . . Investigating . . . And you are in my sights . . .

MAN WITH HAT
So . . . you have just broken in here . . . no permission . . . and you are investigating?

INVESTIGATOR
You got it . . . And let's be clear about something . . .
An INVESTIGATOR doesn't need permission . . . OK?

MAN WITH HAT
Do you have some identification . . . And for the record I haven't stolen any Greek words. I don't know any . . .

INVESTIGATOR
If I find just a whisker of proof you are in big trouble . . .

MAN WITH HAT
Uhhh?

INVESTIGATOR
In France, we don't stand for this kind of thing . . .
You got me? . . . We don't allow it here in France.
(Moves close to the bath and ostentatiously sniffs the air)
And you don't smoke in bathtubs in France either . . .

MAN WITH HAT
Do you have some identification?

INVESTIGATOR
An INVESTIGATOR doesn't need identification.

MAN WITH HAT
So . . . You're just walking freely through the house?

INVESTIGATOR *ignores the question and walks away, leaving the room.*

CUT

9. INT—LAVISH ORNATE ROOM IN THE PALACE (PRESENT DAY)

INVESTIGATOR moves to a table covered with notebooks and sketchbooks . . . He picks up some plays by Sophocles and Aristophanes.

INVESTIGATOR
What's all this? . . . What's all this?
Ah!!! Got it . . . Oedipus . . . Of course.

CUT

10. INT—UPPER DOME OF PALACE (PRESENT DAY)

INVESTIGATOR confronts a young woman who he suspects has a neurotic identification with the 'Sphinx'.

INVESTIGATOR
I'd like to see your office if you permit.

SPHINX
(*Ironically*)
Sure . . . I love it when people intrude on my creativity.
Anyway . . . Who the fuck are you?

INVESTIGATOR
I'm an INVESTIGATOR . . .

CUT

11. INT—A GRAND OFFICE INSIDE THE PALACE (PRESENT DAY)

INVESTIGATOR
Well . . . Well . . . Well . . . So where does all THIS come from?

SPHINX

Huh!!! . . . I made this . . . It comes from me using my 'intellectual property'.

INVESTIGATOR

YOUR intellectual property?

SPHINX

Yes . . .

INVESTIGATOR

And where did you nick this intellectual property?

SPHINX

Very simple . . . from life . . .
From things transmitted and rewritten from ancestor to ancestor up to the present day . . .
From History . . . Even before that . . . from pre-history.

INVESTIGATOR

Do you think it's good to steal the intellectual property of Greece?
(2 beats)
Poor Greece . . . In this terrible state . . . Hmm? . . .
I believe you have also been changing the role of the SPHINX?

SPHINX

She was forgotten . . . Erased from history . . . I am bringing her back to life in my new play.

INVESTIGATOR
(With contempt)

Yes . . . Yes . . . Of course you are an actress as well . . . And you have given yourself the role of the SPHINX . . . Of course!

CUT

12. EXT—SEASHORE—DAY (PRESENT DAY)

BCU [Big Close-up] of the SPHINX looking straight out to us with a seductive stare.
On the sound we hear voiceover (VO) of HÉLÈNE CIXOUS.

HÉLÈNE CIXOUS (VO)
The Sphinx is traditionally, in what's been left to us,
a figure of what we don't understand.
Insofar as, when Oedipus answers the Sphinx,
It is only a way, an artifice to enable us to continue along a faltering path,
from one misunderstanding to another.
The spirit of research within us needs to proceed in steps.
But understanding is only one step.
Each step enables us to advance to another stage of incomprehension.

SPHINX speaks out in sync to camera.

SPHINX
The SPHINX is always sad, because she is never heard . . .

CUT

13. EXT—A VILLA—GREECE (PRESENT DAY)

Oedipus is relaxing by a luxurious swimming pool.
Oedipus is nonchalant as he drinks a glass of champagne.

SPHINX (cont. VO)
She is in love with man, but man's unconscious never listens.
So this sadness is a deep sadness . . .
A sadness beyond language.
As she is in love with man . . . Her human part suffers.

CUT

14. EXT—SEASHORE (PRESENT DAY)

BCU of the SPHINX as she speaks out to us.

SPHINX
And that's why the SPHINX, is always sad.

CUT

15. EXT—ATHENS STREET, DEMONSTRATION ARCHIVE

CU of a burning television news broadcast van.
The voice of THEODOROS TERZOPOULOS, a theatre director of Classical Tragedy.

THEODOROS TERZOPOULOS (VO)
Today, God does not exist. In God's place we see The Bank . . .
In the place of the city what do we see? Ruins . . .
Not just architectural . . . Human ruins . . .
What is a city without Man?

CUT

16. CHAPTER HEADING

Act One: Sleepwalking to Eternity

17. EXT—RUINS IN AN ANCIENT LANDSCAPE (ANCIENT GREECE)

OEDIPUS confronts TIRESIAS who is a cross between an American hippy and a biblical blind seer.

OEDIPUS
Tiresias? Tiresias?

TIRESIAS drops out of the scene to speak directly to us.

TIRESIAS
(*Confidentially to camera*)
Tiresias was an airhead who went and sniffed the vapor coming up through the rocks and got really stoned . . .
Then he came down to town and started babbling and people thought that there was some kind of great message there and pretty much made of it what they would . . .
But he made a living out of it so he didn't complain, and he didn't have to work.

OEDIPUS
Speak, from your strange world. Let me hear the truth.

TIRESIAS
It's terrible to see the truth. When the truth brings only pain to he who sees.

OEDIPUS
You're perverse, unhelpful to our city. You're withholding the truth.

TIRESIAS
You have buried the truth, the truth that haunts your psyche.

OEDIPUS
What is this . . . drivel? This garbage. If you know something tell me, I command you.

TIRESIAS
I'd rather not be the conveyor of pain for you.

OEDIPUS
Are you determined to betray us, to destroy Thebes? . . .
You scum . . . You rabid dog . . . I am your King . . .
It is your duty to tell me what you know.

TIRESIAS

You rage unaware that the insults you fling at me will soon be flung at you . . .

OEDIPUS

What gibberish . . . What treachery.

TIRESIAS

(*Firmly as he turns and moves away*)
All men of power remain blind to the deeper currents of events surrounding them.

CUT

18. INT—THE PALACE OF THE SPHINX (PRESENT DAY)

SPHINX *is sleeping but is disturbed by distant radio voices.*

JOCASTA (VO)

Oh generations of men, you are nothing. I count you as not having lived at all . . .

HÉLÈNE CIXOUS (VO)

Greece is our past and our future. It's the cradle of a great part of our thinking, our political orientation.
We forget . . . I think it's extraordinary that Europe forgets that we owe Greece half of our political vocabulary.

DISSOLVE

19. EXT—AEGEAN SEA (DREAM)

Dissolve from sleeping SPHINX to the wake of a ship as it weaves its way through the Aegean islands. Sequence of shots of SPHINX writing notes as she sails past islands. Voice of ÉTIENNE BALIBAR, French philosopher.

ÉTIENNE BALIBAR (VO)
It starts with Thucydides coming through centuries to us . . .
I think that Thucydides is one of the greatest political thinkers in Western tradition . . . A tradition of political thinking in which coexists the conscience of one's own 'tragic dimension'.

Sea journey intercut with reconstructed footage of an ancient Trireme being rowed through the same sea. The voice of ARTHUR I. MILLER, physicist, comes through on the radio as the sea dissolves back to the sleeping SPHINX.

ARTHUR I. MILLER (VO)
(Heard on a crackling radio)
Time lines advance but not necessarily in a causal way . . .
One can have anachronistic events . . . Events that at first may seem irrational but can be linked through meaningful interpretation.
What Greek philosophy does is to give you alternative narrative lines.

DISSOLVE

20. INT—SPHINX'S GRAND OFFICE (PRESENT DAY)

INVESTIGATOR continues to confront the SPHINX.

INVESTIGATOR
I represent an institute of authenticity.
An institute of Letters . . . of Words . . . and of Sense . . .
Because Madam we are here in France . . . We are not in America.
I won't let you get away with this.

SPHINX
(Shrugs contemptuously)
I don't care because nothing can stop me.

INVESTIGATOR
You will be dragged in front of a tribunal.

                             SPHINX
A tribunal composed of . . . ?

                           INVESTIGATOR
Of Philosophers . . . Actors . . . and Writers . . .
And they are not happy.

                             SPHINX
Ha! I detest tribunals.

                           INVESTIGATOR
Madam you truly are the SPHINX.

Close in on INVESTIGATOR staring at the SPHINX.

                                                        CUT

21. EXT—AN ANCIENT AEGEAN SEASHORE (ANCIENT GREECE)—(a piano sequento)

This shot, which is 5 mins in length without a cut, passes through 2,500 years of narrative time from the age of Sophocles through to the present day. Most of this sequence is VO with two inserts of sync dialogue from CREON.

                        INVESTIGATOR (VO)
Many things are monstrous.
But there is nothing more monstrous than Man.
When winter approaches and the south wind blows,
Man rows out across the darkness of the sea in his swift-winged boats.
On through mighty waves crashing to the left and to the right
He keeps the course intended
And those most ancient of the Gods he withers away before him.
He traps with snares gentle dreaming birds
And he mercilessly kills them.
He has learned speech and developed original thought
And with pride he builds his cities.

Enter CREON, dressed in modern attire. He walks along the seashore and takes up Hölderlin's poem extract 'Antigone' in sync, looking to the sky as if speaking to the Gods.

CREON

With just a chisel, He can bring to life to cold marble.
With nothing more than a simple paint brush,
He can give a blank wall breath.

Camera tracks and pans out over the Aegean Sea, taking in distant rocks and islands.
(This is part of the sea route to ancient Troy and the Black Sea Greek settlements.)

JOCASTA (VO)

Oh generations of men, you are nothing.
I count you as not having lived at all.
Was there ever a man, ever a man on this earth, who could say he was happy? Who knew true Happiness?
Not an image, a dream, or an illusion that would disappear.

The shot arrives back to the shore now facing the opposite direction.
Re-enter CREON.

CREON

Never without resources . . . Never an impasse as he goes forward to the future.
Only from death . . . From death alone he will find no rescue.
Though mighty and skilled in all things.
He inevitably comes to grief on the rocks.

A number of evocative shots of ancient seashores with rocks close the sequence.

CUT

22. EXT—AN ANCIENT TOWER BY THE SEA (ANCIENT GREECE)

ANTIGONE and ISMENE confront each other on the central issue of the original play.

ANTIGONE
We Greeks always bury the dead . . . even those of our enemies . . .
Creon's power must be defied . . . Tell me all you know.

ISMENE
I have not heard a word. I know nothing more.
Whether luck will improve or ruin is still to come.

ANTIGONE
I am drawn to that body . . .
Our brother . . . Our own flesh and blood.
I have no choice despite Creon's laws . . .
Tell me Ismene . . . Are you with me or are you a coward?

ISMENE
I am what you are.

ANTIGONE
So will you share the labour? Will you care for the body?

ISMENE
What you're asking for is a Political Act.

ANTIGONE
He was our brother!

ISMENE
Creon is all-powerful here. We must bide our time . . .
Or we too will die the worst death of all and our souls too will be unreleased . . . Don't rush to extremes . . .
We must obey the ones in power, at least for now . . .
Circumstances will change . . . This is inevitable.

ANTIGONE
All right . . . All right . . . I'll do it myself . . . You're a coward.
We have only a short time to honor the living, but an eternity to honor the dead . . . Commitment . . . Commitment is what we need.

ISMENE
(Imploring)
Your own impetuousness will betray our true cause . . .
To restore our father's reputation and to do away with arbitrary dictatorship.

ANTIGONE
(With contempt)
Go back to your shadows, to the darkness where no man can disturb you.

CUT

23. EXT—ATHENS STREETS, TAXI (PRESENT DAY)

We find the INVESTIGATOR sharing a taxi ride in Athens with the French philosopher ÉTIENNE BALIBAR.

INVESTIGATOR
I will be continuing my investigation.
Layer by layer I'll get to the bottom of this.
Étienne . . . How did this situation come about?

ÉTIENNE BALIBAR
The Greek financial crisis exploded in 2010. I immediately had the feeling that this affair concerned us directly, and, that it would have consequences for a long time on the situation in the whole of Europe . . . We have to be more than jointly responsible.

I believe we have to go there, to Athens, to understand what is happening, not only from the point of view of the effects of the crisis and the disastrous and devastating treatment that the European monetary system has inflicted upon them . . . But also, of course, from the point of view of the Greeks themselves and their initiatives . . . What we are witnessing is, in effect, a laboratory and oppressive economic experiment.

CUT

24. EXT—METROPOLITAN COMMUNITY CLINIC, ATHENS (PRESENT DAY)

The Metropolitan Community Clinic provides free health care for the unemployed and those in poverty. It is run by volunteer doctors and nurses. Most are from the Athens area but some from abroad. We see a variety of shots inside and outside the clinic showing its daily business.

DR. GIORGOS VICHAS

Recently, a patient of ours with a very serious health problem—he would die if he wasn't hospitalized—was treated at the 'Laiko' hospital . . .

When I told the director of the hospital that this patent had neither money nor social security to cover the cost of his treatment in order that they don't make up a bill . . . She told me that his fee would go to the Tax Office. This effectively meant that he would go to jail for non-payment.

I asked the director . . . If the law leads someone to their death, do you still respect that law? Unfortunately her answer was yes—the law is above everything . . . / . . .

. . . / . . . At that point 'Antigone' came to my mind, and what I asked her . . . And this we asked her publicly through a press statement . . . Was whether these people in charge today—on whom the life of our fellow human beings depend—serve the model of 'Antigone' or that of 'Creon'?

What was clear to us at the clinic from the beginning was that we are going to serve the model of 'Antigone' . . . With this model we move on . . . No human law can be above moral law.

CUT

25. EXT—A BALCONY IN ANCIENT THEBES

We see the outlines of ANTIGONE and ISMENE through a curtain which moves gently in a breeze. Their debate continues.

ISMENE
Why sacrifice yourself when there is so much to do . . .
You're on a hopeless quest . . . the State cannot afford to appear to be defied.

The State is power . . . Power is real . . .
You know as well as I that property determines who makes law.

Camera moves through the curtain and into close-up of ANTIGONE. Then into increasingly closer two-shot observation of ISMENE and ANTIGONE.

ANTIGONE
Creon is trying to turn back the tide of history . . . to deny us any kind of equality . . . to destroy our sacred and human rights.

ISMENE
Creon is a corrupted human being. His blood is like acid that flows through corroded veins. His power is already beginning to wane.
We must use reason and see things in their right perspective.

ANTIGONE
You are using reason and arguments . . . and dialectic where there is no resolution that is possible.

ISMENE
(Emphatically)
The philosophers have told us that the dialectic is not some idle play of the mind, dear impulsive sister. It describes how things move—always advancing through contradictions . . .

ANTIGONE
(With deep contempt)
Shut up Ismene, you are making me hate you. The dead has its dialectic too, it's crying for its release.

ISMENE
(With resignation to the inevitable)
Then go. I do not fear the dead . . . Go to this act of impetuous rebellion.
I know you act from a true heart but you let your feelings overpower your reason.
(With empathy reaching out to her sister)
Wild irrational as you are my sister . . . You are truly dear to the ones who love you.

ANTIGONE
(Speaking trance-like from her innermost thoughts out across time)
What is a life, if loyalty matters little?
What is a life if a corrupt state and corrupt judgement carries all?
What is a life if fear rules every thought?
What is a life then?
(Turns to camera)
. . . Nothing.

CUT

26. EXT—ARCHIVE FILM CLIP OF ANTIGONE BURYING THE BODY

We hear the voice of the poet Hölderlin (spoken) over this sequence.

HÖLDERLEIN
Antigone. Oh! Unfortunate one. Born of the unfortunate father, Oedipus.
What drives you? And where to?
You have disobeyed the King's law, in a thoughtlessness that gripped you.

CUT

27. EXT—ATHENS ROOFTOPS—DAY (PRESENT DAY)

The Greek economist ANTIGONE LYBERAKI reflects, in two brief interviews, on the economic consequences of the austerity measures put on Greece and on Greece's own responsibilities for its economic situation. In this first interview, she approaches these issues with a view to Sophocles's Antigone.

ANTIGONE LYBERAKI
Even economists have to think about ethical questions, because they are very essential to the decisions that we take.

I personally would go for Antigone's point of view, but I think that the main message of the play is that there can be more definitions of right—of a right decision—and that one has to be very careful not to focus exclusively on the one or the other.

Societies progress only when all of us realise that we have to pay very close attention to the different definitions of what is right and what is wrong.

CUT

28. EXT—SEASHORE (PRESENT DAY)

The SPHINX is staring straight into the camera. She puts a spell on us . . . Mesmerizing us the viewer.

SPHINX
The SPHINX has already been in love. It's a great secret . . . But that's why she always returns in different forms.

29. EXT—A VILLA BY THE SEA (PRESENT DAY)

OEDIPUS is standing, looking out to sea then turns to face us as the SPHINX continues her VO.

SPHINX (VO)
She's in love with Oedipus . . . So she returns . . . She returns and returns in many different forms . . .
Yes . . . She's still in love with all the forms that Oedipus takes . . . Modern . . . Ancient . . . She's there . . . She's there.

30. INT—SPHINX HOME (PRESENT DAY)

The INVESTIGATOR continues his interrogation of the SPHINX.

INVESTIGATOR
You have written that Oedipus did not solve the riddle.

SPHINX
Oedipus and the Sphinx are bound to each other . . .
They need to be together . . . Eternally together . . .
Oedipus cannot be allowed to solve the riddle and thus destroy the Sphinx.
The Sphinz is ephemeral. A being that reflects the depth of historic forces.

INVESTIGATOR
(Emphatically)
The whole of western Civilization depends on Oedipus solving the riddle.

SPHINX
She's been abandoned by history. This true feminine presence . . .
Abandoned by Sophocles . . . Abandoned by all the Greeks . . .
I am going to rewrite her real story with Oedipus and her deeper purpose.

CUT

31. INT—PARIS—HÉLÈNE CIXOUS STUDY (PRESENT DAY)

HÉLÈNE CIXOUS
I don't think that we need to have a real answer about the Sphinx; we are lucky enough to have what the Greeks have presented us with, because they have presented us with allegory. We NEED allegories, we need fables.

Those who help us, and the great writers who help us are those who give us answers that are allegorical.

Then it is up to us to interpret further and further and further, but not of course in a way that would be final—ever.

CUT

32. EXT—BOAT JOURNEY TO ITHACA (ANCIENT GREECE)

Cavafy's great poem is spoken VO under a sequence of shots signifying the ancient mythical journey to Ithaca.

TRAVELLING PLAYER—MALE
When Ithaca calls you, hope the voyage is long and full of adventure, of discovery . . .
Laistrygonians, Cyclops, even angry Poseidon—don't have fear of them.
You won't come across these things if you keep noble thoughts . . . / . . .
. . . / . . . As long as a rare anticipation moves your spirit . . . You won't meet Laistrygonians, Cyclops, or wild Poseidon unless you carry them with you inside your soul.

FEMALE VOICE
Hope that this voyage is a long one, with many summer mornings, when with such pleasure you arrive in new harbours never seen before.
Hope you stop at Phoenician ports, to buy fine things: mother of pearl, amber and ebony, sensual fragrances of every kind . . . as many as

you can . . . May you see wondrous Egyptian cities, to take from their scholars great knowledge.

MALE VOICE

Always hold Ithaca in your mind.
Your destiny is to arrive there. But do not hurry your journey.
It is better that it lasts for years . . .
So by the time you reach her you are old, rich with all you have gained.
BUT . . . Do not expect Ithaca to make you wealthy.

FEMALE VOICE

If Ithaca had not called you, you wouldn't have set out.
Now she has nothing more to give you.

MALE VOICE

If you find Ithaca poor she won't have deceived you.
Now so full of experience and wisdom, you will have finally realized . . .
What all these 'Ithacas' mean.

CUT

33. CHAPTER CAPTION

Act Two: Ghosts of Democracy

34. EXT—ATHENS LOOKING OUT FROM ACROPOLIS (PRESENT DAY)

The INVESTIGATOR is set on a rock high above the skyline of Athens. He is reading to himself out loud from Aristophanes The Frogs. *The text is an extract and is amusing him greatly. It at first appears to be a text full of nonsense until the scene develops.*

INVESTIGATOR

The Frogs, 'Frogs'.
(Laughing out loud as he reads)

Sorry old man, I really can't help it. A lion skin over a yellow nightdress? What's the idea?
(*Laughing*)
Why the buskins, why the club, what's your regiment?

CUT

35. INT—ATHENS THEATRE (PRESENT DAY)

The TRAVELLING PLAYERS are rehearsing the play The Frogs. *We drop into the play between lines 1265 to 1290.*

MALE PLAYER 1
That's cheap wine that you're drinking, . . . It lacks taste.

FEMALE DIRECTOR
Recite another line for him, and watch out for mistakes.

MALE PLAYER 2
OK . . . 'Now I've returned to this land.
My father's power will save me . . . It will answer my prayers' . . .

FEMALE DIRECTOR
OK . . . Start again from where I interrupted you . . .
Where the ghost of Euripides speaks . . .

The INVESTIGATOR breaks into the rehearsal . . . in much the same way as he broke into the film itself in his first scene.

INVESTIGATOR
(*Initially speaking in French*)
Excuse me . . . I'm doing a little investigation . . . I see you're working on a text by Aristophanes, *The Frogs* . . .
My investigation involves texts, ancient texts, Greek texts. Ah Ah . . . So you see I am here to check what you and others are doing . . .
And . . . I'm under the impression that what you're reading doesn't reflect the original text . . . I don't know how this is possible because

I can tell you that in France we take this very seriously . . . Very seriously indeed . . .
I need to check your reading of this great play . . .
And I mean . . . LETTER BY LETTER . . . WORD BY WORD . . .

FEMALE DIRECTOR
(Changing from Greek to English)
Excuse me . . . I don't speak French.

INVESTIGATOR
OH! OK . . . OK . . .
I'm sorry. I'm just saying that you are going to read *The Frogs* by Aristophanes . . .

FEMALE PLAYER 1
The Frogs yes.

INVESTIGATOR
Right OK . . . Well . . .
The problem is that, you know it sounds very bizarre for me when you . . . when you read these lines OK . . . It doesn't sound like the original. It sounds . . .

FEMALE PLAYER 1
Oh it's the original . . .

INVESTIGATOR
Sounds . . . to me like you're distorting the text.

FEMALE PLAYER 1
Perhaps you don't know the language, that's why.

INVESTIGATOR
Well I do know the language, you know . . .

FEMALE PLAYER 1
Ancient Greek perhaps?

INVESTIGATOR
Pardon? Yes! Yes.

FEMALE PLAYER 1
No no no, we read it and are rehearsing it in Modern Greek . . .
We play it in Modern Greek.

INVESTIGATOR
Why in Modern Greek?

FEMALE PLAYER 1
Because everybody must understand it.

INVESTIGATOR
Ah . . . The Greeks should understand ancient Greek!

FEMALE PLAYER 1
Ancient Greek?

INVESTIGATOR
Yes!

FEMALE PLAYER 1
No.

INVESTIGATOR
(Shocked by this revelation)
My God . . .
OK . . . Please proceed . . . But make sure it is exact.

MALE PLAYER 1
Great Lord of the Greeks, listen to me.

ALL PLAYERS
Hurry . . . Hurry . . . We fear we can hold out no longer.

Whilst the rehearsal continues, we hear the voice of THEODOROS TER-ZOPOULOS *on the sound track.*

THEODOROS TERZOPOULOS (VO)
The value of Aristophanes, and of this particular play, is certainly great. In *The Frogs* he demystifies the tragic poets and he gives us really a lesson in democracy. That he could do this to these monumental plays reflects 'democracy' in ancient Greece.

Loud crashes and bangs in the background . . . This is the 'music' that underscores the players . . . As in ancient Athens.

CRASH

FEMALE PLAYER 2
By great Zeus! Which way's the crapper? I can't hold out! These crashes are bad for my kidneys.

BANG

MALE PLAYER 1
You can't go to the toilet till you've heard the next part. It has great music.

FEMALE PLAYER 2
Well get on with it, but no crashes this time please.

CUT

Time moves on to free discussion of the play with the INVESTIGATOR. The PLAYERS conversely begin to train the INVESTIGATOR in Greek pronunciation.

MALE PLAYER 1
(To INVESTIGATOR)
It's a bit difficult.

ALL PLAYERS
To-flat-a-frat-to-flat-a-thrat

MALE PLAYER 1
A fox to dog the Sphinx . . . A Sphinx to do the fox.

ALL PLAYERS
To-flat-a-frat-to-flat-a-thrat

MALE PLAYER 1
The prophet bird swoops with a vengeful spear.

ALL PLAYERS
To-flat-a-frat-to-flat-a-thrat

MALE PLAYER 1
Through the skies his milky way doth spiral.

ALL PLAYERS
To-flat-a-frat-to-flat-a-thrat

MALE PLAYER 2
The allied force assembled to assault great Ajax.

ALL PLAYERS
To-flat-a-frat-to-flat-a-thrat

THE PLAYERS and THE INVESTIGATOR practice this last line taking the INVESTIGATOR through impossible tongue twists until he finally gets it right.

INVESTIGATOR
To-thrat-o-fat-to-trat-a-wat
To—clat-a-flat-fat-brat
Do—flot-a-flit-trrrrrr
Trrrrr-a-flaaa-trat-trat-trat

ALL PLAYERS
Well done . . . Goodbye

INVESTIGATOR
I will be continuing my investigation and, layer by layer . . .
I'll get to the bottom of this.

CUT

36. INT—ATHENS CAFÉ (PRESENT DAY)

The INVESTIGATOR has tracked down a prominent journalist, KOSTAS VAXEVANIS, who has revealed in his magazine the depth of corruption in Greece amongst the elites.
The INVESTIGATOR'S questions are unheard but implied.

INVESTIGATOR
Do you think that Greece, its writers and its artists have lost the sense of values they once did have? If that is the case . . . Why?

Interview with KOSTAS VAXEVANIS—journalist.

KOSTAS VAXEVANIS
Philosophers, poets, artists, thinkers have lost their pace, lured by the sirens of the markets. We must rediscover human values.

We must rediscover collectivity. We must rediscover how people exist closer to one another. Not in a way where one builds a swimming pool next to his neighbour's house, and the neighbour is envious.

I think that Greece has all the potential to rediscover the values which thousands of years ago were first established here, but we have exchanged those values, for a political amorality, for an economic amorality, for Machiavellianism.

All our old values we must rediscover. Greece has the potential. But in order to use of this potential, it must rid itself of the political system that governs it. It must throw away the system of corruption, which in Europe and the World presents itself as the salvation.

I don't know which political power will do it, but it can't be done by those who brought Greece to the point it is today.

CUT

37. INT—GREEK FILM ARCHIVE (PRESENT DAY)

The INVESTIGATOR tracks down various Citizens of Athens who effectively form a 'chorus' commentating on events. His questions are always unheard.

INVESTIGATOR
Tell me what are the effects of the austerity policies imposed on Greece now.

CITIZEN OF ATHENS (VALERIE KONTAKOS)
The things that are happening in terms of reductions of public services . . . In healthcare facilities . . . In education . . . In almost all spheres of public life . . . Are the result of everything being privatised . . .

So there is no more social care, no more social services, and it's forced us into a period of readjustment . . . It leaves us with everyone feeling that the only way they can make it is on their own . . . It's a total privatisation, to the smallest level.

CUT

38. EXT—GROUNDS OF THE ACROPOLIS (PRESENT DAY)

The INVESTIGATOR is walking through ancient shrub land. He is very disturbed by where his investigations are taking him. The camera follows him and then drops down to the ground where lines of ants are moving on pre-set paths.

CREON (VO)
Men make their own history, but they do not make it as they please. They make it under conditions existing already . . .
Under circumstances given and transmitted from the past.

39. EXT—PALACE GROUNDS (ANCIENT GREECE)

CREON is demonstrating his grasp on power whilst seducing the SPHINX

CREON
We live in a world of rulers and slaves and most people are moved by the basest of motives.

40. EXT—POLITICAL DEMONSTRATION—ATHENS (PRESENT DAY)

CREON (VO)
That is why the tradition of all dead generations weighs like a nightmare on the brains of the living.

CUT

41. INT—ATHENS APARTMENT (PRESENT DAY)

The INVESTIGATOR tracks down another Citizen. His question remains unheard.

INVESTIGATOR
Is there any value in Europe and its culture?

CITIZEN OF ATHENS (CHRISTOS KARAKEPELIS)
If Europe loses the welfare state . . . Which originated in Pericles's democracy . . . Nothing will be left but barren economism. This is not our vision of Europe.

If Europe has something to offer the world . . . It is a modern concept of citizenship through faith in diversity . . . But on the contrary . . . recently Europe's oligarchies—the political elites, and the Brussels palace—have opted for populism.

This populism is now employed by local political and economic elites to undervalue the Greek people and treat them disparagingly . . . They apply this contempt every day in labour relationships, in our relationship with reality, and with a more policed state . . .

I think the most vicious problem in Europe today is this gaze of the powerful towards the powerless.

CUT

42. EXT—ANCIENT GREEK LANDSCAPE (PRESENT DAY)

The TRAVELLING PLAYERS are rehearsing a reading of Cavafy's poem 'Waiting for the Barbarians'.

The reading of the poem is intercut with an interview with ANTONIO NEGRI who the INVESTIGATOR has tracked down to a secret apartment perhaps in the most ancient part of Rome.

FEMALE PLAYER 1
What are we waiting for in the forum?

MALE PLAYER
We wait because the Barbarians are coming today.

FEMALE PLAYER 1
Why aren't the senators legislating?

MALE PLAYER
Because the Barbarians are on their way, what's the point of making laws now? When the Barbarians turn up, they'll do the legislating.

Cut to ANTONIO NEGRI interview. The INVESTIATOR's questions unheard.

INVESTIGATOR
Who are these Barbarians?
How can we tell who is what?

ANTONIO NEGRI
I think that when we use identity to talk about nations . . .
Classes . . . Power in general . . . Racial stereotypes . . .
We always arrive at results that are disastrous.

Cut back to TRAVELLING PLAYERS.

FEMALE PLAYER 1
Why have our consuls and magistrates come out today wearing their scarlet togas?
Why are they carrying their elegant canes inlaid with silver and gold?

MALE PLAYER 2
Because the Barbarians are coming today and things like that dazzle them.

Cut back to Rome. INVESTIGATOR's question remains unheard.

INVESTIGATOR
Where does our concept of identity come from?

ANTONIO NEGRI
If you think of someone as 'black'—being a slave for centuries—it's only by overturning this identity and recognising we are cosmopolitan, that we're different, singular, that we have richness in ourselves. Because others recognise it . . . Because we 'love' each other . . . That's the real phenomenon . . .

It always sounds ridiculous to talk about 'love'!
It's assumed we're religious or some ridiculous server of Eros.
It's not THAT! It's joint responsibility. It's ethics born from love . . .
Pure love [amour-propre].

Cut back to TRAVELLING PLAYERS.

FEMALE PLAYER 1
Why this unexpected restlessness? Why this confusion?
People's faces . . . why so solemn?
Why are the squares emptying so fast? All going home so deep in thought?

FEMALE PLAYER 2
Night has fallen and the Barbarians haven't arrived.
And those, returning from the border report the Barbarians are no more.

MALE PLAYER 2
So what's going to happen to us now without 'Barbarians'?
The Barbarians always gave us a way out.

CUT

43. EXT—PARIS ROOFTOPS (PRESENT DAY)

MARTIN McQUILLAN (*literary critic and cultural theorist*) *has been tracked down by the* INVESTIGATOR *and is quizzed by him about the origins of Greek thought. Question unheard.*

INVESTIGATOR
How did Greek drama and philosophy originate?

MARTIN McQUILLAN
Greek thought is not a pure thing that springs autochthonously from the origins of Greece. It is something that has been informed by thought that moved from . . . / . . . . . . / . . . North Africa. It is thought that moved across Europe . . . Thought that has been enriched, and made porous, and hybrid, by a series of encounters.

CUT

44. EXT—ATHENS ROOFTOP NIGHT (PRESENT DAY)

The INVESTIGATOR *has followed* MARTIN McQUILLAN *to Athens and has caught him reading* The Frogs.

INVESTIGATOR
Well . . . Well . . . Mister . . . It looks to me like you've been reading *The Frogs* by Aristophanes.

MARTIN McQUILLAN
I've been reading *The Frogs*.

INVESTIGATOR
Have you been distorting them?

CUT

45. EXT—ATHENS BY NIGHT (PRESENT DAY)

The SPHINX is moving through dark streets of Athens. INVESTIGATOR has returned to Paris to further question ÉTIENNE BALIBAR (philosopher) who offers on the sound track his political analysis. Question unheard.

INVESTIGATOR
Are we beginning to see the end of capitalism and the crimes it has inflicted on Man?

ÉTIENNE BALIBAR (VO)
I'm extraordinarily mistrustful of the idea that capitalism is on the brink of collapse, on the brink of mutation. That's what Marx thought back in 1848.

He announced it at the end of *The Communist Manifesto*, and Marxists have often believed it and repeated it at various times. Only to find each time, not that capitalism is immortal, but that capitalism finds in its own crises the way to reorganise itself on other bases.

These radical transformations that have brutal aspects would obviously have consequences for capitalists themselves . . . But others always end up paying the price.

What interested me was to deduce a certain number of consequences, especially to explain why, or ask the question: 'Why left-wing Europe—to whom I belong—in its different components was just so very blind and unarmed against this situation?'

CUT

46. EXT / INT—ATHENS CAFÉ (PRESENT DAY)

The investigation returns to KOSTAS VAXEVANIS—journalist. Question unheard.

INVESTIGATOR
Why did the crisis hit Greece so hard?

KOSTAS VAXEVANIS
Greece was systematically deprived of its production, and lost its sense of real economy. The EU subsidised cultivations that had nothing to do with Greece. They subsidised the uprooting of olive trees. They subsidised the cutting of Greek fishing boats in the Aegean Sea. All on the pretext of central planning in Europe.

What was the result? The creation of several parasitical phenomena without any control . . . People were directed to cultivate various useless things, only to get the subsidy . . . Often they would cheat since there was no control, in order to get the subsidy. It was more profitable to throw away tomatoes, and get the subsidy, than to cultivate quality tomatoes for people to eat here, in England, or in Germany.

In those years that followed, the 'taps' opened, and people were driven to a false sense of euphoria, taking loans for everything: for holidays, to get married, for dandruff.

They made Mr. Papademos the head of the Bank of Greece—the man who ordered the Bank to lend without limits, and without collateral, without guarantees—the same man who as Prime Minister said the loans taken thoughtlessly by the Greeks were to blame. The very man who gave these loans.

CUT

47. EXT—NIGHT—ATHENS GRAPHITE STREETS (PRESENT DAY)

INVESTIGATOR questions Martin McQuillan. Question unheard.

INVESTIGATOR
Are we about to witness the demise of the capitalist system?

MARTIN McQUILLAN (VO)
Capitalism has always been in crisis, it's the nature of capitalism that it is continuously in crisis. It's a crisis for Europe; it's a crisis for European countries, for the European Union. There's no crisis for capital, capital will just move its money elsewhere. Capitalism will always reinvent itself, it will leave behind the wreckage that it leaves behind. Capitalism itself will survive, it has the resources within itself to do that.

CUT

48. EXT—ATHENS ROOF TERRACE, DAY (PRESENT DAY)

ANTIGONE LYBERAKI
In retrospect it is clear that the signs were all there . . . After we joined the Eurozone, we entered a phase of very fast growth, but it was a growth that was unsustainable, in the sense that it was fuelled by consumption and not by production, by innovation, or . . . you know . . . by exports. So this consumption was basically supported by cheap credit because it was so easy to get loans . . . This was true for the public sector, and it was also true for the households and the private sector. So somehow the consumption exploded and at the same time, the production base shrunk, became much smaller. Competitiveness also plummeted . . . / . . .

. . . / . . . This meant that we entered the crisis with a triple deficit: the fiscal deficit; the indebtedness or the debt problem; and also the competitiveness deficit. It meant that we were too expensive for the quality of the goods that we were producing . . . But at the time, nobody wanted to stop the party.

Politicians were adamant at the time that the Greek economy was very well protected by its previous growth rates . . . Whereas in fact . . . These growth rates were based on an untenable situation and created this enormous debt problem that we are facing.

CUT

49. EXT—SEASHORE (ANCIENT GREECE)

OEDIPUS again confronts TIRESIAS. The text is adapted from Oedipus Rex, *Lines 390 to 395, but is applied to the arrogance of the elites of Europe today.*

OEDIPUS

It was I, Oedipus . . . The outsider . . . I, who saved this city, rescued the economy, with no help from sorcery.
A free market, abolition of all worker protections, re-enslavement of the masses . . . Yes TIRESIAS . . .
It was the arrow of my own intelligence that hit the mark . . .
I took the power . . . Saved the city . . . *(2 beats)* . . . And won the bed of sweet Jocasta.

CUT

50. CAPTION

WHEN GREAT PROSPERITY COMES SUDDENLY AND UNEXPECTEDLY TO A STATE . . . IT USUALLY BREEDS ARROGANCE.

51. CAPTION

IT IS SAFER FOR PEOPLE TO ENJOY AN AVERAGE AMOUNT OF SUCCESS, THAN SOMETHING THAT IS OUT OF ALL PROPORTION.

(Thucydides 460–400 BC)

CUT

52. INT—ATHENS APARTMENT (PRESENT DAY)

We are in the study of an apartment somewhere in Athens. INVESTIGATOR continues his interviews with Citizens of Athens. Here he is with YANNIS SAKARIDIS. The question is unheard.

INVESTIGATOR
Why do people seem to be silent?

YANNIS SAKARIDIS
I think the middle class here, they are not fully aware of the crisis, and it's very difficult to apprehend that. It's something that you don't want to lose things, even in your mind, and you don't want to lose things in your relations, in your everyday life. So you act like nothing happened, or you try to act like nothing happened. But actually things are changing and you have to adapt, think about your life, and adapt.

CUT

53. EXT—FOREST—SOMEWHERE NEAR ATHENS (ANCIENT GREECE)

ISMENE is being tutored by the director of the TRAVELLING PLAYERS about false dreams and expectations. She adapts Cavafy's poem: 'As Much As You Can'.

FEMALE DIRECTOR
(With sadness)
If your life can't be lived as you desire . . .
Try as much as you can not to degrade it.
Not to degrade it by excessive attachment to the world, by too much excitement and talk.
Don't go dragging it around exposing it to the daily noise of social gatherings and parties . . .
Or, in the end, it will start to greet you as an impoverished gate-crasher.

(10 beats. CU on ISMENE as the poem registers)

CUT

54. EXT—SCHLIEMANN'S HOUSE ATHENS (PRESENT DAY)

The INVESTIGATOR is sitting on steps beneath the remarkable architecture of, what is now, the Museum of Money . . . Built by Schliemann . . . Schliemann is the man who discovered ancient Troy. INVESTIGATOR is reading an anthology of Cavafy's work. On the sound track we hear the voice of THEODOROS TERZOPOULOS, the renowned theatre director of classical tragedy.

THEODOROS TERZOPOULOS (VO)

And now we are in the present time. We live here in Athens. We say that we live through a tragedy. It is a tragedy or a drama? In 'Tragedy', we never see the terrible events. We never see a murder, a suicide.

CUT

55. INT—ATHENS THEATRE (PRESENT DAY)

The investigation takes us into the private Athenian theatre where THEODOROS TERZOPOULOS presents many of his plays. Question unheard.

INVESTIGATOR

You have directed many tragedies on stage here and throughout the world. Is what we witness in Athens today a public and social replay of these tragedies?

THEODOROS TERZOPOULOS

We are not conscious of living through a tragedy? Because modern Man is not conflictual. He is passive. He is an obedient instrument of various situations—economic, political, ideological—and He lacks power, the energy, and most of all the conflictual mood that is creativity.

He is not creative anymore. He is passive. He is the receiver of many bad things, many bad messages. He is the passive receiver of the bad political discourse, of the bad television program, the television serial, of events in this life which really has sank to a very low level . . . / . . .

. . . / . . . I dare say that our times are post-dramatic, not even dramatic. Because even the elements of drama, of a family drama, of a political drama, all these pieces have come apart, have disintegrated. We are trying to recompose them—to create an image—and what we are actually creating is a post-dramatic image.

56. EXT—POLITICAL DEMONSTRATION—ATHENS (PRESENT DAY)

THEODOROS TERZOPOULOS (VO)
I could say that the body today could really be a political response, a tool.

57. INT—THEATRE (PRESENT DAY)

THEODOROS TERZOPOULOS
The body can be the bearer of energy, of memory, of anger, of laughter, of all these situations which have been repressed. It is vital that a body is creative and active, not passive. And an active body is really dangerous for today's capitalism.

THEODOROS TERZOPOULOS looks straight into the camera. He is set against a wall of the stage area which is an old exterior wall 2,500 years old. Slowly he raises a ceramic plate and after a moment of silence . . . smashes it.

CUT

Act Three: 'Dead Souls' Are Calling

58. INT—LONDON SCIENCE LABORATORY (PRESENT DAY)

The investigation now switches to London. Here the renowned high energy physicist ARTHUR I. MILLER is questioned about the nature of the SPHINX and the nature of 'Time' itself. Question unheard.

INVESTIGATOR
Many have an identification with the Sphinx . . . Why is the Sphinx so powerful in the mind? What are its modern-day equivalents?

ARTHUR I. MILLER
The Sphinx, a long time ago, signified what happened in the past and what will happen in the future.

One manifestation of the Sphinx right now is at CERN. The various particle detectors that are there, that can see into the past and certainly see into the future, and these high energy detectors can take us into deep secrets . . .

What is the real riddle of the Sphinx?
What is the riddle of nature?
How is energy produced?
What are the real sources of energy and what is this thing called 'Dark Energy'?

59. EXT—NIGHT—THE AEGEAN SEA (ANCIENT GREECE)

ARTHUR I. MILLER (VO)
. . . The Sphinx suggests answers to questions such as . . . What is our universe really like?

HÉLÈNE CIXOUS (VO)
In science we are always before the Sphinx. In astrophysics or in biology, we arrive at a certain stage and yet again we don't understand, and that's life. The Sphinx is the signifier of that.

CUT

60. EXT—ANCIENT SEASHORE—DAY

The SPHINX is standing on a rock in the sea. OEDIPUS stands alone on the shore. She calls to him.

SPHINX
Oedipus, what walks on four legs in the morning?
Two legs in the afternoon?
And three legs in the evening?

OEDIPUS
I don't know.

We pull back to reveal a second manifestation of the SPHINX who also poses a riddle for OEDIPUS.

SPHINX 2
What is greater than God?
What, if eaten, brings a slow death?
What has a poor man got but a rich man never has?

OEDIPUS
Nothing.

SPHINX
Oedipus . . . continue with your journey . . . and your story.

CUT

61. EXT—AN ANCIENT TOWER BY THE SEA (ANCIENT GREECE)

OEDIPUS is confronted by TIRESIAS.

TIRESIAS
(*To camera*)
Oedipus is fucked. There's nothing he can do about it. He has no way out and he's not gonna win. But I think also that he has it in his power

to get out of this mess, if he just keeps his mouth shut and doesn't go looking for trouble. The trouble is he's looking for trouble all the time.

OEDIPUS
Is this conspiracy Creon's or yours?

TIRESIAS
Creon is not your downfall. You are your own.

CUT

62. EXT—DUSK—MONTAGE—ROCKY SEASHORE (ANCIENT GREECE)

63. EXT—DUSK—LARGE ROCK FORMATION—SEASHORE (ANCIENT GREECE)

A sequence of shots signifying the close of day. Tiresias is seen walking alone through this rocky landscape.
On the soundtrack we hear the voice of MANOLIS GLEZOS. MANOLIS was a 'Resistance' hero in Greece. (He was the man who tore down the swastika from the Acropolis during the Nazi occupation.) Throughout the last sixty years, he has fought battles for 'Direct Democracy'. Three times condemned to death, he escaped and now is one of the truly great voices of contemporary Greek politics. The INVESTIGATOR is unheard and his questions must be assumed.

MANOLIS GLEZOS (VO)
There was a ritual in Greece. They were calling Tiresias to tell them about the future, what was to happen in the future . . .

I call out to my comrades whom I knew closely, whom I held in my arms. Who were lost in battles, in demonstrations, in executions. I call them all to discuss about what the future holds for our country.

I don't need Tiresias.

64. EXT—ATHENS ROOF TERRACE. ACROPOLIS IN BACKGROUND (PRESENT DAY)

INVESTIGATOR is in discussion with MANOLIS GLEZOS and KAT-ERINA, a translator and friend.

MANOLIS GLEZOS

I need my comrades to talk with. The ones I lost. Let me explain what that means: . . . On the eve of every demonstration . . . On the eve of every battle . . . On the eve of every execution . . . We used to get together and we were saying to one another: 'Manolis, Kostas, Pavlos . . . if you live . . . if "the good bullet" misses you . . . don't forget me.'"

And these comrades told each other their dreams . . . About Greece . . . About the world . . . And even personal things . . .

We used to say 'I have not drank any wine but, you will drink wine for me . . . I have not walked in the forest to hear the wind blow through the leaves—you will do that for me. I have not walked by the sea to the hear the sound of the waves, you will do that for me. And when you meet people on the street and you say good morning . . . You will say good morning for me'.

So right now, when we are talking, I am not alone . . . It's also the voice of all these companions. Their dreams and their visions.

CUT

65. INT—APARTMENT ATHENS—DAY (PRESENT DAY)

The investigation moves forward . . . INVESTIGATOR finds PETROS SEVASTIKOGLOU, a Citizen of Athens, in his study. Question unheard.

INVESTIGATOR

Can you give me an indication of what is not being spoken about . . . About the real effects on people in Greece now?

PETROS SEVASTIKOGLOU

Unfortunately we have a lot of loss. I have friends dying from cancers, from heart attacks and I'm sure it's not a chance . . . It's after two or three years without work . . . without being able to pay bills or the rent. People died from this crisis—a lot.

CUT

66. EXT—SEAFRONT (ANCIENT GREECE)

OEDIPUS *is alone staring arrogantly into the camera.* TIRESIAS *a figure in the distance.*

OEDIPUS (VO)

A free market . . . Abolition of worker protections . . . Re-enslavement of the masses . . . It was the arrow of my own intelligence that hit the mark.

CUT

67. INT—CINEMA FOYER—ATHENS (PRESENT DAY)

Another of the Citizens, NIKOS CORNELIOS, *who make up our chorus, is answering the* INVESTIGATOR. *Question unheard.*

INVESTIGATOR

Could events turn violent?

NIKOS CORNELIOS

We can see the crisis from various points of view . . . From a political and economic point of view it is a war . . . A war of capital against labour . . . That means victims like in every war . . .

CUT

68. INT—ROME APARTMENT—DAY (PRESENT DAY)

ANTONIO NEGRI *indicates to the* INVESTIGATOR *just how deadly the whole thing could become in class 'war'. Question unheard.*

INVESTIGATOR
You did things in the past?
Some of these things were really dangerous.
Do you think the present situation requires similar acts?

ANTONIO NEGRI
When I was young and I was 'condemned' for having done things you weren't supposed to do . . . One of those things I did was to pass weapons to the people who were fighting the Greek colonels . . . In fact I sent a lorry full of weapons and explosives . . . I hope I won't have to do that again.

CUT

69. EXT—ROOFTOP ATHENS (PRESENT DAY)

MANOLIS GLEZOS continues his account of 'Resistance'. He holds a book of letters collected from Resistance members.

MANOLIS GLEZOS
Here we have a letter, let's see it first from its emotional side; what it says is: 'Dear mother, I greet you. Today I go to be executed'. Notice the difference, it doesn't say 'they are taking me for execution', it says 'I go, I offer myself to be executed'—there is a big difference in quality.

It goes on to explain for which reason . . . It says 'going down for the Greek people'—and the word 'LAOS' which is 'people' is in capital letters, to be emphasised. Which means that this could be also for the German people, for the English people, for any kind of people.

This is a letter by my brother, he was three years younger than me. He was in his first year in the academy for teachers. He was only 19. And you will notice that in just these two lines, he says it all.

I have here many more letters. They are all in the same spirit. I mention my brother because in a very succinct way he shows it all in this act.

Now the question that arises in view of the suffering of the Greek people during the Nazi occupation is this . . . By what right does Germany inflict its current policy . . . this austerity policy . . . against Greece?

CUT

70. EXT—SEASHORE WITH HIGH ROCK OUTCROP (ANCIENT GREECE)

A large crowd of Theban citizens is present to witness the trial of ANTIGONE. The crowds are behind our viewpoint but are present on the sound track. They react to the debate. ANTIGONE and ISMENE are pushed forward to hear judgement from CREON. As the women approach the 'Rock of Judgment' we hear the voice of HÖLDERLIN reciting from his 'Antigone'.
CREON sits king-like on the top of the rock. He is all powerful.

HÖLDERLIN (VO)

Antigone . . .
What drives you? And where to?
You have disobeyed the King's law . . .
In a thoughtlessness that gripped you.

CREON

You have committed the gravest crime . . . (*beat*) . . . All deficits must be redeemed . . . All debts paid . . . All defiance must be answered . . . Even the innocent must pay and pay they will.

You, Antigone, daughter of Oedipus the patricide, sister of Polynices the traitor . . . You have committed treason . . . And the punishment for that is death. No exceptions . . . Father, brother, makes no difference.

You are bound by the law—the law of the state—and the state . . . Is me.

What justice could there possibly be if I made an exception for you?

ANTIGONE
You are no court. The people must hear my case. The case of justice.

CREON
If you disavow me as a judge, how can I let you speak?

ANTIGONE
The God of Death, who waits for us all, now waits for me. No husband for me. No music at my wedding. Only death will possess me now.

CUT

71. EXT—AEGEAN SEA—THE SUN SETTING (ANCIENT GREECE)

The trial concludes . . . The crowds are heard being forced to disperse . . . We hold on the fading sun.

CUT

72. EXT—METROPOLITAN COMMUNITY CLINIC, ATHENS (PRESENT DAY)

The investigation returns to contemporary Athens and asks questions about the value of cathartic release in drama. Can it heal?

DR. GIORGOS VICHAS
In ancient times, medical centres were called 'Asklepieia' after Asklepios. What Asklepios, and the doctors that came after him, believed was that for a therapy to be complete a patient doesn't only need a doctor, medicine and a kind of hypnosis, but a very important part of therapy was to experience dramatic tragedy . . . To experience ancient tragedy. Negative feelings must not spread internally. They can produce powerful self-destructive effects. The results can be devastating . . . Like the 4,000 recent suicides . . .

DR. GIORGOS VICHAS *is joined by a second medical volunteer MAR-THA FRANGIADAKI. She is dealing directly with therapeutic needs amongst patients tramatised by the crisis.*

MARTHA FRANGIADAKI

Catharsis is necessary . . . It is helping to heal people . . . And one thing we're trying to do here is catharsis in both senses of the word . . . In support and solidarity with the people and the sense of the word of 'Resistance' against things that shouldn't be happening.

CUT

73. INT—ATHENS CAFÉ—DAY (PRESENT DAY)
The investigation returns to our journalist KOSTAS VAXEVANIS. Question unheard.

INVESTIGATOR

So who should we interrogate to dig deeper?

KOSTAS VAXEVANIS

So today they say that we must comply with the markets. Who are the markets? What are these markets? The markets are the ones who back in 2008 caused the whole planet's real economy to collapse. These markets that now promote the rescue?

Europe is not the dream of Mrs Merkel, nor of the Bundesbank . . . Europe is not the skyscrapers of the City of London . . . It is the people of England and their culture. It is the philosophy of the Greeks. It is the poetry of the French. It is the culture of the Italians. This is what the European Union is. It is not plans around a table about how some will get richer.

CUT

74. INT—PARIS—SPHINX HOME (PRESENT DAY)

INVESTIGATOR
You say that you re-create things? Madam . . . It's plagiarism!

SPHINX
You may say I'm stealing words . . . Ha . . . Stealing . . . But who invented words? . . . Who invented the air? . . . Who invented breathing? . . . Who invented light?

CUT

75. EXT—A PLACE OF EXECUTION IN A CLEARING IN A FOREST (ANCIENT GREECE)

ANTIGONE, CREON, ISMENE and a group of guards are standing to witness the final sentencing of ANTIGONE.

ISMENE
(Making a final plea for reason)
Are you sure you want to go through with this?

CREON
I have no choice.
It's not me who decides, it's the law invested in me . . .
I merely represent that law.
It's not me who decrees this execution . . .
It's not you . . . It's not them . . . It's the law.
What would a man be if he disobeyed that logic?
However cruel it might seem.

ISMENE
But one word . . . One word from you can change it.
Your pride is wounded Creon . . . Only time can heal this.
Open up the dark chambers of your mind; let yourself identify with the other players in the drama. Empathise . . . Empathise.

CREON
Empathise? Rubbish! What worse can come?
I see this execution as the first step in a great act of expansion. Our city can only grow from rigorous will, not self-doubt. We will achieve a nation of power and wealth only from ruthless determination.

ISMENE
Greater cities than yours have fallen into decline and that decline comes when least expected. Only then will you learn from your mistakes but it will all be too late. What will soothe you then Creon . . . ?

CREON
Enough! Your wailing hurts my ears. If a man could wail his own dirge before he dies, he'd go on forever! (*laughs . . . beat*)

Take her away . . . Wall her up alone. Let her scream against the dark until her mind explodes. There will be no release for her but death.

ANTIGONE
(*Speaking out to people in the future*)
I'll soon be there. Soon embrace my own.
The great growing family of our dead . . .
I reviled, go down before my destined time's run out . . .
What laws of the mighty Gods have I transgressed?
I descend alive, to the caverns of the dead . . .
I must make prayer to the Gods before they take me.

CREON
Take her away! We've wasted enough time.

CUT

76. CAPTION

IN ACTS OF REVENGE, MEN REPEAL GENERAL LAWS OF HUMANITY. LAWS, THERE TO GIVE HOPE OF SALVATION TO ALL IN DISTRESS.

77. CAPTION

THEY FORGET THERE MAY COME A TIME WHEN THEY TOO WILL BE IN DANGER, AND WILL NEED THEIR PROTECTION.

(Thucydides 460–400 BC)

78. INT—ATHENS CAFÉ—DAY (PRESENT DAY)

INVESTIGATOR asks one more question of journalist KOSTAS VAXEVANIS. Question unheard.

INVESTIGATOR
Why are the facts not published?

KOSTAS VAXEVANIS
If you open Greek newspapers right now, you will not see a single column about the dirty role the banks play in Greece . . . About how much money they have stolen, and how they were recapitalised with the money of the Greek people . . . Not one column. The reason is that the official sponsors of all media in Greece are the bankers . . . Either by loans . . . Or with the advertisements they place . . . Therefore journalism is not free in Greece. It needs to urgently recover its power . . . It needs to become free again.

CUT

79. EXT—SEASHORE (ANCIENT GREECE)

Again OEDIPUS confronts TIRESIAS for the truth about the plague that is destroying Thebes. Now accusing him of treason.

OEDIPUS
With whom or what are you conspiring?

TIRESIAS
Unknowing, you demand an answer from me, an answer you will not want to hear. And soon now you will face your own dark secret.

CUT

80. EXT—ANCIENT STREET OF THEBES—DAY (ANCIENT GREECE)

OEDIPUS stands dejected leaning against a crumbling wall. JOCASTA approaches as a ghost. She is speaking out beyond OEDIPUS and beyond our viewpoint. Only as she finishes her dialogue does she turn to cast a passing eye on OEDIPUS.

JOCASTA
Mortal man shouldn't fear . . . Chance reigns supreme . . . Knowledge of the future is denied to us . . . Better to live carelessly from hand to mouth . . .

This union with your mother . . . Fear not . . . Men often in their dreams approach their mother's beds . . . The man who sees this as mere phantasy lives out his life most at ease.

CUT

81. EXT—ATHENS STREET—DAY

Demonstration archive, CU of burning television news broadcast van. We are now surrounded by the smoke and close up to the roaring flames. Additional explosions errupt. We hear the voice of THEODOROS TERZOPOULOS in VO.

THEODOROS TERZOPOULOS (VO)
When you enter the area of tragedy, you become a fundamentalist . . . You can't get out.
You enter both a very creative space and at the same time a prison from which you can't escape . . . / . . .

. . . / . . . I put a lot of emphasis on Tiresias's presence but now I see the whole thing as a deep hallucination . . . A nightmare . . . It was a wild projection of a dark material from the unconscious.

CUT

82. EXT—CREON'S PALACE—A BALCONY (ANCIENT GREECE)

The GHOST OF OEDIPUS confronts CREON.

GHOST OF OEDIPUS
You listened when it suited you, and proclaimed your power righteously. Will you listen now?

CREON
Tell me . . . Am I on course? Or have I wavered?

GHOST OF OEDIPUS
You're dead on course.

CREON
I owe you much, I know.

GHOST OF OEDIPUS
Yes . . . You're poised on the razor-edge of fate.

CREON
You're making my blood freeze.

GHOST OF OEDIPUS
Listen to me, hold your thoughts, and listen . . .
Last night I heard a strange voice on the wing beats of the birds—unintelligible, barbaric, a mad scream. They went crazy, began killing each other . . . and then I felt the presence of the Sphinx and she made her prophecy: . . .
. . . It's you Creon . . . You're the cause of all this . . .
Your arrogance has broken sacred laws.
Your inhuman use of power has driven even the sharks mad.
Now the birds cry out no clear sign to me.
They're gorged with the flesh of their victims.
They excrete their foulness . . . Carrion from her corpse and the Gods will no longer listen . . .
Our happiness is dead . . . Hope is gone . . .
So we wait . . . Helpless now for the tide of history to pass over us.

CUT

83. EXT—SEASHORE—DAY (PRESENT DAY)

BCU TIRESIAS speaking out to us.

TIRESIAS
Most days go by with only slight variations . . .
The really apocalyptic days you don't even notice . . .
It's only later that you look back and think . . .
'That was the day, that was the day' . . . Then you remember.

CUT

84. EXT—AN ANCIENT AEGEAN SEASHORE—DAY (ANCIENT GREECE)

We track along the seashore a repeat of the seashore earlier in the film. Voices return from earlier in the drama bringing to us fragments of text as if carried on the wind.

TIRESIAS (VO)
Then you remember . . .

ANTIGONE (VO)
He is our brother . . .

ISMENE
What you are asking for is a political act . . .

CREON
It is the law of the State and the State . . . Is me . . .

CUT

85. INT—SPHINX HOME (PRESENT DAY)

BCU *The Sphinx sleeps. Through an open window we hear the sounds of Athens street life.*
BCU *INVESTIGATOR speaking direct to camera as if emerging from the SPHINX'S own unconscious.*

INVESTIGATOR
Give back to Greece what you have stolen from Greece! Now! Greece must have it back . . .
What belongs to Greece must be returned to Greece.

CUT

86. PORTRAITS (PRESENT DAY)

A series of portraits of some of our Greek helpers on the film. Artisans and assistants. Each portrait lasts for 5 seconds and is in silence with the person looking straight into the lens.

87. CAPTION

THOUGH THEY MIGHT HAVE BEEN CAST DOWN BY
  FORTUNE,
THEY WERE STILL, IN THEIR OWN DEEPER SELVES,
THE SAME AS THEY HAD ALWAYS BEEN.

(Thucydides 460–400 BC)

END CREDITS

END

Étienne Balibar, philosopher

Hélène Cixous, writer

Antonio Negri, social scientist

Manolis Glezos, resistant

Theodoros Terzopoulos, theatre director

Kostas Vaxevanis, journalist

Credits

OXI: An Act of Resistance

WRITTEN & DIRECTED BY
Ken McMullen

EXECUTIVE PRODUCER
Martin McQuillan

PRODUCED BY
Ken McMullen through SCAPE FILMS London

CAST
(in order of appearance)

Travelling Players   ALEXIS GEORGOPOULOS
THEMISSTOKLIS MICHALACOS
EVGENIA GEORGOPOULOU

Jocasta ELENI KALLIA
Investigator DOMINIQUE PINON
The Man with the Hat BRET ROBERTS
Sphinx GABRIELLA WRIGHT
Oedipus LEX SHRAPNEL
Tiresias DON MOUSSEAU
Creon JOHN SHRAPNEL
Antigone JULIA FAURE
Ismene DELLA SABA
Friedrich Hölderlin (VO) JOCHEN WINTER
Second Sphinx CONXI MAURI SAMARRA

DIRECTORS OF PHOTOGRAPHY
GREECE
Stuart Biddlecombe
PARIS
Marion Boutin

EDITOR
Justinian Buckley

SOUND RECORDIST
Tim Barker

ASSOCIATE PRODUCERS
ATHENS
Katerina Iordanoglou
LONDON
Juul van der Laan
Conxi Mauri Samarra
PARIS
Suzy Foster

MUSIC
ORCHESTRAL COMPOSITIONS
Adrian Munsey

PERCUSSIONS AND AMBIENCES
David Cunningham
ADDITIONAL SCORING
The Cabinet of Living Cinema

CREW

First Assistant Director	TOM COLEY
First Assistant Camera / Focus Puller	SAM SPURGEON
5D 2nd Unit Photography	JUUL VAN DER LAAN
D.I.T. / Boom / Wild Tracks	JUSTINIAN BUCKLEY
RED 2nd Unit Direction	STUART BIDDLECOMBE & JUSTINIAN BUCKLEY
Stills Photographer Skopelos	JOANNA HESELTINE
Unit Driver Athens	GRIGORIA KATSIKAROU
Location Finder	SAM McMULLEN

INTERVIEWEES
ATHENS

Nikos Cornelios
Martha Frangiadaki
Manolis Glezos
Christos Karakepelis
Valerie Kontakos

Antigone Lyberaki
Yannis Sakaridis
Petros Sevastikoglou
Theodoros Terzopoulos
Kostas Vaxevanis
Giorgos Vichas

INTERVIEWEES
PARIS

Étienne Balibar
Hélène Cixous
Martin McQuillan
Antonio Negri

90 ～ Credits

LONDON
Arthur I. Miller

RED / Camera Equipment	DIMITRIS STAMBOLIS / N-ORASIS
Production Advisor (Paris)	PASCALE LAMCHE
Translations	KATERINA IORDANOGLOU
	SUZY FOSTER
Additional Translation	SAM McMULLEN
Demonstration Footage Athens	KEN McMULLEN
'Antigone' Film Clip, Kind Permission	IOULIA MERMINGA
Legal Services for SCAPE	JAMES WARE
	HERMIONE ROSE WILLIAMS

Kingston University London

Finance Advisor	ANDREA WHITING
Insurance Advisor	JEANETTE BARRY
Music Supervisor	DAVID CUNNINGHAM

MUSICIANS
Orchestral music composed by Adrian Munsey
Arranged by Geoffrey Alexander and John Bell
Performed by the City of Prague Philharmonic Orchestra
Conducted by John Bell
and
The Medici Quartet
With Mary Scully (double bass) and Andy Crowley (trumpet)

Recorded at Bandarov Studios, Prague
and Abbey Road Studios, London
Engineered by Gareth Williams and Toby Wood

David Cunningham
Solo performance and compositions

The Cabinet of Living Cinema
Music written by Kieron Maguire, Camilo Tirado
& Francesca Ter-Berg
Music produced, recorded & mixed by Camilo Tirado
Kieron Maguire—Viola
Francesca Ter-Berg—Cello
Camilo Tirado—Percussion

SPECIAL THANKS TO
ATHENS
The Greek Film Archive / Professor Maria Komninou
Theatre Attis
Elleniko Metropolitan Clinic
Titania Hotel

Theatre of Neos Kosmos
Monetary Museum
Cyceon Café Elefsis

SKOPELOS

Restaurant Agnanti
Ioannis Andriotis
Café Aramis
Kyra Leni Bakery
Restaurant Blo
Dream Cars
Magic Cars
Konstantakis
   Charalampos
Sukey Fenwick
Taverna Filsvos
Eleni Giannopoulou
Moschoula
   Giannopoulou
Michael C.
   Hesseltine
Christine Holliday
Agios Ioannis

Ioanna-Maria
   Kantartzis
Ioannis Kantartzis
Mama Mia Kiosk
Evangelia
   Koliopoulou
Charalambos
   Konstantakis
Georges Kostopoulos
Eliana Koumnioti
Ismene Koumnioti
Vassilis Kukorinis
Maria Kyriakaki
Port Authority
   Loutraki
Giorgos Michelis
Ioannis Palaiohogos
Father Alexios
   Papastamoulos

Café Bar Petrino
Argyris Polychroniou
Eleni Polychroniou
Kostas Polychroniou
Nina Polychroniou
Vagelis Polychroniou
Argyris Polychronis
Hotel Selenunda
Andromachi
   Stamatakis
Nikos Stamatakis
Nikos Triantafyllou
Dimitrios Tsaknis
Taverna Vagelis
Zafiroula Varlami
Dimitris Vogiatzakis

PARIS
Hotel La Louisiane / Monica and Staff
LONDON
Kingston University London
Prof. Armand D'Argan
Legal Café
Gernot Fuhrmann / Audiotactics Sound Design
Beatriz Gómez Navarro
Ram Tripathi Samaveda

Filmed on location in Athens, Paris, London and

Memories, Dreams, Ghosts and Friends

Free Associations on the Making of a Feature Film

Ken McMullen

'OXI' *is the word for 'No' in Greek. OXI is also a sign of resistance, painted on walls and monuments. It has reappeared for centuries in times of crisis and of occupation in Greece and is now appearing again.*

Prologue: Who Is Directing What?

Creativity is frightening. It involves long periods of being lost and then found again. It would have been impossible to fully script a film like OXI. Events were changing fast in Athens, and many different perspectives were being offered on the nature of the 'Crisis'. OXI would not be a documentary but would fuse fact and fiction to give us a view into the internal life of Greeks as well as the economic and political realities. There were some constant points of reference for the film. As a starting point, OXI would draw on the Theban plays of 400 BC, and scenes from these would be adapted to reflect the contemporary political conditions. The city of Athens itself would be a physical text both in its historic buildings and in its newly painted radical graffiti. In contrast, the Aegean island of Skopelos would be used for the filming of the classical scenes.

In the making of any film or art work of depth, the meaning of the work can only be a set of hazy concepts, changing as the process develops. In spite of all protestations, machinations and pretentions, preconceptions don't work. Likewise, the person living through great social and historical events is rarely aware of the significance or movements of changes beneath the surface. For the artist, consciousness is limited to a fraction of what we can know about our times and our work. Perhaps the best we can hope for is to draw on the enormous reservoirs of unconscious material and energy and, if we are lucky, to merge this with, and underscore, the consciously proposed 'departure point' (the intentions behind the work).

Often it is the accidental happening that gives a view of what is going on beneath the surface. Something seems to be going wrong; but is it, or is it merely challenging our initial idea? All creative endeavours must be open to incorporating the 'positive accident' and to allowing the process itself to be our guide. It is inherent in any medium that resistance will refuse the imposition of a fully formed concept upon it. As with the medium of politics, so with the medium of film. In the words of the great Sam Beckett, 'You can ask an author the intention of the work but you cannot ask the meaning'.

The free associations written here come from many of the complex, contradictory and mostly unspoken considerations and inspirations behind the film. Some are deadly serious in their intent. Others vary between the sublime and the ridiculous, between actual events and fictions, between historical truth and the psychic truth experienced by those deeply involved. They may offer the viewer some unusual insights into the making of *OXI: An Act of Resistance*.

Political and philosophical intentions:
- *OXI* will be a film that would respond to the crisis in Greece. It should support the Greek working class against perceived injustice.
- *OXI* must be a radical film not just in content but also in form. To be built using many different registers of content (windows within windows), these to include: Fiction in the form of dramatic reconstructions of Classical Tragedy; Actuality footage; a Chorus of Citizens; Narration and Commentary; Poetry and Evocation; a Dream framework within the drama; a Series of silent portraits of Greek workers who helped on the film.

- *OXI* would not submit to conventional rules of cinema but would work in an organic way with its material. The film was to use a montage of styles to strike a blow both at preconceptions and political conditioning.
- The aim will be to give insight into the existential reality of human existence in times of crisis.
- *OXI* would contain many archaeological and cultural references. These to be planted . . . embodied in the work. But they should not be 'in your face', self-conscious cleverness. *OXI* should offer the viewer the chance to be their own investigator. Travelling beneath the surface of the manifest narrative to discover primary elements for themselves. For example, we will use Schliemann's house in Athens with all its signifiers, the ancient sea route to Troy, the prehistoric fort of Selenunda and its imperial Roman ruins. The film should offer the possibility to touch treasures and concepts that, for the most part, are out of reach. There would be echoes of Jacques Derrida, Sigmund Freud and Karl Marx, among others.

Cinematic and technical intentions:
- The film would be shot using a high-end 4K digital camera for the main shoot—this in contrast to my general approach in previous films where 35mm and 16mm were the chosen forms. We would exploit, interrogate and take advantage of the opportunities offered by digital shooting.
- The final print/DCP was to be 2K resolution. Due, however, to the 4K origination of the material, it would be possible to exploit the advantage of allowing for movement within the frame during postproduction. The edit would therefore be both temporal and spatial. The surface area of the image would allow for tracks and repositioning within the 4K visual field. The time restraints and the terrain of the locations would in any case have made it impossible to set tracks and crane positions.
- Prime lenses would be from earlier analogue days in cinema. We acquired a set of Super Baltars Primes (lenses from Pinewood Studios of the kind used on such films as *The Godfather*). Adaptor would be used on the 'Red Three' that was to be the main camera.

This aimed to give the visual field a more integrated look towards the look of 35mm cinema.
- Actuality shots would be introduced using material that would be drawn from street footage I had shot using a small pocket-sized Canon camera . . . these to be integrated into the main drama. We would have a textural mix in the final film. But how would it work and what would we find?

Acting, style and narration intensions:
- There must be various styles of acting in OXI, drawing on deep traditions and techniques.
- Greek actors will open OXI with a scene from Sophocles's Antigone—a primary scene about dictatorship in which Creon is critized by his son Haemon for exercising blind use of power in sentencing Antigone to death. Creon's determined use of power will be spoken straight to the camera, directly out to us 'mere mortals' of the audience. The scene would be performed as a string of monologues, each character encased in their separate realities ignoring the other's arguments. It is a scene that has been played out throughout history by tyrants, dictators and their like. Comrades . . . Watch this scene more than once if you can . . . Allow it to unleash its power . . . Do not blink . . . Breath deeply . . . Stare into Creon's eyes . . . You have seen him before . . . 'The stranger and the enemy . . . You've seen him in the mirror'. Ah! So Plato sneaks in.

In the work with actors, I will reflect on the great mystery of transference. Reflect on the story of Polus, the slave, who during the fifth century BC emerged out of slavery to become one of the greatest actors of ancient Athens. He was famed for playing Electra, and it was reported that on his last performance, at the age of seventy, he had affected the audience in a strange and disturbing way . . . A great sense of grief . . . A terrifying sense of loss . . .The scene concerned the death of a child. Though Polus had played the role many times before, on this day he had projected something extraordinary onto the audience. When asked how this had been done, he is reported to have explained that that night was the anniversary of his own child's death and he had had this child's ashes placed in an urn, a prop in the production, as an act of remembrance. Without any obvious reference to this fact, his performance had silently passed on his own pain to the audience.

I also reflect on Socrates, who had interpreted the power of an actor's transference as the actor being captured by the author's text so profoundly that evocation was at work beneath the words. Ah!!! Greek wisdom. Can such transference be brought about in *OXI* when shooting the Greek scenes?

A different approach to the playing of the classical tragedies would involve British and French actors who would take us into a sharp use of naturalism. Their exchanges, persuasions, judgements and consequences should produce a different sense of reality to the Greek scenes. These scenes would be played out among undisturbed locations, ancient in themselves, appropriate settings for these mythical texts. As with Polus's prop, the locations themselves would weave their spell and act as another 'concrete' text beneath the manifest dialogue. The French actor Dominique Pinon would bind the elements of the film's different narrative registers together by improvising his way through splinter scenes where he will investigate the courses and causes of the Greek financial crisis and search out its most contentious issue . . . **'Who owes what to who'?**

And so Comrades . . . Money scarce, time limited, travel complicated, we must begin. ADVANCE . . . **ADVANCE** . . . We must make it now for if it is not done now, it never will. There will only be 12 shooting days, the maximum the budget allows. They would be: Athens 3 days, Paris 2 days, Skopelos 6 days, London 1 day. The full meaning of this intense engagement with technique, myth and reality would become clear and brought to light through the processes involved in the making of the film. Remember Comrades . . . that while we embrace myth we are not mystics . . . Not 'Consciousness before Being', as Hegel proposed but 'Being before Consciousness', as the great Karl proposed turning Hegel's dialectic on its head. Indeed how conscious can a director be in such a situation?

SIDE NOTE: Of course, much of these thoughts must remain unspoken. To begin, people who are supporting the film must trust that there will be a concrete result. A work that will be able to reach out to an audience as a resolved piece of cinema . . . We were lucky. The backers and particularly the executive producer were cool.

Part 1: Alternating Perspectives

'So . . . All this really does exist' . . .
'What I see here is not real'. . .

When Freud first visited the Acropolis in Athens in 1904, he reports that he was struck by an uncanny sensation of alienation, a fleeting, transitional sense of reality which both disturbed and puzzled him and which, for the next thirty-two years, he relegated to the back of his mind. Recovering the 'memory', he finally commented on this in an open letter to Romain Rolland in January 1936, giving it a title, 'Disturbance of Memory'. Whether Freud's 1936 account of the sequence of the incident bore any likeness to the 1904 experience seems unlikely since all memory has the quality of being the recall of something that did not take place . . . (A fact that Freud himself was well aware of and that Jacques Derrida had discussed in depth in my earlier film—*Ghost Dance*). Nevertheless, Freud's dual, contradictory statement strikes powerfully all who find themselves confronting things that are both happening in front of their eyes and that should not be happening. All external situations are layered with many alternating perspectives. In the economic world, we all know what money is, but economists cannot agree. We all know what borrowing and lending is, but political and historical analysis tells us we don't have a clue.

'Who owes Who What? Does Debt exist or is it not real?' Only the most pedantic among us can state their absolute conviction on issues of money, debt and indebtedness. For the rest of us, muddling through from day to day, knowing and not knowing . . . the most human of experiential dilemmas . . . the comprehension of such things is transitory and forever changing through an internal dialectical process that often translates things into their opposite.

So . . . In his memory of that moment standing on the Acropolis in Athens back in 1904, Freud thirty-two years later is recalling a memory of something that did not actually take place but which nevertheless brought to consciousness the extraordinary insight into the way we perceive the reality of the world around us . . . assuming, that is, that it is possible to perceive objective reality at all without intervening projections and filters of prejudice.

As a note, it is worth commenting that Freud came to the conclusion that his sense of disturbance had resulted from the fact that he had surpassed his own father in his travels, achieving something that his father could only dream of (i.e., standing on one of the great monuments of the ancient world and confirming that it really did exist).

In Freud's late work *Beyond the Pleasure Principle*, he goes on to offer an insight that is perhaps more disturbing to our understanding of 'crisis'. In this work, he opens a door to disturbing perennial motivations always active within each individual and within the greater social organism—an insight ignored in general economic and political analysis. Freud concludes that deeper instinctual forces in the human psyche are in permanent conflict . . . directed far beyond our consciousness by irresistible historic forces, instincts of Libido and Thanatos . . . The battle is between the 'Life Instinct' and the 'Death Instinct' and inevitably it is the 'Death Instinct' that always wins in the end . . . returning us finally to our previous, long lost, inorganic state . . . Ah!!! 'Exist . . . Not Real'. Yes indeed . . . All preordained? Ah!!!

But Thanatos in the ancient world was the bringer of a peaceful death while the other, more frightening Gods, came to give us more dreadful ends. Now, there are no Gods, there are only the Banks . . . And out of dark recesses of the auditorium, accompanied with a mighty clash of symbols 'strutting and fretting their hour upon the stage' . . . Dressed in fine suits and designer dresses . . . We present for your consideration . . . **The Troika** . . .

Yes . . . Like a bunch of walking cutthroat razors. There is something not of Thanatos, but of the murderer, in the way Greek history and the depth and magnificence of Greek culture is being repressed by this shoddy chorus of self-assured 'economists'. With a look of 'consideration' on their punitive faces, they announce to the powerless of Europe their favourite maxim, '**Austerity**'. . . 'Lost Territory' . . . 'Sterility' . . . 'You all must pay' . . .

F. . . . .rs
'So . . . All this really does exist' . . .
'What I see here is not real' . . .

In April 2012, following a retrospective of my work at the Greek Film Archive and, following through on some thoughts of staging the Theban plays, I was staying in Athens and had climbed the Acropolis once again to sit and look out over the troubled city. The city that was now suffering, not plagues or invasion as it had done for over 2,500 years, but the full force of a program of economic emasculation . . . . Ah!!! That name again '**Austerity**'. . . and the reply again . . . **F. . . . .rs**.

Down below that mighty rock, in Syntagma Square, there had been many demonstrations outside the Greek Parliament, and I had filmed some incidents on a small camera I often carry around with me. I had been close to an explosive incident when the television news van was blown up with a Molotov cocktail. (*That was close, Readers . . . a little too close . . .The shot though appears in the film as a major signifier.*) This day was different. As I walked back to the hotel, I moved through some small groups of quite depressed and quietly agitated people near the Square. Something on their faces brought Freud's comment, '*What I see here is not real*', to my mind. There was a look on people's faces that was different to the usual post-demonstration groupings. People seemed dazed and shocked. I noticed a young man with tears and asked him if he was okay. That was the first that I had heard about the suicide of Dimitris Christoulos, a pensioner and retired pharmacist, who shortly before had walked into Syntagma Square, apparently picking a relatively solitary spot, where he pulled out a gun and shot himself. On a note he left behind, he had written that he could not face the prospect of 'scavenging through garbage bins for food and of becoming a burden to my child'. Dimitris Christoulos had had serious health problems and, like many pensioners and unemployed in Greece since the imposition of 'Austerity', he struggled to pay for medicines . . .

Surely '*What I am hearing here is not real*'. But it was . . .

I had been witness to some of the effects of the 'Austerity' measures that were being imposed on Greece as I had travelled the country . . . 'So . . . All this really does exist' . . . I say to myself . . . 'Yes . . . *it really does exist Ken . . . It is not a film or a daydream . . . Many people here are suffering unjust and profound humiliation and depravation*'. Like many people here, I find myself questioning my own sense of reality. Of course, politicians, just like all individuals when facing crises, will find defence mechanisms to hide from awkward realities and to tell us that difficult realities do not really exist . . . Many of those suffering often hide in denial as the only defence against obliteration. In the midst of extreme deprivation, I have heard Greeks laugh. I have seen them shrug their shoulders and imply, 'So?' I have heard their songs in a small taverna out on the island and in the Ouzoris of Volos . . .

'What is going on here cannot be happening. What is taking place is not just'.
Readers, let us protect ourselves . . . These are difficult times, but do not become too depressed. There is more than one dimension to Greek life. Imagination dear Readers . . . Imagination. 'Mythistorema' in the words of the great George Seferis . . . Myth, History, Story all in one . . . Ah!!! Yes . . . MYTHISTOREMA . . . Yes please . . . Give us MYTHISTOREMA I hear you cry . . . Give them **MYTHISTOREMA** . . . And I reply . . . 'Come back Greek friends from the past . . . I miss your mischief and your stories . . . Don't be flattened by the situation. None of us are perfect little prefects, or want to be those self-satisfied Northern Europeans, or self-congratulatory little fascists . . . As for me . . . I want to sit with you . . . There . . . Share your imagination . . . For what is life without imagination? . . . In the words of a young nine-year-old critic . . . 'A blank page'. . .
So . . . raise your spirits and celebrate imagination. Do not let the Troika, the politicians or the bankers steal your own sense of 'Being'. To change the mood of this text, here are some accounts of strange encounters on journeys of discovery in an Athens of previous years. Yes . . . Athens existed even before the Troika. The Athens of adventures and wonderful misdemeanours that still can be found behind the pain. Go to Greece dear Readers and spend some dough. You will meet some remarkable people. It will cheer you up, and you will help your fellow human beings.

Part 2: The Rock and the Acropolis . . .

Some years before.
Now . . . There are those that say it arrived fully intact from outer space . . . This weird historical fact was confirmed and stated with absolute conviction, after a number of glasses of ouzo, by a Greek friend of

mine back in 1981. A man of poetry and loud pronouncements, he had insisted on his preference of the Doric column over the Corinthian. 'The Doric points directly to the heavens' he said, demonstrating this by setting fire to variously shaped rolled-up paper serviettes and watching how high they flew. **WOW** . . . They fly . . . they really fly . . . Up into the night sky, dancing and swirling above the city along with our hopes and simple dreams. 'Health and Safety' I hear the EC Commissioners shout . . . 'Health and Safety . . . You cannot do that . . . No you cannot send fire into the Athens air' . . . 'Want to bet'? . . . **Whoosh**.

Having won this architectural debate with himself, he then, with added gravitas, moved on to his belief that the Aegean Sea, the 'wine red sea' (*where during later years traditional fishing boats would be ordered to be destroyed as part of an EC 'Rationalisation' directive*) was deeper than the Ionian Sea. The water was both purer and definitely Greek. His new subject of debate being demonstrated by pouring glasses of water over his and anybody else's head within reach. I caught a few drops, but I was not as wet as our American friend who had one glass poured down the front of his shirt and the other down the back as he sat staring straight ahead like a dope, soaked on the inside with ouzo and soaked on the outside by the mighty Aegean and Ionian Seas . . . Poor Fred, not quick enough to get out of the way, now sitting with a dumb look on his face which said 'Parents . . . why did you send me to this crazy country . . . they are all poets' . . . *Sit back, dear Reader, the water stays in the story and there is more* . . . Ah!!! Now . . . The real action . . . Sound, Camera, **CLAP**, **ACTION** . . . Gathering a pile of plates and reciting Seferis's 'Argonauts', the plates started to fly . . . **Crash** . . . **Crash** . . . Trying to rise and climb on the table with more plates in his hand, our dear friend fell off his chair and sat in poetic shock, a startled look across his chops, before shouting from the floor in an urgent mixture of Greek and English, pointing at the distant Acropolis . . . '**ZEUS** . . . Help . . . it moved . . . By the swinging sword and the wafting wings of mighty Zeus himself, it moved' . . . 'I swear it moved' . . .

Slowly rising from the floor, staring straight ahead his head tilted on one side and ignoring us mortals around the table, our friend sallied off alone in a deep philosophical stupor . . . out he wandered into those darkened, haunting streets of the Plaka and for a while his voice could be heard fading in the distance . . . 'It moved' . . . 'It moooooved' 'By the swinging sword of mighty Zeus' . . . (A phrase remembered long after our friend's name was forgotten.) Yes . . . There he went off into the blanket of that warm and sensual Athenian night his voice audible for a while . . . 'Moooooved' . . . 'Mooooving' . . . On he marched, imaginary swinging sword in hand, till the lights were turned out in the taverna and the ancient streets returned to silence . . . I had learnt a lot . . . Seferis was to have a profound influence on me along with Cavafy and I learnt that plates were for breaking. I learnt about the mighty mythical seas around Greece. I still remember his lesson in Greek architecture and its pillars. 'Jesus I love this country' I thought. Where are you now dear friend? Did you ever get home? I want to hear again your poetic pronouncements . . . I can take the water and dodge the flying serviettes but I want to keep learning . . .

On the same streets now, people are rummaging through garbage bins for food. Store windows are boarded. Occasional Molotov cocktails fly where once only burning serviettes rose into the sky . . . But Myth still emerges . . . 'Give us MYTHISTOREMA'. You cry, . . . 'Don't scare us or depress us . . . Do not dwell on financial figures . . . We do not care . . . Fuck the debt . . . What about the debt owed to Greece? . . . To the poets and playwrights . . . Down with financial straightjackets . . . Give us our **MYTHISTOREMA**'.

'Give us libido', the Readers cry . . . 'Enough of Thanatos and of melancholy . . . Give us fantasy, enough of reality. We are fed up of being told financial facts' . . . 'Readers and viewers . . . Directors should not fantasize. Film is a technical artwork on a massive scale . . . Directors should never stop thinking about the way the film can be brought to resolution . . . Directors cannot know this in advance as has already been pointed out but they must appear to have the answers. They can daydream but must not get too immersed in fantasy . . . they should always know the difference . . . Reality is a dreadful teacher, dear Readers, but here now, staring out at the Athens of 2013, I daydream back to another earlier encounter and one more detour to take us back to happier times . . . Yes, . . . let us bring back Eros . . . Bring back Magic, Myth and Story . . . Ah!!! **MYTHISTOREMA**'.

I have been told more than once that the giant rock on which the Acropolis sits emanates strange electrical fields out of its very core. They say it has rays that can push a couple into a passionate sexual frenzy without inhibition (*a statement I was earnestly told by a young German woman who loved Athens, a naturalist, who professed to be not only a serious trigonometrist, but also a leading expert in rays, electricity, levitation and such matters*).

'I hate Nazis', she said. 'I am going to make reparations for the terrible Nazi occupation' she whispered as she demonstrated her naturalness to the Acropolis . . . She knew her history and her politics . . . She was a stunning activist, and what she said she meant. . . Ah!!! The thought of it . . . Yes . . . Mein Liebling . . . I believe you . . . I always will . . . Down with the swastika . . . Rip it to bits . . . I see the rays . . . Tell me again and lets repeat the whole scene Mein Lieber . . . You are not to blame for those Nazi fuckers . . . You are here with me . . . Ah!!! Lovely . . . **Hold it** . . . **CUT** . . . Stop right there . . . Really Ken . . . I mean **REALLY**. . . **SLAP** (author is slapped) . . . 'This is a serious book . . . You are a director. Directors must stick to the script and the rules of cinema . . . **CLOSE UP; LONG SHOT; DON'T CROSS THE LINE**. You are also an academic. For the sake of Zeus himself, and all his swinging swords, **MAKE SENSE**' . . . 'I know . . . I know . . . OK . . . Sorry' . . . But that was back in 1992. Now it's 2015 . . . It probably never happened . . . Honest . . . Though for some reason I do keep being drawn back to that city and that country, and I do still know some German words'.

The Acropolis . . . Oh yes!!! It was true . . . Where, with total impertinence, for a short time during the Second World War, the swastika had indeed flown. Yes . . . Right there . . . The arrogant fascist invader had imagined it would fly for 1,000 years. . . **F. . . . .rs** . . . Before being ripped down by a real contemporary Greek hero of ours, Manolis Glezos. He must appear in the film . . . He doesn't have to tell that story for he doesn't like to tell of his own heroics, but he will tell us other moving accounts . . . Of his comrades . . . Of their dreams . . . Of their desires . . . And of their deaths.

So . . . bringing us back to concrete reality . . . The Rock has been there since times immemorial and the Acropolis was built by mortal men, men who in the ancient world assumed that in some distant future, it would still be there to help us and to ease our simple fears . . . There to tell us . . . Yes . . . don't be afraid . . . We were once here too and now we watch over you . . . And when you feel lost and very much

alone, always remember the wisdom of the Oracle . . . 'Know yourself'
. . . 'All things in balance' . . . 'Nothing in excess' . . . Yes . . . Yes . . .
I will try . . . Honest . . . And the film . . . Can a film strip away the
conditioning processes that we are all subject to? Give us fresh insight.
Allow us to breathe and our imaginations to work on the material?
Can a film manage to bring together the contradictory parts of our own
selves, our daydreams, angers, desires and fears? Ah!!!

Part 3: Justification and Self-Delusion

The justification offered by our self-important economic wizards for
their attack on the working people of Greece was that the Greek working
class **'deserved it'** . . . Easy? Hey? Why it's their fault . . . They are
not like us you know . . . They are **untrustworthy** . . . Just look at the
charges of corruption and Greek irresponsibility that were being constantly
bandied about by the press in Europe . . . **But**, I can testify to
the work and generosity that I have seen in Greece, the people working
on the subway and buses of Athens and Thessalonica, in the shops and
cafés, in the universities, in the Film Archive in Athens, in the workshops
of Volos, on the ships and in the fields . . . So **I don't believe you.**

What about asking . . . 'Who gave and who took the loans in the
first place that have bankrupted the country?' Loans taken on behalf
of a people who had no say in the negotiations and in many cases
received no benefit . . . I have heard all the counter arguments to my
position such as 'The Greeks are all corrupt . . . It is part of the culture,
they will never change' . . . The endless stream of repetitive arguments
keeps being bandied around but I stand firm I say . . . **'OK F. . . .rs** . . .
If this were so and you knew that then . . . **Why give the loans in the
first place'?**

At this point there is an interruption from a member of the audience . . . 'McMullen, you are an apologist for Greek irresponsibility. It
is clear that you yourself are an irresponsible artist/filmmaker and you
identify with them . . . But we can tell you from experience . . . They
are all born liars.'

I respond by saying the first thing that comes into my head . . . 'You
may be right that I identify with my Greek friends . . . but . . . Remember
this you priggish prat . . . You continue to confuse imagination with

fabrication . . . Why should the Greeks suddenly adapt your puritanical point of view? It is your lot that are projecting your destructive envy onto a people that you imagine have achieved a better quality of life than you . . . You are pathologically jealous of their poetry and their philosophy'.

'Typical of you and your weird version of economics and politics tinged with Freudian, Marxist, Anarchist, Free Association Thinking' the interrupter shouts.

'Fuck Off' I shout back. 'And Fucker . . . It is no good calling me names since I do not belong to any organization nor do I follow any dogma . . . unlike you Fuck-brain . . . a so-called Free Market operator when there is no free market . . . a self-justifier when there is no justice . . . a fabricator of facts for your own convenience . . . Yes Fucker . . . But let's look more closely, and then we will be forced to ask . . . **Who are the liars now?**'

Someone whispers in the director's ear . . . 'I don't know if we can give you money for this film given your approach to the subject and your delinquent attitude.'

EDITOR'S NOTE: *Hold on . . . Relax . . . Take five dear Readers. The film will be made and the director will take a deep breath and try not to swear for a while. But it is hard when he thinks of the self-entitlement of the European ruling class . . . He will offer some other counter insights into Greek mischief. For there has probably always been mischief . . . Mixed with a bit of* **'MYTHISTOREMA'**.

It is plain to see that the burden was falling not on the elites and oligarchs who had moved substantial amounts of their money out of the country but on the working people of Greece. In some cases it became clear that many of the debts had been induced by collusion, pure criminality, deals done with other European partners and their companies . . . often offering large accompanying payoffs in Swiss accounts. Can it really be so simple? Surely the world is more complex, but there it is . . . 'So . . . All this really does exist' . . .

Part 4: The Context, the Drama and the Ghosts

'Why fear the future,' says Jocasta in *Oedipus Rex* . . . 'Not a man alive knows a day ahead. Live for today' . . . Now . . . Simultaneously, I had been hearing on the streets of Athens, Thessalonica, Volos, and on the ships going out to the islands phrases and words, along with uncanny explanations, that seemed to come out of a distant past and directly from the Classical Tragedies of ancient Athens . . . There it goes again . . . 'Not a man alive knows a day ahead' said a group of seamen working on the ferry boat out to Skopelos . . . This was the island that was to offer many of the ancient settings for the film . . . Walking among us the ghosts of characters written long ago . . . It was as if an ancient chorus was returning trying to explain the ongoing, bewildering events . . . 'Cinema' is a machine that allows us to see death at work' writes the great Jean Cocteau. A technical Thanatos not to be ignored.

So . . . *OXI* is not a historical documentary but more a product of political and cultural engagement. It will take advantage of evolving events, texts and reflections from a 'history of the mind' compared with those of purely cause and effect. In the words of the mighty but rarely read Jacob Burckhardt, who, writing about Greece back in the 1890s, so influenced Freud himself . . . 'Historical accounts are frequently uncertain, controversial, coloured or, given the Greek talent for lying, entirely the invention of imagination or self-interest'. Evocation then has the potential to make contact with 'material conveyed in an unintentional, disinterested, or even involuntary way by sources and monuments; they betray their secrets unconsciously and even paradoxically through fictitious elaborations, quite apart from the material details'. (*Burckhardt 1898–1902, recounted by Richard H. Armstrong in his book* A Compulsion for Antiquity.)

Freud maintained to the end of his life a distinction between 'material truth' and 'psychic truth' and if such a film as *OXI* is to have value, it must also draw on these two aspects of 'truth'. Indeed, as we approach the critical issue of the financial collapse of Greece, it is necessary to draw on alternating perspectives of reality and to learn from the alternating truths first brought to human consciousness in the Greek Tragedies in the great amphitheatres of the distant past. We must reach out with our twenty-first-century medium to reveal these contradictions in a new light. The mesmerizing, mysterious medium of **CINEMA**.

Part 5: Cinema

QUESTIONS:
What form could such a cinematic response take to 'History' in the making?
What kind of film can this be?
Should a film act as propaganda or should it simply inform if that is possible?
What is this thing called 'Cinema' . . . And yes . . . In a Lacanian interpretation we will think of the word itself . . . 'Cinema' . . . 'Sinema' . . . 'Anima'?
'Cinema . . . Here is a mechanism for producing history. This story is psychological and individual . . . in the sense that I project myself into what I watch, but at the same time it's also collective. Cinema has the role of arranging individuals' stories into a collective story' . . .
'All human societies as a general rule invent a history that they never had . . . In others words . . . what counts is not the historic reality, it's the editing and the way I lay out the blocks of my past, to create what is after all a fiction. It can be a beautiful story . . . or it can be a bad one . . . because human beings only have a future, by fictionalizing it in relation to their past'.
(*Bernard Stiegler in discussion with Ken McMullen 2009*)
OXI must interrogate the nature of motion picture and story itself. Apart from evoking the great dramatic tragedies of 2,400 years ago, it would also include brief, but poignant, philosophical commentary . . . (Étienne Balibar, Hélène Cixous, Antonio Negri) to be inserted into the epic texts and sequences from the 'Tragedies'.
Additionally, current activist commentators from Greece would be given a platform in the film to take us deeper into what is the greatest living European drama of our times. These 'real' participants must merge with the fictional characters so that the boundary between them blurs. The unconscious will find utterance in these contemporary characters. The ghosts of historic figures will reemerge in their new costumes as journalists, political commentators, contemporary philosophers, and a detective, the prerequisite of any good investigation. Their 'analysis' will be our commentary . . . contentious, committed, unforgiving . . .

QUESTIONS:
Is commentary and narration the best way to advance political understanding? Must a film about such a crisis be so depressing?
While deadly in its critiques, the film must go further than pure journalism. It must draw up a subterranean text more akin to the novel than the newspaper . . . A borderline between fiction and reality in order to express a deeper reality . . . It must integrate flashes of humour and the absurd into this deeply disturbing political reality highlighting the multifaceted nature and fragility of the human condition, not just in Greece, but also in all places that are vulnerable to blind economic forces . . .
The developing work will not be a sound bite or a piece of the evening news . . . It must scrape away the veneer of academic and bourgeois commentary and take us deeper into the nature of these events, seeing them as symptoms of an interplay between unconscious historic and contemporary social forces, the fusion of which is releasing an unexpected energy of resistance . . . *OXI*

Part 6: Precedents

It is inevitable that a director will always draw on earlier screenplays for inspiration, in spite of aiming for complete originality, for these are latent in the fabric of his own history of making films. Think of all the people as characters. Some of them real and some pure fiction. Draw on theory and literature such as on Sophocles, Shakespeare, Bulgakov, Pushkin, Dickens, Gogol, and the many others who have left their trace. Draw on those too with whom you disagree. Yes, on the remarkable Fukuyama and other advanced capitalist thinkers . . . even those. Read theory lightly, though there is however no economist worth reading who hasn't him- or herself read Marx . . . Held the dialectic . . . Grasped its power . . . Thesis, Antithesis, Synthesis . . . Pure Greek poetry . . . Yes . . . Greek . . . Marx is one of the few who saw all economic systems as transitory . . . Tribalism . . . Feudalism . . . Capitalism . . . And then??? . . . Fuck what's next? . . . Corporatism? Monopoly Capitalism? Fascism? Why did you leave us, Karl, when you had only finished the first volume of the nine you intended? Why did you get distracted? Now we have to complete them ourselves . . . Help . . . We don't like the dark . . . Reach out to us Karl . . . Put down the old pint pot, leave the maids alone, stop watching Arsenal. We need your guiding light. Not some fuck-faced Stalinist and not some self-appointed wizard of the free market . . . We need some facts on which to base our fictions . . . Tell us again, Karl, that great text of yours and put it into perspective . . . Readers do not be afraid . . . It is not a stranger breaking in . . . it is the spectre of Marx approaching.

Out of the blue the ghost of Marx appears to the writer and in a voice ringing with gravitas:

'Men make their own history, McMullen, but they do not make it as they please; they do not make it under self-selected circumstances, but under circumstances existing already, given and transmitted from the past. The tradition of all dead generations weighs like a nightmare on the brains of the living'. Thank you, Karl . . . (*Readers, that was Marx's,* Eighteenth Brumaire of Louis Bonaparte *[1852] spoken to me on 20 March 2015*).

Phew!!! To think of it . . .

Christ, this text is getting crowded. Here comes Fukuyama. Here comes Galbraith. They are all coming for their moment on the stage . . . Knock. Knock . . . Quiet Readers . . . Be seated . . . Who is this? By Zeus, it is Leon himself dropping out of my last screenplay and whispering in my ear . . . Readers please bear with me as I recall the lion-like Leon's great speech. Direct from 'THE SOLOIST', another of my unmade films . . . There are lots . . . One day dear Reader when we have thrown off our chains, they will all be made. Yes. And you will be first to see them. But how difficult it is for us mortals to see the historic process. Give him your ears . . .

TROTSKY
(Ringing with gravitas)
The Laws of History have nothing in common with simple cause and effect—unevenness is the most general law of the historic process. The historic process is a natural process, full of contradictions, ebbs and flows—it is built on tremendous reservoirs of energy, and when the conditions fuse it sends all who stand in its way into the ashes of time. (Beat.) The masses learn to handle the fire of revolution by burning their hands and jumping away. Revolutions take place according to

certain laws. This does not mean the masses in action are aware of the laws of revolution, but it does mean that changes in mass consciousness are not accidental. It is this that makes prophecy possible.

And now they have returned, these ghosts of reason past, what a shallow lot these contemporary leading economists appear to be. Ah!!! Here comes dear old Uncle Engels. Speak Uncle . . . The Readers are holding their breath. Speak Spectre.

'All great world-historic facts and personages appear, so to speak, twice.

The first time as tragedy, the second time as farce'.

Well done, Uncle Engels . . . 'Goodbye Fuckers' we say out loud to the Troikas of the world. 'You will soon only appear now as farce'.

Now that's off my chest I am almost ready for the film. But hold on dear Readers . . . One more association has popped into my head which may explain more . . . I was once told by the great drama teacher Jack Garfein that all the scenes, the whole drama and all the whole works of Shakespeare pass through our daydreams in one form or another in any one day . . . In ONE DAY. All of them appear . . . Coriolanus, Brutus, Cassius, the Richards, the Henrys, Hamlet, even some extras, here comes the Master, the Margarita and all the 'Dead Souls'. They seep through in disguise affecting our continuing relationship to the external world . . . Desire, Murder, Fear, Regality, Revolution, Always there . . . We know them all. Fuck . . . Help . . . Karl . . . KARL.

Part 7: The Director

'You want accuracy, but not representation. If you know how to make the figuration, it doesn't work. Anything you can make, you make by accident'. 'I want a very ordered image, but I want it to come about by chance'. (*Francis Bacon*)

Is there actually a director for any film, or are directors being directed unknown to themselves and if so by what? Can this be defined? Why must we pretend that everything is conscious from the beginning? I never fixed the result when painting. I have had some very insightful teachers: Heinz Koppel, Bill Clark, Bill Coldstream, Marion Milner, Joseph Beuys, Stuart Brisley, Tadeusz Kantor and Francis Bacon among many others. They taught me to work with the process and not be captured by preconception. Sounds easy, but it is a far more difficult task than at first appears. Some living, some dead, I converse with them, in my thoughts as I approach the film. I won't be able to discuss this with anyone around me, but there it is. Silently, as they pass by I reach out and ask for guidance and strength. They reply firmly and the work continues.

'In my case all painting is an accident. I foresee it and yet I hardly ever carry it out as I foresee it. It transforms itself by the actual paint. I don't in fact know very often what the paint will do, and it does many things which are very much better than I could make it do.' (*Francis Bacon*)

A filmmaker, who is not shooting 'by numbers', like the painter, who is not painting by numbers, can only guess at what the end result will be. What sequence will work best where, and what meanings will montage release? What edited scenes will fall to the cutting room floor? What to do with each actor's performance? Obvious things like how to adapt to the demands of changing weather? What meanings are being discovered as the film and its many processes develop? What is film if not the process of forming a piece of concrete thought?

Perhaps the only answerable question a Director can be asked . . . Are you positioned with your resources to advance the project and to see it through to resolution?

OXI: An Act of Resistance was not going to be an easy film to make and, because it radically crosses boundaries of genre, it will not be an easy film to describe in a world that largely demands categorization and conformity. The quest is to find a new and radical sympathetic cinematic form. A form that will allow the audience to draw up into consciousness their own unconscious theatre. By placing both classical tragedy and contemporary politics into a single dramatic journey, we will pass through time and location seemingly finding echoes and precedents in events that happened long ago. There will be moments when choices are made. Taking the initiative on decisions is the only point of freedom a director has.

'All painting is an accident. But it's also not an accident, because one must select what part of the accident one chooses to preserve'. (*Francis Bacon*)

So . . . Some things **are** conscious then . . . But who are our characters? How do we know them? Let's return in time to a discussion in Paris in 1993.

Part 8: Conversation: 1993, KM with Jacques Derrida

Twenty years ago in 1993 I had been producing a play in London, an adaptation of Sophocles's three Theban plays. In the course of preparation, I had talked in Paris with Jacques Derrida with whom I had previously worked. We had previously discussed ghosts and unconscious communication but would now focus on the reinterpretation of Oedipus . . . Meetings were established and the discourse filmed. The idea was to incorporate Derrida's answers directly into the play projected onto large sails positioned above the stage. Actors, sometime using dance and mime, would freeze as the short inserts from Derrida appeared. Here is what he said printed in the dialogue form spoken at the time. Read it as script. Pause for '(*Beat)*'.

Abstracts from transcripts of a day with Jacques Derrida:

KM
   I have a question to ask you Jacques.

JACQUES DERRIDA
   Sure . . .

KM
   Let me use the present tense . . .
   (*Beat*)
   Who is Oedipus?

JACQUES DERRIDA
   Ah!!!

(*Beat*)
   In order to interpret Oedipus cinematographically, we have to know how (as either object or subject) we are going to play Oedipus.

(Beat)
   For example, if I say:
   'I am Oedipus' . . .
   Such a reply to the question:
   'Who is Oedipus?'
   must be economical for the purposes,
   and constraints . . . of Cinema . . .
   Yet it must be provocative
   at the same time . . . It must provoke you.
   What I am referring to, when I say:
   'I am Oedipus'. . .
   is not only the narcissistic 'I/me',
   but also the 'I/me' in general.
   Whoever says 'I/me' will have
   had the Oedipus experience . . .
   the experience of seeing . . .
   What he should not have seen.

(Beat)
   Now, as you know, cinema started
   at the same time as psychoanalysis . . .
   and Benjamin has some very
   strong statements about this,
   i.e., that for some unfortuitous reasons,
   Cinema shares the same . . .
   contemporary birth date
   as Psychoanalysis.
   Which means that, at a time
   when Psychoanalysis . . .
   or . . . in fact Freud, made the
   Oedipus paradigm . . .
   in Greek tragic theatre . . .
   (a major reference for Psychoanalysis) . . .
   Freud probably didn't realize that Oedipus'
   place was not in fact the theatre,
   but the Cinema . . . not the Cinema of today . . .
   The Cinema of the future.

Certainly not even the Cinema of the
beginning of the 19th century, and
not the cinema of today, but tomorrow.
That is where Oedipus' future lies.
And because of, or indeed thanks to,
the technology of cinema,
this Oedipus will probably no longer
resemble the Oedipus that we know,
and who has been interpreted
for centuries and centuries.
It's as if Oedipus had been waiting
for the arrival of the cinema,
in order to be able to say:
'I am the Cinema . . . I am the camera.

(Beat)
And, once again, this technical,
or technological, experience,
could be Oedipal, simply because, from
the start, the figure of Oedipus . . .
will have been a figure of
interiorisation, or subjectification.

(Beat)
Oedipus is the moment when man
develops his own conscience . . .
and is able to make his
own identifications,
thanks to his memory . . .
which is an internal process . . .

(Beat)
The blinding of Oedipus . . .
no longer being able to see . . .
is another internal relationship with oneself,
i.e., you no longer need an image . . .
Let's say that, in order

for man to say 'I/me',
he will have to be capable of
doing without the screen . . .
or, at least, to have an internal screen,
without the help of technology.

(Beat)
My dream is for Man to be
able to efface technology!

(Beat)
KM
Fuck . . . so Oedipus is really there.
Ready and waiting in the wings . . . Getting ready to pounce . . . ready to murder our psyches . . . waiting for his moment and his moment is coming . . .
Soon . . . Soon now . . . In his new dazzling costume . . .
The costume of 'Cinema' . . . the great Sin with an 'S' . . . Our seductive Anima . . . Sinbad himself.

(Beat)
Fuck . . . It scares me Jacques . . . It scares me.

(Beat)
JACQUES DERRIDA
It scares us all . . . All of us Ken.

Time code:10:03:49:00

KM
Jacques, I want to ask you about that other character that haunts our psyches.
Again Jacques I want to use the present tense.
Who is Antigone?

(Beat)
JACQUES DERRIDA
   As far as Antigone is concerned, man . . .
   Oedipus, me, the father, the brother . . .
   probably dreams of this
   'desire without desire' . . .

(Beat)
   It is so sublime,
   that he strives for what lies beyond desire
   or, at least what desire implies . . .
   the possibility of conflict . . .
   As Hegel said . . .
   A relationship without desire . . .
   Is probably a relationship which,
   although it doesn't abolish
   sexual differences,
   turns this difference into something
   other than opposition and conflict . . .
   . . . A totally pacified desire . . .

(Beat)
   This is probably what man dreams of . . .
   when he dreams of Antigone . . .
   She is the figure of
   rebellion against the state . . .
   And, mingled with this dream,
   is the dream of an Antigone
   who takes care of my death.

(Beat)
   She has already started
   to watch after me,
   in every sense of the word . . .
   So, I love Antigone . . .
   She is the priestess of my death . . .
   Which obviously makes Antigone . . .
   the other absolute . . .

(Beat)
    She is both the other absolute
    and my dream . . .

(Beat)
    So, to get back to what we
    were talking about earlier:
    The interior screen . . .
    The screen which is no longer outside . . .

(Beat)
    Antigone teaches me the impossible,
    i.e., . . . How I can love my death . . .
    How I can love the figure of my death . . .
    which is an impossible impossibility . . .
    And it's this impossibility that
    I love in the figure of Antigone . . .
    The impossible . . . possible . . .
    Which bears the name ANTIGONE . . .

Time code: 10:06:31:00

KM
    So there they are . . . Oedipus and Antigone . . .
    Stalking our psyches . . . Waiting . . . reaching out to us . . .
    How can we react? What can we say or do?
    Can we respond?
    Tell me what you make of this question . . .
    What is improvisation?

(Beat)
JACQUES DERRIDA
    Ah!!!
    Improvisation is the most difficult
    thing one can do.
    Even when one 'improvises' for
    the camera . . . or the microphone . . .

One is taken over . . .
Something else does the talking for us . . .
Something that is already
instilled in us . . .
That comes from the back of one's memory,
one's social and cultural conditioning.
The people we've already talked about:
Antigone, Tiresias, Oedipus . . .
are already instilled in our minds . . .
These names prevent us from improvising . . .

KM
Sure . . . I know this . . . I feel this straightjacket . . .
Can we speak spontaneously at all?

JACQUES DERRIDA
We can't say what we like . . .

KM
No . . . I know that . . . What a pity . . .

(Beat)
JACQUES DERRIDA
Ha . . . Apart from . . . An utterance . . . a slip . . .
a 'correct slip' . . .
We're obliged to reproduce stereotypical discourses . . .
Things that have been said and done before . . .

(Beat)
But, I do believe in improvisation . . .
I defend the right to try to improvise . . .
But with the feeling that . . . It is impossible.
Where improvisation exists . . .
I can't see myself . . .
I'm blinded to myself . . .
Only someone else can see me . . .

(Beat)
   At this moment . . .
   I can't see what is improvised here!
   10:07:59:00 (Number of minutes and frames)

The issue of originality, both in the acting and in the writing or speaking of texts, stalks the whole making of *OXI*. How can we play these scenes with originality? Do we see things for what they are? Are we so deeply preconditioned that we cannot see facts for facts and fictions for fictions? Given the film's subject, this may not be surprising. In acting out classical scenes, it is fairly obvious we are drawing on words and characters from long ago, but it was surprising hearing ancient texts come alive when shooting the actuality footage or in the 'interviews' with witnesses. So many references came to mind in the shooting of the film that often seem to have come from nowhere. References that must have sprung from deeply internalized and imprinted words. Even in the locations and the observation of concrete reality where the filming would take place, there seem to always be prompts at work. (*Remember at all times when shooting motion pictures that location is a primary text in itself.*)

It is difficult to see the Acropolis as a place outside of text, even when standing next to it or walking around inside its great pillars. Likewise sitting on the steps of Schliemann's house . . . (the house of Troy) . . . in central Athens. The sensation of 'Real' and 'not Real' so powerfully described by Freud can also be underscored by a variant written by Charles Dickens . . . 'Reality and Originality' . . . There is a story mentioned by Dickens about when he visited the ancient ruin of Hoghton Towers in Lancashire one 'sunny April day'. Dickens was exploring ideas on the position of narrator in his text 'George Silverman's Explanation'. He writes . . .

'Upon myself, it has made the strangest impression of reality and originality!!! I feel as if I had read something (by somebody else) which I should never get out of my head!!! It is very curious that I did not in the least see how to begin his (the narrator's) state of mind until that sunny April day' . . .
   Ah!!!

Readers . . . I hear you asking for dark secrets . . . unspoken and unspeakable . . . to the incest always present in cinema . . . to the gossip of the set . . . without ever forgetting all that incest in the original plays . . . Reflecting on the simple fact that on film sets since the beginning of motion pictures the question that stalks the set . . . excites, persists and causes chaos . . . 'Who is in bed with who? Which lucky fucker has a secret liaison? Did she? Did he?' . . . Most probably' . . . What idiots we mortals are . . . Ah!!! And thank the Gods for that.

Part 9: Oedipus: Who Is Fucking Who?

Disgusting say the voices of the Troika . . . You must concentrate on 'Austerity'. Really? This cannot be true? Asks the economic prude . . . Yes . . . Yes . . . They did . . . all of it and even more . . . Oh!!!

So . . . What happens when we ask the question to the text?

Let's not be priggish Comrades . . . We are dealing with real human instincts and desires . . . Behind that mask of responsibility and reason someone is always present . . . Our friend . . . Our master . . . Ourselves . . . **Oedipus** . . . Always present . . . In everyone . . . Even there inside the Troika . . . The Three . . . The Holy Trinity . . . Someone must have been at it . . . Incestuously? It was always incest from the start.

Bear in mind innocent Readers that there are always four people watching when two people have intercourse. Peering out from inside our psyches. What's more, these internalized parental figures bring their internalized figures and so on and so on . . . Always an audience watching in the unconscious . . . Waiting to announce their presence . . . And so we ask in a voice shaking with gravitas . . . How many Troikas inside the Troika?

There must have been an offstage incestuous sexual relationship between Haemon and Antigone. After all . . . He is defying the laws of the King, his own Father in taking her side. In the opening scene of the film, Haemon pleads with his father, Creon, to reverse his decision to execute Antigone. Haemon is speaking from the position of both lover and future spouse of Antigone, notwithstanding the fact that he was also her first cousin. The power of his attachment to Antigone, no doubt deepened and fired by incestuous familiarity, takes Haemon into the position where he defies his father. He has chosen the woman over the man, an act almost incomprehensible in ancient Greek culture. *'Are you saying that . . . all this really is going on?'* . . . *'What has happened was not real'* . . . What was going on beyond the frame? Out of sight . . .

Stop the text . . . Hold the writing . . . Readers, an amazing object has been uncovered in the last few days in a dark and dusty cave in the mountains of central Greece . . . What is it? What can it be? Open the box . . . Move the dirt, the rust, the bones and the stones . . . Jesus Jack it's a newspaper from Thebes dated 1 April 1000 BC. 'What does it say?' you cry . . . 'Can you read ancient Greek?' . . . 'Tell us now. Don't hold back' . . . Readers hold your breath and indignation. I am as shocked as you will be . . . On translation the report appears to say . . .

Records have come to light that definitively confirm by witness account that Antigone and Haemon had indeed already had intercourse and that Antigone had also engaged in an even greater incest with her brother Polynices. It is also completely clear from witness statements that Oedipus was born of Jocasta when she was just fourteen, and therefore, when he committed his incest with his mother, he was sixteen and she was 30. Having had royal privileges and never having worked she was still striking in appearance . . . Long legs . . . Golden hair . . . Some say she outdid all others. Witnesses also attest to the Sphinx appearing in many forms, both as beast and beauty, and that far from murdering those who didn't answer the riddle she promptly made love to them . . . In some cases fucking them to death . . . It is also confirmed by three witness statements that Ismene, the innocent, was thrown into confusion after the slaughter on battlefield of the two brothers, Polynices and Eteocles, since she had had intercourse with both of them on many occasions with Antigone looking on. For it is a well-known fact that the palace in Thebes was 'all go' and that all siblings slept in the same bed in the same room at the same time . . .

We must stop there . . . The facts get even murkier. Stated and confirmed by our correspondents on the spot. Peering into the darkness of the ancient bedchamber. Vulgar addictive behaviour . . . Wicked indeed . . . Voyeuristic . . . Believe them or not at your peril . . . Or better still . . . when the lights are dimmed . . . Look into your own darker fantasies or sit back, turn off the lights, watch a piece of cinema.

Before dismissing the above reports out of hand, remember that we are told by Sophocles that Oedipus fucked his own mother to produce Antigone, Ismene, Polynices, and Eteocles. And so it goes on . . .

Readers . . . Does anybody see the day for what it is? See the depth of the crisis and the ongoing dialectical reality? See their own internal contradictions? Are any of us capable of distinguishing between our own projections and perceptions? . . . Workers of the world . . . Throw off your preconceptions . . . You have nothing to lose but your outer clothing and your internal conditioning.

Reflect on this dear Reader . . . While Haemon seems justified in accusing Creon of defying the laws of Gods, it is in fact he who is defying the primary law of nature regarding incest . . . So we have a complex series of shifting realities and contradictions. They are all at it and all have their dark secrets. Could Creon be the real victim of the play in spite of his orthodox views and misogyny? Judge for yourselves dear Reader by revisiting the opening scene of the film.

Printed below is the scene printed in the shooting script and given to the actors.

1. EXT—AN ANCIENT GREEK VILLAGE—DAY

CHORUS
Listen to your son . . .
Learn from what he says . . .
Haemon, you learn from your
father too . . . You both have spoken wisely.

(Beat)

CREON
(With increasing irritation)
So . . . men of my age . . . are
supposed to learn from men of
his?

HAEMON
You should look at my merits, not
to my years.

CREON
Am I to rule by the judgment of
others . . . or . . . by my own?

HAEMON
No city belongs to one man.

CREON
(*With incredulity*)
Don't men in power own their cities?

HAEMON
You would make a good monarch . . .
of a desert.

CREON
SHAMELESS! An open feud with
your father!

HAEMON
I only attack your abuse of
power.

CREON
Is respecting my own interests an
abuse?

HAEMON
What are you protecting when you
defy the Gods?

CREON
(*Furious now at his son's refusal to submit*)
O . . . DASTARD NATURE! . . .
A WOMAN overpowers you.

Adapted from Antigone: Lines 800 to 825

What has Antigone done to deserve the fate being handed down to her? Well, to say the least, she has committed treason against a vulnerable state. She has buried the body of her brother, who had committed treason against Creon . . . Why was Antigone loyal to the dead body of Polynices? Is she not really acting out the role of a fanatic determined to attack the State and is Ismene possibly the voice of reason? And Creon the real victim of the play? This cathartic question can only be approached dialectically. The film must give us options of interpretation . . .

Yes, she is right . . . No, she is wrong . . . Creon is a monster . . . Creon is a victim . . . But Creon is no innocent, either. His reason for sentencing Antigone to death is a statement of pure self-interest. 'You have defied the law . . . the law of the State . . . (Beat) . . . and the State . . . (Beat) . . . is **me**'.

So Antigone, drawn by the power of sibling love, defies her duty to the State and threatens the edifice of law, without which the State could not exist. The closer we read Sophocles's texts of *Antigone* and *Oedipus*, the more striking it appears that one of the driving forces of the whole narrative was not only political but potential murderous incest and regressive infantilism . . . Can we get some sense of this in the way scenes are played out? These disturbing alternating psychological realities are often left out of the staging of these scenes.

Perhaps with careful visual construction, mise-en-scène, and a kind of performance that speaks out from the past directly to us, we can reempower the text with untouched perspectives. A film must always offer insights into issues happening today. Sophocles lived at a time of terrifying consecutive crisis in Athens. *OXI* must revisit the texts reflecting the contemporary crisis.

The Theban plays were always being rewritten and reinterpreted. Bertolt Brecht's powerful adaptation of *Antigone* written in 1947, not long after the war, addressed the issue of 'humanity standing up to barbarity'. Some years later, Brecht wrote a prologue, directed straight at the audience, explaining who these characters were and what he wanted them to represent. Tiresias, Antigone, Creon were given new interpretations. Brecht rewrote much of the dialogue and many of the dramatic situations, but the play was still called *Antigone*. Like Brecht's

Antigone, OXI must use our contemporary political reality as its backdrop. Dialogue must be adapted and scenes reinterpreted.

What happens when we take a look at current events, the imposition of economic laws and collective defiance? What motivates those imposing their power? Are we simply regressing to a preverbal stage of our own human development when we accept all the rationalizations by European economists, rationalizations that offer no insight into the unconscious dynamics and play of historic forces at work on the streets of Athens? There is an unstated game of murder and incest stalking our times . . . The unconscious dynamics, both of the forces at work in society and of the forces at work in the psyche of the single individual, were being fused in the furnace of crisis on the streets and squares of Athens. I had known a Greece in earlier times; in fact I first heard of this land called Greece in my childhood and it always sounded sunny and full of games. I even knew some ancient Greeks in person, or so they told me they were. But then I grew up in the great international metropolis of Manchester. Ah!!! Those were the days when a hero was a hero and a God was a God.

Back in time to times more innocent? Let us find some inspiration in the mischief of some Greek games.

Part 10: The Game

My friends . . . The first Greeks

I don't want to paint a sunny picture of the Greeks as all-embracing sweetness, suffering little innocents. I can certainly attest to the extraordinary sense of 'the game' that Greek friends of mine since childhood have introduced me into . . . But what imaginative power . . . What characters . . . What stories they told.

The first Greeks, as far as I was concerned, were not ancient Greeks or the Greeks of Greece but Greek acquaintances of mine, born in the UK of Greek parents, living in our great metropolis . . . Manchester . . . 'Roman' Manchester . . . The Manchester of the 1960s . . . From where I took so much inspiration and where I first read extracts from *Capital* under the guidance of our great teacher Mr Eckersley, who told social history by taking us around the city and showing us industrial history while reading out large chunks of Marx and Engels. It was all there in front of our eyes. Wow . . . Teach us again . . . Ah!!! Back then in early parts of my life, I learnt things. I learnt a lot from my Greek friends . . . Different to Marx . . . Innocent and guilty . . . Geniuses of the imagination . . . Brilliant at adaptation . . . Ah!!! Greek Mancunians . . . where are you now? Tell the Readers.

Manchester, aged 11
My best friend in my first year in secondary school was a boy called Constantine Ziliakos. True, we engaged in some matters economic (we ran an illicit exchange office in school for the transfer of foreign coins). Now, Constantine was very fortunate because he lived exactly three miles and twenty yards from the school, which meant he was entitled to a free bus pass (three miles minimum was the rule). But while he lived just around the corner from me . . . I lived two miles and 1,750 yards from my school . . . I didn't get the bus pass. I had another friend as well, David Brightbug we called him, who lived a little bit closer towards the school . . . He didn't get the bus pass either. Now Constantine, who was very good at art, came up with a brilliant idea that we should all copy his bus pass and so David and I spent a good three weeks in the Arts room at school copying, under Constantine's instructions, his bus pass. The forgeries were good, in fact very good, and we were very proud of them. For the following three weeks travelling up and down, spending our bus fares on other things more important, like the James Bond book *Dr. No* and other pieces of rubbish . . . So confident were we, we started taking buses everywhere, out to Salford, out to Main Road where Manchester City played; sometimes we just went for the fun of it. Until that dark afternoon, when Thanatos himself got on the bus in the living form of a ticket inspector. We dutifully flashed our passes, but, BANG, a lightening bolt from Zeus, or 'by the holy Mother of Jesus', as David said, the eagle-eyed inspector noticed that we were all called Constantine Ziliakos, and since David and I didn't look at all Greek, the game was up . . . Swish . . . We managed to skip it fast . . . Ah . . . but . . . The lesson was there . . . I was learning.

At school at this time I first encountered Greek plays though Constantine assured us all that they were all bullshit . . . My learning stopped for a while. Until . . .

London, aged 24

On to the Slade to do a postgraduate in Fine Art at Slade where I met the brilliant Georges Papadopoulos . . . a student who was UK born of Greek parents. On his first day he proclaimed to us all in a loud and deep theatrical voice . . . 'The Object is Dead'. . . and harangued us all for still painting. 'For fuck's sake Georges . . . Who the fuck are you' said Chris, an Anglo-French genius . . . 'I am Georges Papadopoulos and I am a revolutionary Conceptualist . . . I need say no more' . . . Ah!!! . . . So it goes . . . Two years went by with many illuminating discussions and arguments . . . and not just arguments . . . Ah!!! Yes it was also a time of wonderful sexual freedom. The studios were not only used for painting . . . every studio a hot incestuous paradise. Many bodily fluids were daily exchanged between the Slade, the Royal College of Art and Royal Academy of Dramatic Art . . . Ah!!! (**SLAP** . . . Author is unreasonably slapped for giving away the secrets that everybody always knew) . . . So back to arguments on Conceptualism, on the value of Plumb Lines, Perspective, Concrete Object, Concrete Cinema, World Cinema, Literature, UNTIL . . .

One week before the end of the course with a final exhibition looming and no concrete work to show, Georges, suddenly with a flash of recognition of the fact he had no work . . . pompously announced . . . 'Back to The Object' and promptly made six enormous canvases using strong wood and heavy sailcloth which he took down to Gower Street and asked the road repair teams there to cover them with black tar. He then lifted the canvases at various angles as the tar cooled and carted them back to the Slade with much help from anybody that he could rope in . . . (Imagination, Organization, and Genius in total harmony) . . . Problem . . . His exhibition space was too small for these giant painting to all fit. So he exhibited three and left the rest outside in the rain announcing . . . 'Process is all'. He was awarded his HDFA Slade (the highest award in Fine Art at that time).

Georges is now a brilliant artist and teacher of drawing in London.

I was learning even more . . . Learn and the world learns with you . . . Said Georges . . . And we did.

So . . . Did all that really take place. What I see now is all tinged with a golden grad.

Part 11: Scene Missing... Scene Missing...

There is always something missing.

So much is hidden from ourselves. Deep hidden catharsis which, if we can touch, should be handled carefully. In the course of making the film, a number of scenes were shot and then finally, in the last stages, edited out and sent to the silence of the lost. It's worth noting that in Greek tragedy we never see the murders or all those dramatic things and horrors. We are only told about them and see the consequences. In the same way, it may be that lost scenes nevertheless have a presence through absence. One example is the terrifying scene from *Agamemnon*, which was acted out so brilliantly by our Greek actors but could never find its place in the film when completed. Nevertheless ... The memory of the scene haunts my reflections on the making of *OXI*. Here is the full scene as shot intercut as it was in the original edit with the scene from the volunteer hospital in Athens with the doctor speaking on 'catharsis'. The scene then was intercut between drama and actuality.

EXT—VILLAGE STREET—AGAMEMNON: LINES 1375 to 1395

DR. GIORGOS VICHAS (Greek VO—subtitled)
In ancient times, medical centres were called 'Asklepieia'. What Asklepios, and doctors that came after him, believed was that for a therapy to be complete, a patient doesn't only need a doctor, medicine and a kind of hypnosis—but a very important therapy was tragedy, ancient tragedy.

CLYTEMNESTRA (Greek—subtitled)
I said things before to suit the moment. Now I'm not ashamed to speak the opposite. How can anyone deal with enemies who claim to be friends? Enclose them in a net of misery with no escape.

DR. GIORGOS VICHAS (Greek VO—subtitled)
They believed they had to release negative feelings.

CLYTEMNESTRA (Greek—subtitled)
I stand where I killed him. I did it. I will not deny it. He could not escape his fate.

DR. GIORGOS VICHAS (Greek VO—subtitled)
A very important tool was theatre. Something we must also do in Greece today.

CLYTEMNESTRA (Greek—subtitled)
I stabbed him twice. With two groans his limbs relaxed, and as he fell, I added a third blow. A gift to Hades, the place of the dead. As his lifeblood gushed forth, I felt his blood cover me.

DR. GIORGOS VICHAS (Greek VO—subtitled)
Negative feelings must not spread internally, and have self-destructive effects, like the 4,000 recent suicides. These negative feelings must be externalised. The most creative way to release them—and make people fight—is 'Art'.

CLYTEMNESTRA (Greek—subtitled)
He filled the cup in his house with so many cursed calamities. Now he has come home to drain it off.

EXT—METROPOLITAN COMMUNITY CLINIC, ATHENS

MARTHA FRANGIADAKI
Catharsis is necessary, it is helping to heal people, and one thing we're trying to do here, it is catharsis in both senses of the word: in the sense of the word of support and solidarity with the people, and the sense of the word of resistance against things that shouldn't be happening.

Agamemnon's terrifying scene with the recall of its extreme violence is relayed to us, through memory of the event, outside of the palace . . . the cauldron of political incest, where the most violent and lascivious acts apparently take place somewhere in the wings of the theatre. Not on stage. But is it these hidden actions which prompt our actors into delivering lines written by those we will never know or meet and passing on their psychic reality? Who then is responsible for these words,

and who should pay the price? The actor or the hidden forces that drive the play forward? . . . Who should pay the price for the economic and political meanderings of contemporary Greece? Are the actions not as violent, are the desires not as lascivious? Do we ever catch this Troika lit on stage during their plotting? And what is cinema but a medium to be seen only in darkness . . . a regressed state? When memories of past events emerge from their amnesia, we should always reflect on a statement by the Polish critic, Jan Kott,
'Memory has only one tense . . . the Present'.

Epilogue: Repetition

'So all this really does exist' . . . 'What I see here is now real'.
Viewers of OXI, Readers, Comrades . . . The time has come to bear witness to the 'Repetition Compulsion' . . . Another manifestation of great Thanatos . . .
'Lets hear the same story again'. I hear you shout . . . 'Yes please . . . All over again' . . . Ah!!! . . . 'Don't change it . . . I'll cry if you change it' . . . But I say that this time there must be a twist . . . 'I hate it when the story changes', People scream . . . It must change and it will. So . . .
When Freud first visited the Acropolis in Athens in 1904 he was struck by an uncanny sensation of alienation, which puzzled him and which he left in the back of the mind for thirty-two years. He finally commented on this in an open letter to Romain Rolland in January 1936, giving it a title 'Disturbance of Memory'.
By going to the Acropolis, he had travelled further than his father ever did in his own lifetime. He had outstripped and defeated his father and seen things his father could not see. In that moment, he had unconsciously murdered his own father . . . Ah!!! The most primitive instinct of man . . . Is it possible that what holds back our understanding of the ritual sacrifice of Greece is the unconscious fear and wish of killing our own Father, and of destroying a country which was indeed the 'Father of Western Civilization'. MURDER of the paternal wisdom . . . MURDER . . . That part of ourselves that is Him . . . Is indeed the

making of a motion picture a direct attack on the Father's knowledge?
Yes . . . Yes . . . Yes . . . **HELP**.
'Think on' said my Grandfather . . .
'Think on' said my Father . . .
Think on dear Reader . . .
'Think on' . . .
Such was the advice . . . I hope I always will.

What is written here all took place.
What you have read here is not true.
    Free associations on the making of OXI . . . Only, of course, a fragment has been revealed.

Spartan Helotry

Martin McQuillan

3 January 2013

The graffiti around the city of Thessaloniki have taken on a more direct tone of late. Amid the usual declarations for gangs, lovers and rival football teams, there is a strong strain of political aphorism. In the middle of Platia Dikastirion, the public square a few blocks from my hotel, a message written in English reads: 'Refugees Welcome, Tourists Fuck Off'. Austerity-crippled Greece may have more reason than most to encourage the tourist trade, but the sentiment speaks of exasperation with the international community after the imposition of consecutive rounds of painful 'fiscal discipline': Those who have nothing, like us, are welcome; those who bring their wealth to play by the Aegean Sea are not. Academic visitors are not quite tourists or refugees: They have something to bring other than holiday euros, but equally they have somewhere to return to. I am here for a symposium on narrative. Stories interest me and so does the state of universities. I am compelled to ask, then, what is the story of Greek universities during these most austere of times?

In August 2011, at the height of the tourist season, the Hellenic Parliament passed, with an overwhelming majority, a higher-education reform bill, Law 4009. For some, the bill heralded a brave new dawn of efficiency, accountability and competitiveness long overdue in an underperforming sector. For others, it represented a violation of the Greek constitution and the dismantling of hard-won rights as the first step towards the privatization of the country's forty universities and technical institutes. The provisions of the bill include: the shortening of undergraduate degrees from four or five years to three; the appointment rather than the election of rectors; the reduction of student voting influence over university governance; curriculum oversight of academic departments by faculties; more powers for the Hellenic Quality Assurance Agency for Higher Education; the linking of funding to institutional performance; and the incentivization of private donations, sponsorship and the hiring of facilities. The bill also abolishes the right to asylum on university campuses—something enjoyed since 1982, when memories of the generals' rule of the country from 1967 to 1974 were still raw but which, by making campuses police-free zones, had enabled petty crime and rough sleeping in some places. In recent years, campuses served as refuges when street protests gave way to violent clashes with the police.

The bill is also said to address the disparity between healthy participation and anaemic graduation rates in the country. According to Universitas 21, a global network of research universities, Greece, along with South Korea, Finland and the United States, has one of the highest higher-education participation rates in the world. However, Organisation for Economic Co-operation and Development statistics reveal that the country also has one of the lowest rates of graduation and graduate employability in the European Union.

The bill also targets that bête noire of austerity, 'waste': Greek students receive free textbooks and free lunches. However, the government is at pains to stress that privatization is not on the agenda.

If all this sounds to British ears like a mild dose of real-world corporatization, it is worth pausing to reflect that despite all the economic problems Greece has—it recently received another 40 billion euro (32 billion pound) tranche from the EU and the International Monetary Fund as its de facto structured default gathers apace—no one here is suggesting that the cost of higher education should be transferred from the state to the student. No one is talking about the introduction of tuition fees for Greek undergraduates, which normally would be page one of the neoliberal playbook.

Nevertheless, there is a familiar story unfolding here. Austerity begins with a demand to cut back on public spending. It follows that the state must give up responsibility for some things it has previously provided. Given all the demands on an ever-shrinking public purse, some statutory (pensions and care for the elderly), some conventional (the military, the Olympics), the nation will need to prioritize its commitments. Starting with the most inessential first and working down the list, cuts are enacted and parts of the public realm are given over to the private sector.

In the UK, universities lost their place in the queue for the public purse long ago when vice-chancellors first agreed to tuition fees as a way of funding higher education. Despite the safeguard of requiring a parliamentary vote to raise the cap on fees, there has been a slow but inexorable progression, one-thousand-pound 'top-up fees' in 1998 to sector-wide nine-thousand-pound charges today, which has flipped the ratio of public–private financing in UK higher education to 30 to 70 in favour of 'graduate contributions'. While the coalition's troubled vote on fees in December 2010 brought students out on the streets and wreaked lasting political damage on the Liberal Democrats, the rise was in reality achieved through incremental progression, by which the once politically impossible became the politically inevitable. English universities have been like the allegorical frog that is boiled alive without knowing it as the temperature of the water is raised a few degrees at a time.

Austerity was the primary justification given during the vote on tripling tuition fees. Vince Cable, the business secretary, somberly pronounced that the UK didn't want to 'end up like Greece'. However, as an indication of the bad faith behind such pronouncements, it is worth considering that the bill for higher education in the UK is expected to be 4.2 billion pounds in 2014–2015, while the total cost of the quantitative easing (QE) programme to date has been 375 billion pounds. Since student finance is also a form of government debt (for a fraction of the QE outlay so far), why wasn't the cost of the student loan book folded into the scheme?

Greece, of course, cannot do what the UK has done: As a member of the eurozone Greece cannot devalue its currency, or quantitatively ease or inflate away its national debt. Instead, the Greeks, like the Irish, have had to issue ever-stricter austerity budgets, cutting public-sector salaries and pensions while raising taxes.

The take-home pay of Greek academics has been cut by 25 per cent in the past four years, with further cuts expected. They consider themselves relatively fortunate. Walking back to the hotel after the first day of the conference, I witness an evening march by workers who have not been paid for sixteen months (at which stage they cannot meaningfully be described as 'workers' any more). Direct funding to universities has been cut by 20 per cent and is expected to be cut further; with a freeze on hiring at most institutions, staff workloads are expanding as the workforce shrinks. The narrative symposium is being held at the Thessaloniki Museum of Byzantine Culture because the cleaners at the Aristotle University of Thessaloniki are on strike and rubbish is piling up all over campus. In this sense, academic visitors retain a tourist-like status: We are to be spared the sight of bin bags and protest. The cleaners are in dispute over the transfer of their contracts to a private company. Strikes have become habitual: I am told an informal agreement has been reached that they will be reserved for Wednesday afternoons in an attempt to keep public institutions functional.

The calculation of the Greek government is somewhere between the shock doctrine and the frog. The reforms all come at once and are extensive, but they also open the door to the long road of managerialism and self-corporatization. Why protest in the street over directly imposed reforms when appointed managers will willingly enact reforms gradually in time? Law 4009 has met with resistance from Greece's students and rectors, some of whom have publicly pronounced their refusal to implement it. This should also give British readers pause for thought. Yiannis Mylopoulos, the rector of Aristotle, was one of the last to hold out against implementation but folded when the government threatened to withdraw all state funding from his university.

Only Athens Polytechnic, it is said, remains noncompliant. The institution, Greece's premier school for mathematics and engineering, occupies a special place in the imagination of Greek higher education and politics. It is where, at 3 a.m. on 17 November 1973, the generals sent in a tank to break a student occupation. Some thirty people died that night, sparking a chain of events that would eventually lead to the fall of the military junta and the restoration of democracy in July the following year. The date is observed as a national holiday for all Greek educational establishments: wreaths are laid and the day ends with a march from the Polytechnic to the American Embassy in Athens.

If it is hard enough to imagine English vice-chancellors standing together to oppose government reforms; it is harder still to imagine Imperial College London or the London School of Economics wanting even to recall the history of their students' protests against the Vietnam War or Rhodesia. It is for these hardwired, historical reasons that the Greek government wants to attenuate the student voice in university governance but at the same time will not (yet) contemplate tuition fees. What is on offer is a slow-burn management approach that opens the door to a long corridor of reform through assurance and audit, as the legacy of student activism recedes into history.

Austerity should not target the university; on the contrary, when the economy is shrinking, education and training should be national priorities. In practice, it would seem that austerity abhors only the *public* university. As the plight of the University of California system demonstrates, the public university is always near the top of the austerity regime's list of the nonessential, with a public commitment to the arts and humanities prominent among the items to be cut.

Lord Browne of Madingley's identification of the arts, humanities and social sciences as 'non-priority subjects' echoes Ronald Reagan's pronouncement, during a presidential campaign speech while governor of California, that the Golden State had no interest in 'subsidising intellectual curiosity'. The present governor of Florida, Rick Scott, has said that the state has enough anthropologists and has increased fees for arts and humanities degrees at Florida State University to discourage take-up and incentivize students to opt for science programmes. James Dyson, the British industrial designer, has called for special treatment and fee waivers for engineers in England and recently claimed that too many people are going to university to study 'French lesbian poetry'. Such sectarianism seems thankfully absent in Greece. When I express admiration for the ability of my host, Effie Yiannopoulo, to fund a humanities symposium at this time, she replies wryly: 'We have had three governments in three years—no one has been around long enough to realise there was still money in the humanities pot.'

While the Greek constitution declares the state to be the only legitimate provider of higher education, the country has a growing private market, much of it the result of British universities franchising degrees for private colleges. Austerity is at ease with the private provider. Who could argue against thrifty students and free enterprise? The sting comes when private institutions repatriate profits derived from publicly funded loans for tuition fees. This is the mess that the Obama administration is trying to unpick in the United States; this is the future that the UK government is actively encouraging.

The University of Law is the first for-profit, private equity–backed university in the UK, but any capitalist worth his or her salt knows how to extract income from a corporate structure with or without the 'not-for-profit' nomenclature that, for example, the New College of the Humanities avows. Greece is not the basket case on this one.

In the past, healthy numbers of Greek students came to study in the UK as demand for higher education significantly outstripped the supply afforded by the country's forty public institutions. It would seem that this traffic is likely to grind to a halt in the face of nine-thousand-pound fees for home and EU students and will be redirected towards less expensive, American-run private universities in Eastern Europe.

The regimes of austerity have meant different things in the Greek and UK academies. While Greece holds on, for now, to direct funding and a belief in the public university, its higher education budget is in sharp decline. It is not certain that the imported cult of managerialism will reverse that. The financing of universities in England is a piece of legerdemain by which government borrowing is redescribed as private debt, the sort of off-book accounting for which the Conservatives in opposition criticized Gordon Brown. Unlike the Greek rectors, Universities UK (UUK) has said little in public about this. It is its belief that over a period in which public spending will decline, the new finance arrangements will actually put more money into English universities (which is not something it wants to draw to the attention of the Treasury). However, UUK has not calculated for the decline of undergraduate student numbers in the face of nine-thousand-pound fees. The next round of Universities and Colleges Admissions Service figures this month will severely test these assumptions.

'Crisis' and 'critic' are both derived from the same Greek root, *krinein*, 'to judge'. When the story of the global financial crisis comes to be written, how shall we judge the dramatis personae? The politicians, bankers and plutocrats will all survive, no doubt, but they have brought tragedy to Greece. Like Oedipus, they might say that they did not know what they were doing. The crime of Oedipus may have been committed in ignorance, but he still gouged his own eyes out when he realized what he had done. Who will be the brave, suicidal Antigone who defies the state for the sake of an ethical duty they hold dearer than compliance with the sovereign's wishes? After she is gone and all is lost, King Creon laments his own 'mistakes made by a foolish mind . . . Oh the profanity of what I planned.'

What would Aristotle make of it all? Of narrative, he famously noted that all plots have a beginning, middle and end. Previously we have understood a 'crisis' to be something that will pass when the normal order of things is restored. The trauma of the present crisis is the feeling that the worst is yet to come, for the UK, for Greece and for our universities. There is no end in sight.

I am told that when it is clear, you can stand at the harbour in Thessaloniki and see all the way to Mount Olympus. Today I cannot see beyond the hazy smog.

Post-Structuralist Politics

Martin McQuillan

26 March 2015

One of the most remarkable things about events unfolding in Greece is how many members of the Syriza government are academics—cue national newspaper headlines in January, 'How British Universities Helped Mould Syriza's Political Elite'.

Finance minister Yanis Varoufakis—who describes himself on Twitter as an 'economics professor, quietly writing obscure academic texts for years, until thrust on to the public scene'—has a PhD from the University of Essex and has taught at the universities of East Anglia, Cambridge and Glasgow. MP Costas Lapavitsas is professor of economics at Soas, University of London, while Syriza central committee member Stathis Kouvelakis taught political theory and philosophy at King's College London.

There is, of course, a long history of professors entering government as technocrats or leaders. Mohamed Morsi, for example, went from head of a science department at Zagazig University to become the Muslim Brotherhood's first president of Egypt, while Barack Obama taught at the University of Chicago Law School. What is significant about Syriza is that they draw a key membership from university departments that have histories of engagement with critical theory and heterodox political economy. It will be interesting to read Essex's impact case studies for the 2020 research excellence framework.

There is a similar situation in Spain. The Spanish political party Podemos is often compared to Syriza, as an anti-austerity party that is eclipsing an existing social democratic party. With regional and national elections scheduled for the winter of this year, the party is currently polling at 25 per cent of the vote. Podemos draws heavily from the academic scene in Madrid. Party leader Pablo Iglesias was acting head of political science at the Complutense University of Madrid and is an expert on psychoanalysis and cinema. Deputy leader Íñigo Errejón is a postdoc in the same department. Unlike the Greek academics forming Syriza, who were trained or employed in UK and U.S. universities, Iglesias and Errejón are 'precarious lecturers'—staff who have never had full-time tenured posts and survive on fixed-term and hourly paid work.

The Spanish academy has a genuine problem in this respect. A generation of *'funcionarios'* in their fifties occupy most of the permanent positions in Spain's universities. As tenured 'civil servants' in a heavily controlled and subsidized system, their employment is guaranteed regardless of personal performance or student recruitment. On a recent visit to a Catalan university, I discovered a school of the humanities that had fifty undergraduate students and fifty *funcionario* staff.

Spanish students are required to pay 2,000 euros (1,400 pounds) in annual up-front tuition fees, and the financial crisis has resulted in a serious squeeze on students in certain subjects, especially in regional universities. Despite years of harsh austerity, neither the government in Madrid nor the regional authorities, which co-fund Spanish universities, have taken any steps to address the issue of the *funcionario*. There has been a go-slow on granting similar employment rights to a new generation of academics, and it is hoped that natural retirements will 'see out' the last of the tenured. There is a generational conflict in Spanish universities as precarious lecturers, some now in their forties, watch senior colleagues enjoy the benefits of extended gardening leave during a period of national financial hardship. Youth unemployment in Spain is currently running at 55 per cent.

It is not surprising that the leaders of Podemos should emerge from a generation of academics who are locked out of a system that was designed by the Franco regime to ensure stability through middle-class loyalty to the state. The precarious academics behind Podemos have nothing to lose. Like their equivalents in Greece, they are strongly committed to reform of public institutions that would root out nepotism and irrational gerontocracy. The question of university reform is central to the platforms of both parties.

In Greece, Syriza have already reinstated the (mostly mature and part-time) students who had been removed from higher education through a recent change in the law. It is also committed to dealing with endemic problems of privilege and sclerosis within the Greek academy. The interests of Syriza lie in returning economic growth to a functioning post-crisis society. They recognize that this will require social mobility, intergenerational justice, and wider participation in higher education.

Rather than the usual graduates of the Harvard Business School and in PPE (Philosophy, Politics and Economics) at Oxford, the academics leading Syriza and Podemos are experts on Jacques Lacan and Jacques Derrida. The Greek minister of education, Aristides Baltas, is author of a book on Spinoza and Wittgenstein. It is unusual for academics in the critical humanities and theoretical social sciences to find themselves occupying political office (although Slavoj Žižek did run unsuccessfully for the presidency of Slovenia in 1990).

Michel Foucault declined François Mitterrand's offer of the post of cultural attaché in New York, and Derrida was close to the election campaigns of both Mitterrand and Lionel Jospin. That generation of thinkers did not cross the line between the critical academy and the exercise of government.

Inspired by the work of academics such as the late Ernesto Laclau, professor of political theory at Essex, and Étienne Balibar, anniversary chair of philosophy at Kingston University, a new generation of critical thinkers is choosing to cross that frontier in response to regimes of austerity. They do so not out of an understanding that social science research is of value when it can be utilized by the state in an 'impactful' way. Instead, they act out of a necessity that is fundamental to their own academic work, risking theoretical positions against the problems of the world. In doing so, they are likely to experience the same frustrations and compromises of government as their predecessors. How they respond to this—in more or less intelligent ways—will be the measure of how true these professors-turned-politicians remain to their academic ideals.

False Economy

Martin McQuillan

They have signed *our* I.O.U. and we can no longer not acknowledge it. Any more than our own children. This is what tradition is, the heritage that drives you crazy. People have not the slightest idea of this, they have no need to know that they are paying (automatic withdrawal) nor whom they are paying . . . when they do anything whatsoever, make war or love, speculate on the energy crisis, construct socialism, write novels, open concentration camps for poets or homosexuals, buy bread or hijack a plane, have themselves elected by secret ballot, bury their own, criticize the media without rhyme or reason, say absolutely anything about chador or the ayatollah, dream of a great safari, found reviews, teach, or piss against a tree . . . This story, the trap of who signs an I.O.U. for the other such that the other finds himself engaged before having known a thing about it, even before having opened his eyes, this children's story is a love story and is ours—if you still want it. From the very first light of dawn. (Jacques Derrida, *Envois*, 10 September 1977)[1]

The Purloined Future

What then, to paraphrase Derrida on Marx, is the state of the debt?[2] When in 2008 we began to speak of a 'credit crunch', what we really meant was a 'debt crisis' in which repayment of substantial loans became attenuated and banks and other financial institutions became insolvent.

However, this situation is considerably complicated and not merely a case of a few large debtors defaulting on payments. Allow me to spend a little time unpacking this because it is the aetiology of everything that has fallen out from it, including the bankruptcy of global financial institutions and sovereign states. Debt and its converse credit are not the fortunate or unfortunate outcomes of banking practices; they are the very point of banking and indeed of capitalism itself, perhaps of all economy as such. The classical purpose of a bank is to lend money on the basis of the deposits of its so-called customers (individuals and companies who have placed their money in the bank for security reasons). Using depositors' money or money borrowed at a low rate of interest from another bank, the bank lends to others at a greater rate of interest, and as long as these loans are repaid on schedule, the bank will theoretically initiate an infinite chain of profit. In so doing, banking as such both introduces credit into the economy, enabling growth, employment and wealth creation and initiates indebtedness, which ties individuals to the bank and the system of capital in general. If one is predisposed towards this sort of thing, then credit and debt are not merely necessary, they are essential to the operation of the entire capitalist system.

Once the bank lends money to an individual or company, that money is deposited back in the bank, again for what Rousseau's discourse on inequality might identify as security reasons. On this basis, the bank has increased its deposits base by leveraging its capital but without any actual 'new' money coming into circulation. The bank, having increased its deposits, is free to repeat this process ad infinitum within the limit of retaining the cash ratio required by law for capitalization. In this way, banks generate their large balance sheets of assets (loans and advances) and liabilities (customer accounts) from a relatively low deposit base and minimal cash ratio. This is a form of phantasmagoria that makes the commodity fetish look like a concrete tower block. At its height in 2008, the Royal Bank of Scotland had assets of 1.9 trillion pounds (greater than the entire GDP of the sovereign guarantor of the United Kingdom, making it then the largest company by asset size in the world).[3] At this point, we might invoke the distinction that Aristotle makes in *Politics* between economy and chresmatics, the former being the management of goods essential to the maintenance of life, the latter being the originary ruin of the former as the accumulation of wealth for its own sake.[4] In this sense, it no longer makes any sense to speak of economics in relation to banking; perhaps today some universities should rename their business schools, trapped within the curriculum of orthodox economic theory, along Aristotelian lines.

The banking business model is unique within capitalism because it requires minimal equity (the difference between assets and liabilities) and, accordingly, banking is, despite appearances, a less-than-secure enterprise. In this situation, banks must manage the risk of loan defaults, and one might say that the business of banks is precisely the management of risk. Banks are placed at risk when liabilities begin to exceed equity in an unmanageable way. In 2008, at the start of the financial crisis, Barclays had sixty times more assets (due loans) than equity (the difference between assets and liabilities). The median leverage ratio of banks in the United States in 2008 was 35 to 1, and 45 to 1 in Europe. What this meant was that only one-thirty-fifth of U.S. bank assets had to go bad before the banks would be insolvent, and one-fortieth in Europe. That is, if only 2.5 per cent of loans were defaulted on, then the European banks would collapse. This is exactly what happened with the subprime mortgage collapse in the U.S. housing market when it became clear that money had systematically been loaned to those with little prospect of making their repayments. Banks sitting on over-leveraged positions as this market began to unravel began to collapse in a domino principle, from Bear Stearns to Lehman Brothers in the United States and Northern Rock to HBOS in the UK, resulting in bailouts for the system by central banks (i.e., the state) as the guarantor and lender of last resort. These collapses and the so-called credit crunch in personal finances arose when banks then quickly attempted to deleverage by contracting their assets without harming their equity ratios. This means offering less credit and calling in as much debt as possible; since this is the exact opposite of the banking business model, the entire system came close to collapse when financial institutions even stopped lending to each other, viewing one another as risky prospects and potentially bad debtors.

Banks are equally keen to obviate risk within the banking system, and to this end financial markets have developed sophisticated financial products to do just this. The trade in derivative products (options and futures) exceeds tenfold the total value of the world's economic output. The derivatives are designed to hedge risk, to take insurance out against uncertainty by fixing prices in the future. However, like the leveraging of a bank's capital, trade in derivatives generates financial transactions based on, but far in excess of, the original asset price, and when those transactions begin to unfurl, derivatives have the opposite effect of not hedging risk but magnifying it. It is for this reason that J. P. Morgan pioneered the credit default swap (CDS) that allows one to both leverage capital and hedge it against risk. Swapping positions in the market is a relatively recent method of alleviating potential uncertainty by mitigating exposure to risk, which makes it much more likely that you will be able to repay the money borrowed from the bank for your business activity, making you a sounder debtor and so able to borrow more money, and so on and so forth. Credit default swaps enable financial institutions to sell the risk of a loan going bad. They allow banks to lend money and then to insure themselves against default by someone else taking on the risk associated with the debt. Suitably insured, the bank can be relaxed about having to hold onto capital reserves and so can continue to lend again and again based on its assets register (which we recall is really the outstanding loans owed to it). Regulators accepted the argument for CDSs because they were thought to spread risk throughout the financial system rather than concentrate it in one place, thus making individual banks safer prospects. The first difficulty with CDSs is that they are designed to produce an economic impossibility (i.e., make lending risk free) the profit derived from an investment is unfortunately directly related to the risk involved. The second difficulty is precisely that they spread risk throughout the system in undetectable and unmanageable ways; this risk is further multiplied by the practice of securitization in which bundles of debt are sold to offshore shell companies which take on the bank's risk, broken up, reengineered, sold again to investors and so on, with each resale deliberately designed to disguise the more risky aspects of the debt. The shell company allows the bank to remove the loan from the bank's balance sheet and so seeming to decrease the asset-to-equity ratio, making the bank look less leveraged and more credit worthy, allowing it to lend more money, which again will be risk free through further CDSs. As Derrida says in *Donner le temps*,

'The counterfeiter will have figured out how to indebt himself infinitely, and will have given himself the chance of escaping in this way from the mastery of reappropriation. He will have figured out how to break indefinitely the circle or the symmetry' (150). In other words, the producer of counterfeit money can never lose; counterfeit money is risk-free money. The practice of repeated packing and securitizing debt makes it practically impossible to keep track of the quality of that debt. AIG collapsed and was bailed out by the U.S. Treasury at the cost of 173 billion dollars because it underwrote the insurance for the majority of the world trade in credit default swaps. If AIG had not been bailed out by the Treasury, Goldman Sachs, Merrill Lynch, Deutsche Bank, Barclays, BNP Paribas, Société Generale (the list is long and distinguished) faced astronomical loses. The market capitalization of AIG was only 2 billion dollars, meaning that it cost eighty-five times its value to bail out.[5] When governments (or central banks) bail out commercial banks, they do so not by transferring capital from their own reserves but by selling their own debt, or more strictly speaking, their own capacity of repay debt, in the form of bonds. The more secure a nation you are, with a good credit rating, the lower the interest paid on bonds but the safer the investment for bond buyers. The more stretched you are as a nation-state, the more it will cost in interest payments to attract bond investors. When the bond market stops believing in a nation's capacity to repay the debt, that country quickly runs into trouble; unable to borrow money in the form of bond issues, it is forced to seek its own bailout to meet its obligations, notably its guarantee to underwrite the debts of its own banks. As a condition of the bailout, international lenders such as the International Monetary Fund and the European Central Bank insist on the nation-state making itself more credit worthy by spending less on public services in order to be better able to repay its international debt. This is the situation we have experienced across Europe, in which the citizens whose borrowed deposits in banks made the entire system possible are now facing austerity measures to prevent the collapse of the system. They are paying the price of someone else having borrowed their money.

Money Worries

This is exactly what Derrida proposes in *Donner le temps*, that any economic exchange involves the production of a certain reciprocity of debt; this is especially the case with the gift. Any gift, however freely given, indebts the recipient to the giver and so initiates further exchanges, perhaps of material goods but also of more abstract considerations such as gratitude and clienthood and so on. The givers themselves are involved not in an excessive generosity without reserve but in a relation of sacrifice in which there is always the return and the expectation of return of a certain credit to the giver. The question of sacrifice in the gift is significant in the 1977–1978 seminar by Derrida because later sacrifice becomes the predicate through which Derrida begins his sustained deconstruction of sovereignty through his analysis of the death sentence and the animal.[6] The business of sacrifice is always that business of the sovereign, the one who is allowed to put to death without legal consequence, whether it is the sovereign who commutes the death sentence or the sovereign human subject which sacrifices animal life in order to support human development. In thinking capital punishment and the continuum of planetary life, Derrida attempts to think an economy without sacrifice, in which no other is subordinated to the utility of any other.[7] The seminar on the gift, then, is an important nascent step in the development of Derrida's thought on sovereignty. Here he distinguishes the 'pure gift (if there is any)' from sacrifice:

> The sacrifice proposes an offering but only in the form of a deconstruction against which it exchanges, hopes for, or counts on a benefit, namely, a surplus-value or at least an amortization, a protection, and a security.[8]

The purity of the gift itself is always a matter of compromise, but what interests me here in the context of systemic debt is the idea that securitization disarticulates sacrifice; namely, it turns a sacrifice from a gift into an offering that expects a return. In the case of, say, credit default swaps, we have a sacrifice (the lending of money) that is immunized against risk and already deconstructs its own sacrificial status. In the case of student loans, for example, the ideological trick is to appear to be making a sacrifice, even offering a gift, by paying the loan up front for the student, but already to have calculated the return in the form of future interest payments, the indebtedness of citizens, the capacity to sell further debt, and the credit for having reduced the sovereign debt.

Rather than the gift itself as the main focus of *Donner le temps*, I would like to turn to the text of Charles Baudelaire that informs the second half of Derrida's seminar to worry through certain philosophical problems (I mean 'worry' here in the philosophical sense that one worries through a knotty topic, rather than 'worry' in the sense that one lies awake at night worrying about the mortgage). The reason for this is to consider the fictional nature of debt, given that as Derrida says 'the symbolic opens and constitutes the order of exchange and debt'.[9] The banking business model that I have described in the first half of this chapter, were it a product of the novelistic imagination, would surely be condemned as an improbable fiction. The relation between accounting and recounting is one of the important subtexts of Derrida's book. I think there are two important strands to follow here, given all that has been said above. The first is the question of counterfeit money versus 'real' money:

> We can no longer avoid the question of what money is: true money or counterfeit money, which can only be what it is, false or counterfeit, to the extent to which no one knows it is false, that is, to the extent to which it circulates, appears, functions as good and true money.[10]

Derrida here is thinking of the Baudelaire text 'La fausse monnaie', the basis of which is the story of two friends who meet a beggar in the street, one of whom gives him a substantial gift, only to reveal to his friend (the narrator) that it is a counterfeit coin. The narrator wonders as to his friend's motives and imagines that he has offered the coin in order to create an event in the otherwise desperate life of the beggar, speculating what may result in the circulation of and speculation on this counterfeit money to the benefit or possible detriment of the beggar. The narrator is horrified to discover that, in fact, his friend is motivated to do the beggar good (and earn the moral credit of alms to the poor) by offering him a large donation but does so secure in the knowledge that he has not given away any of his own real money.

However, the question that imposes itself today is the one of whether a financial product derived from leveraged or packaged debt constitutes real money or counterfeit money; that is to say, the simulacrum of money. When credit derivative swaps are spread throughout the global financial system, how far can we say that this system is based on real money or not? Might we say that the whole of banking depends upon the fictional structure of money, every bit as fictional as Baudelaire's text? The business of what is real and what is virtual in the financial system has surely brought us quite quickly to the border of the gift and of the economy of sacrifice. The future is a fiction invented by those who have lived in the past. The circulation of student loans, say, is a perfect example of counterfeit money become true capital:

> Is not the truth of capital, then, inasmuch as it produces interest without labour, by working all by itself as we say, counterfeit money? Is there a real difference here between real and counterfeit once there is capital? And credit? Everything depends on the act of faith . . . This text by Baudelaire deals, in effect, with the relations among fiction in general, literary fiction and capitalism, such as they might be photographed acting out a scene in the heart of the modern capital.[11]

The untested and risky assumptions concerning the take-up and repayment of tuition fees is precisely the equivalent of the *fausse-amie* who throws a counterfeit coin in the beggar's bowl. It will create an event, but not for the reasons they think, justify to themselves, or hope for return on.

The second and related strand is the question of that which links the modern phenomenon of literature to the financial system and to religion, namely, 'credit', or as '*crédit*' is usually translated from French, 'faith'. An enormous and unspoken act of collective belief is required every morning in order for the stock market to open and for banks to continue trading. Who, other than a true believer, could possibly tolerate the use of their deposit account to fund credit derivative swaps?

> Everything is [an] act of faith, phenomenon of credit or credence, of belief and conventional authority in this text which perhaps says something essential about what here links literature to belief, to credit and thus to capital, to economy and thus to politics. Authority is constituted

False Economy ~ 153

by accreditation, both in the sense of legitimation as effect of belief or credulity, and of bank credit, of capitalized interest.[12]

Derrida is writing here in 1977, four years after the establishment of the Chicago Board Options Exchange, which institutionalized the trade in futures and options, but four years before the introduction of swaps into the financial system and twelve years before the construction of the first credit default swap (engineered by J. P. Morgan to cover Exxon's exposure following the environmental disaster of the Exxon Valdez in Alaska). However, Derrida, like Karl Marx and Marcel Mauss before him, has correctly and presciently located the fictional nature of credit.[13] One accepts a fiction on trust, on the basis that it is nothing other than a fiction; we take the word of the narrator. As literature, it contains within it a system of reference that maintains the literary aporia throughout, accounting at the same time for the truth and the falsehood of the knowledge literature conveys about itself, distinguishing rigorously between metaphorical and referential language and delineating a difference between speech acts in books and speech acts in the real world. The referential system of money, in contrast, would seem to be much more shaky than literature's because it both requires a greater trust and fails to properly delineate the difference between money and counterfeit money, the real and the virtual. Derrida takes this question further in an aside to the final chapter of *Donner le temps*:

> Let us locate in passing here the space of a complex task: To study for example, in so-called modern literature, that is, contemporaneous with a capital—city, *polis*, metropolis—of a state and with a state of capital, the transformation of monetary forms (metallic, fiduciary—the bank note—or scriptural—the bank check), a certain rarification of payments in cash, the recourse to credit cards, the coded signature, and so forth, in short, a certain dematerialization of money, and therefore of all the scenes that depend upon it. 'Counterfeit money' and *Les faux-monnayeurs* belong to a specific period in the history of money.[14]

Derrida is here referring to André Gide's novel, but we should note in passing that in French 'les faux-monnayeurs' comes to stand by metonymic substitution for all fakery and all counterfeiting in general. This might well be an example of a white mythology of credit, one of the coins erased in Nietzsche's pocket whose fictional structure we no longer recognize.[15] The history of banking since Derrida's seminar has not only been based upon the accelerated dematerialization of money from the virtuality of credit cards and cheques into the imaginary structure of credit derivative swaps, but also on the eclipse of the author, if I might play on Roland Barthes for a moment. The entire difficulty of the financial crisis since 2008 has been based upon the inability to distinguish between good and bad debt by the anonymity of debtors when packaged, securitized and swapped. It simply has not been possible to decide whether one was dealing with a reliable narrator or not. In fact, the story of the narrator (i.e., the debtor) had ceased to be important; what mattered was the mediating extra-diegetic narrative of the financial institutions that sold the debt and the credit rating agency that confirmed the provenance of the story. Since both were interested parties, they were by definition unreliable narrators. There is no discrimination between the narratives of debtors, banks, central banks, public expenditure and government; everyone will be given the benefit of the doubt, the assumption behind student loans and sovereign bailouts is that everyone is a good debtor. This is the story that the national governments are telling themselves and the international bond market; much will depend upon this credulity.

The questions of literature and philosophy and debt are closely related. On the one hand, we might look at the way in which debt is a considerable question for literature itself. Here Dickens's *Little Dorrit*[16] might be a good example. The account draws upon the reserves of a debtor in the Marshalsea prison, William Dorrit, who is freed as a consequence of the intervention of Arthur Clennam. Clennam is an ostensibly disinterested Dickensian hero who wishes to see justice done to the Dorrits without expectation of gratitude or return. He pays the debts of Edward Dorrit, the wastrel son, and assists in the discovery of an unclaimed inheritance that enables William Dorrit to leave the Marshalsea. In turn, for this is a Dickens novel, Clennam is ruined by bad investments in a seemingly risk-free stock venture and is imprisoned in the Marshalsea. Clennam's mother reveals to William's daughter Amy (Little Dorrit), that she is heir to a great legacy, but Little Dorrit refuses her inheritance. When Clennam's business partner returns a rich man from an enterprise in Russia, he pays off Clennam's debts. Of course, Clennam's previous motives do not constitute a pure gift, consciously or unconsciously; he acted out of his love for Amy and at the end of the novel they are married as debt-free equals. Dickens's narrative is provocative because the narrator of the novel characterizes Amy as the 'child of the Marshalsea'; that is, the child born into debt and who only ever knows a life of debt, just as Barthes once characterized the subject as '*un bilan de faillite*'.[17] George Orwell criticized Dickens because he thought Dickens was unable see a world beyond individual philanthropy (i.e., a society beyond the pure gift).[18] He was unable to see a welfare state, which would take responsibility for Little Dorrit and educate her, perhaps even send her to a public university rather than have her achieve social mobility through first the inheritance of a gift and secondly through marriage. Given Little Dorrit's socioeconomic origins, she would probably, prior to 2012, have received state-funded bursaries to attend university, and although the Marshalsea was historically situated in Bermondsey within a few miles of the houses of parliament and the site of the 2010 'tuition fees riots' in the UK, Little Dorrit would probably not have been charged with horses and beaten with batons in the pursuit of her future.

This is in contrast to the text by Baudelaire, 'Beat Up the Poor!' ['Assommons les pauvres!'], which Derrida describes as a 'symmetrical counterpoint' to 'La fausse monnaie'.[19] Derrida takes much less time over this narrative, but it is worth dwelling on today. Here the narrator recounts how 'for fifteen days I had shut myself up in my room and had surrounded myself with the most popular books of the day . . . that treat of the art of making people happy, wise, and rich in twenty-four hours'. One can readily imagine the contemporary equivalents of these books on what is now fatuously described as 'well-being'. It is enough to make one sick, 'I had digested—or rather swallowed—all the lubrications of all the purveyors of public happiness—of those who advise the poor to become slaves, and of those who encourage them to believe that they are all dethroned kings'. Neoliberalism would now like the professional classes of tomorrow to be indebted to the state and then to measure their 'well-being'[20] as an indicator of national success: 'It will be readily understood that I was in a dazed state of mind bordering on idiocy'. What intrigues me here is that the narrator, the being (re) counter (as opposed to a bean counter) has been brought to the state of ideologically induced stupidity through reading, and a marathon of reading at that; fifteen days locked in a room on his own, like an academic researching the condition of well-being. He leaves his room 'with a terrible thirst' because 'the passion for bad literature engenders a proportionate need for fresh air and cooling drinks'. Having consumed vast quantities of idiocy, he must now wash it away, exchanging a thirst for non-knowledge with a need for the disinfectant of alcohol and oxygen. In other words, he enters into a credit derivative swap in which he hedges the time spent on bankrupt ideas against his faith in fresh air. He has earned his drink after the sacrifice of solitary reading. As he is about to enter a bar, he comes across a beggar. Unlike the two friends in 'la fausse monnaie', he does not give the beggar alms but, encouraged by the voices in his head,[21] he decides 'a man is the equal of another only if he can prove it, and to be worthy of liberty a man must fight for it'. Accordingly, he beats up the beggar 'pounding his head against the wall . . . sure that in this deserted suburb no policeman would disturb me for some time'. While 'kettling' (to use a term borrowed from London's Metropolitan Police Force) the beggar, a philosophical miracle occurs, 'O bliss of the philosopher when he sees the truth of his theory verified!', the beggar proves himself the equal of the narrator by retaliating and 'proceeded to give me two black eyes, to knock out four of my teeth and . . . to beat me to a pulp'. The narrator describes himself as satisfied as 'one of the Porch sophists' and declaring the beggar his equal, shares out his purse, telling him that should another beggar ask him for alms, he ought to apply the narrator's 'theory' and teach the other the same painful lesson concerning equality. The text ends with the beggar swearing that he understands the theory and vowing to follow this advice.

By any reckoning, this is a remarkable text; how shall we read it? On the one hand, we might take it as a neoliberal allegory of tough love for the poor, who must not be satisfied by handouts but learn to stand on their own two feet and take on board the lessons of a sacrificial economy in which equal status is attained through beating the other to a pulp. On the other hand, and in contrast to 'la fausse monnaie', the moral of this story might be that awakening from the torpor of idiocy-inducing ideology, the narrator has the revelation that not only must he give to the beggar but, as Derrida says in his brief reading of this text, he must give well ('*il faut bien payer*').²² The narrator gives a gift to the poor but does not merely offer money in return for indebtedness or spiritual advancement but goes beyond the material benefit of the gift to give added value in the form of a theory of giving. This would be the excessive violence of the pure gift or a gift without conditions that taught the poor a lesson. In this sense, it is the perfect allegory for school children, university applicants and student protesters whose futures have been mortgaged before their education has even begun and who are for their troubles beaten up by the state that is offering the gift of a student loan. Perhaps, rather than being Dickens's children of the Marshalsea, they will prove themselves the equal of their creditors by being worthy of liberty by fighting for it.

Let me conclude by way of reference to the epigram from *The Post Card* that has overseen this chapter from the very beginning. Here Derrida has in mind the Platonic tradition to which we are all indebted in every aspect of our daily lives. I think the striking sentence in this paragraph is the first one: 'They have signed *our* I.O.U. and we can no longer not acknowledge it'. It is not that we have signed an I.O.U. for the debt that we owe to Socrates and Plato but that they in advance of us have mortgaged our future, signed 'our I.O.U.' for us before we have even began to live in the world. Derrida specifically names this structure as a fiction, 'a story, the trap of who signs an I.O.U. for the other such that the other finds himself engaged before having known a thing about it'. In this way, we are all infinitely indebted to the philosophical tradition before we have even begun to read or started to take up our place of study.[23] Derrida calls this a 'children's story' and a 'love story'. It is certainly the story of our children today who have had their I.O.U. signed in advance by a generation of politicians who have thrown them into debt before they have even begun to read. As we have seen above, to inhabit capitalism is never a question of 'paying off the debt', it is always a case of having had the I.O.U. signed for us in advance of our entry into capital. The task, then, is not to refuse debt but to affirm another register of debt, an infinite and unpayable debt: our debts to the western tradition, to philosophy and to the university. One cannot live without faith or debt. Today we need to articulate a counter-faith: a belief in the public realm, publicly funded institutions, the idea of the university, and a belief in the necessity of critical thought. This would be a catechism so simple that it would be worthy of the term 'a child's story'. If the 'I.O.U.' is also a love story, it is a tale of how we do not fall in love but that love falls upon us, smothering us with its dialectic of our infinite debt to the one we love in advance of any engagement with it. In this sense, it is also the story of university managers and higher-education policy leaders who are indebted to the very idea of the institution they serve prior to any understanding of what the institution might mean. They have had their I.O.U. signed for them in advance of their entrance into the principal's office; in this way their debts and duties are infinite. These vice-chancellors and presidents have a choice today, to accept the credit default swap that passes the debt of the university from state to student or, to affirm the gift of higher education by refusing this sacrificial economy. They may well predominately choose the former and so, like Baudelaire's narrator, beat up the poor, but they will not do so out of the same theoretical motivation. Rather, they will be like the somnambulant friend in 'la fausse monnaie' who thinks they are doing good by offering counterfeit money, seeking advancement while hedging themselves and their institutions against loss. They, like Baudelaire's false-alms giver, deserve our contempt: 'I will never forgive him the ineptitude of his calculation . . . the most irreparable of vices is to do evil out of stupidity'.

Notes

1. Jacques Derrida, *The Post Card: From Socrates to Freud and Beyond*, trans. Alan Bass (Chicago: University of Chicago Press, 1987, 2nd edition).

2. Jacques Derrida, *Specters of Marx: The State of the Debt, the Work of Mourning and the New International*, trans. Peggy Kamuf (London and New York: Routledge, 1994).

3. For details such as these I am indebted to John Lancaster's *Whoops! Why Everyone Owes Everyone and No One Can Pay* (London: Penguin, 2010). The chapters of this book first appeared in *The London Review of Books*; they should be read as an autobiographical novel, as a form of testimony from one who lived through the crash. Other helpful nonacademic introductions include Philip Coggan, *The Money Machine: How the City Works* (London: Penguin, 2002), Charles R. Morris, *The Trillion Dollar Meltdown: Easy Money, High Rollers, and the Great Credit Crash* (New York: Public Affairs Press, 2008) and Frank Partnoy, *F.I.A.S.C.O.: Blood in the Water on Wall Street* (London: Profile Business Press, 2009).

4. Derrida addresses this distinction in Aristotle's *Politics*, 1257b, 1258a, and goes on to suggest that this strategic distinction can only ever be provisional and quickly dissolves in any reading of economy; see Jacques Derrida, *Given Time: 1. Counterfeit Money*, trans. Peggy Kamuf (Chicago: Chicago University Press, 1992), pp. 157–59.

5. John Lancaster, *Whoops!* p. 62.

6. On the animal, see Jacques Derrida, *The Animal That Therefore I Am*, trans. David Wills (Bronx, NY: Fordham University Press, 2008). The seminar on the death sentence is as yet unpublished, however Derrida discusses it at length in Jacques Derrida and Elisabeth Roudinesco, *For What Tomorrow . . . : A Dialogue*, trans. Jeff Fort (Redwood City, CA: Stanford University Press, 2004).

7. In reading the gift through sacrifice, we should also attend to Jacques Derrida, *The Gift of Death*, trans. David Wills (Chicago: University of Chicago Press, 1995). Here Derrida famously asks why he should only feed his own cat when so many other cats across Paris are starving, leading him to suggest '*tout autre est tout autre*' which Wills translates as 'every other (one) is every (bit) other', in an attempt to understand the impossibility of a calculation as to who or what is to be sacrificed to the greater good.

8. Derrida, *Given Time*, p. 137.

9. Derrida, *Given Time*, p. 13.

10. Derrida, *Given Time*, p. 59.

11. Derrida, *Given Time*, p. 124. After Baudelaire's own essay on Constantin Guys, Derrida gives chapter 3 of *Given Time* the subtitle 'Baudelaire, Painter of Modern Life'.

12. Derrida, *Given Time*, p. 97.

13. See Karl Marx, *A Contribution to the Critique of Political Economy*, ed. Maurice Dobb (New York: International Publishers, 1970).

14. Derrida, *Given Time*, p. 110.

15. See Jacques Derrida, 'White Mythology: Metaphor in the Text of Philosophy' in *Margins of Philosophy*, trans. Alan Bass (Brighton: Harvester Wheatsheaf Press, 1982).

16. Charles Dickens, *Little Dorrit* [1857], eds. Stephen and Helen Wall (London: Penguin, 2003).

17. This phrase, '*un bilan de faillite*' means a register or index of debts produced for the assessment of bankruptcy. I am grateful to Celine Surprenant for this reference.

18. See George Orwell, 'Can Socialists Be Happy?' *Tribune*, 20 December 1943. Available as 'Why Socialists Don't Believe in Fun' from *The Observer* 28 June 1998 at www.observer.co.uk.

19. Charles Baudelaire, 'La fausse monnaie', is reproduced in dual-language copy as an appendix to the English edition of *Given Time*. See also, Charles Baudelaire, *Paris Spleen*, trans. Louis Varèse (New York: Norton, 1970).

20. Along with Nicolas Sarkozy in France, David Cameron in the UK has proposed a 'well-being' index to measure national happiness to inform policy decisions rather than, say, the measurement of GDP. Since, as Georges Danton asks 'who is to be happy if not all?', this seeming measure beyond market calculation is of course the most cynical of sacrificial economies. I discuss the question of well-being in relation to Rousseau's 'On Public Happiness' in the introduction to *The Paul de Man Notebooks* (Edinburgh: Edinburgh University Press, 2014).

21. At this point in the text, the narrator invokes the good demon who advised Socrates, 'There is, however, this difference between Socrates' Demon and mine, that his Demon appeared to him only to forbid, to warn or to prevent, whereas mine deigns to advise, suggest or persuade. Poor Socrates had only a censor; mine is a great affirmer, mine is a Demon of action, a Demon of combat'. In this way, we might add to Derrida's list of the debt to Plato and Socrates in the epigram from *The Post Card* with which we began, 'piss against a tree, beat up the poor . . .'

22. Derrida, *Given Time*, p. 139.

23. I am grateful to Simon Glendinning for directing me towards Derrida's text, 'The Right to Philosophy from the Cosmopolitical Point of View (the Example of an International Institution)' in which Derrida discusses Immanuel Kant's 'Idea of a Universal History from a Cosmopolitical Point of View' in a passage Derrida gives the title 'Of Philosophy: Debt and Duty'. I reproduce it here as it seems germane to all that has been said above:

> This enlightenment, and with it a certain sympathetic interest which the enlightened man inevitably feels for anything good which he comprehends fully, must gradually spread upwards towards the thrones and even influence their principles of government. But while, for example, our world rulers have no money to spare for public educational institutions or indeed for anything which concerns the world's best interests (*das Weltbeste*), because everything has already been calculated out in advance for the next war, they will nonetheless find that it is to their own advantage at least not to hinder their citizens' private efforts in this direction, however weak and slow they may be. But in the end, war itself gradually becomes not only a highly artifical undertaking, extremely uncertain in its outcome for both parties, but also a very dubious risk to take, since its aftermath is felt by the state in the shape of a constantly increasing national debt (a modern invention) (*Schuldenlast [einer neuen Erfindung]*) whose repayment becomes unforeseeable (*unabsehlich*) [repayment is *Tilgung*, the annulation, the erasure of the debt, the

False Economy ~ 161

destruction which Hegel distinguishes from the *Aufhebung* which erases while conserving]. And in addition, the effects which an upheaval in any state.

Derrida goes on to say, 'With this citation I wanted to suggest that the right to philosophy may require from now on a distinction among several registers of debt, between a finite debt and an infinite debt, between debt and duty, between a certain erasure and a certain reaffirmation of debt—and sometimes a certain erasure in the name of reaffirmation.'

Translated by Thomas Dutoit, *Surfaces*, http://www.pum.umontreal.ca/revues/surfaces/index.html. [under S 1. Kant's *Streit der Fakultaten* or *The Conflict of Faculties* (Derrida)].

The Godfather

Martin McQuillan

For Ken McMullen

Laguna Beach, 8 May 1998

I didn't have the heart for postcards this time, my stay will have been too sad (death of Jean-Francois Lyotard, with whom I timeshared the same house at Laguna Beach for years—I have been teaching at Irvine, twenty minutes from here, several weeks a year for twelve years—and still other commotions . . .). A letter just before returning, therefore, instead of cards. I would have liked to tell you of my love for Laguna and for those I call, also in 'Circumfession', 'my friends the birds' on their white rock. I took some photos of them for your book. Haven't moved this year, the telephone is hell when the news isn't good . . . Normally I go several times to Newport Beach, past Corona de Mar (Fashion Island or South Coast Plaza, for shopping or to buy French newspapers), once or twice to Los Angeles, which is nearby. Sometimes I leave Laguna Beach for two or three days on a trip I wouldn't admit to (Las Vegas, Death Valley, Boulder City, or the Grand Canyon by night train—the South West Chief, my very own American cinema . . .). Failing always impossible stories—anyway, we won't have the time or place—be content with dreams from Laguna, as promised.

Jacques Derrida, letter to Catherine Malabou, *Counterpath*[1]

In the book *La Contre-allée*, Catherine Malabou reproduces several items of correspondence with Jacques Derrida, written to accompany the publication of her text '*L'Ecartment des voies: Dérive, arrivée, catastrophe*'. In the letter written from Laguna Beach, in southern California, on 8 May 1998, Derrida tells Malabou about his daily routine when teaching at the University of California (UC), Irvine, and of less routine trips on the Amtrak train, the Southwest Chief, that runs from Los Angeles to Chicago. Derrida says (in the form of a letter to be openly published in a book) that these trips to Las Vegas, Death Valley, Boulder City and the Grand Canyon are not ones he would admit to. The confession is a poignant one, in the context of a letter that opens with the sad news of the death of Jean-François Lyotard, his compatriot with whom he shared a house in Laguna Beach. These train journeys are not to be admitted to, not because they are clandestine, perhaps, but because they are not philosophical or academic in orientation. Earlier in the letter, he tells of a visit to UC, Davis, to speak on de Man and materiality; such travel is proper to the philosopher. Even when he does not want to travel, out of exhaustion or inconvenience or fear of the event, a sense of duty, Derrida notes in this letter, always compels him to attend the academic gathering: 'neither courage nor masochism but another law, that no longer belongs to the world, dictates to me the compelling need *to go*'.[2] It is difficult not to recognize the need for academics to 'unfailingly obey some other' that renders us passive in the attendance of events that we would rather not be at. However, the train rides that Derrida 'wouldn't admit to' are of a different order. These journeys, under the cover of darkness, on the night train to Chicago, are not business trips, but travels for pleasure, and so should not take up space in an academic book ('we won't have the time or place'). They are for Derrida connected to the experience of film; he calls the window of the Southwest Chief, 'my very own American cinema'. There is little to be seen out of the window of an Amtrak train in the middle of the night, so this is a curious kind of cinema screen, one on which the projection has yet to begin, as if Derrida had arrived too early or too late in the cinema. Or it is a screen on which Derrida himself projects what he calls 'impossible stories', ones that are 'failing always'. These are stories about America, the iconic tourist sites that he mentions have all been over-imagined in American cinema, as has

The Godfather ~ 165

the figure of the train, from Alfred Hitchcock to Richard Linklater. America has been written in advance for Derrida by cinema, or we might say has been screened in advance, both in the sense of showing a film and the screen that blocks, obscures, or separates us from whatever lies behind it. A screen is there precisely so we do not see, like a movie theatre without projection, or a train window at night that only reflects back our own image: my other self looking back, inspecting, me.

In Benoît Peeters's biography of Derrida, he writes of the young Jackie growing up in Algeria during World War II, between the liberation of North Africa and the Allied invasion of Europe, when American G.I.s occupied the country:

> For Jackie, it was 'a first amazing encounter' with Foreigners from a faraway land. The 'Yankees' ('*Amerloques*'), as he and his friends called them... 'Before I ever went to America, America took over my "home", he later said'.[3]

This is an experience of occupation that in particular is related to the experience, and the pleasure, of cinema. Peeters writes:

> Another favourite pastime was the cinema, as soon as they had enough money to buy a ticket. In Jackie's eyes, this was real time out, an essential emancipation from his family, but also a sort of erotic initiation. He would remember all his life an adaptation of *Tom Sawyer*, especially the scene where Tom is trapped in a cave with a small girl.

If we take Peeters's biography, based on interviews with Derrida, at face value, then it is notable that what connects the experience of the young Jackie during the war with the Jacques Derrida who writes to Catherine Malabou in 1998 is that cinema constitutes an escape, 'real time out' away from his family, or a nighttime train ride that should not be admitted to by the philosopher. Cinema is the night train to America, to dreams of Laguna, and the failing impossible stories of filmic culture. It is also an occupation of the mind, a type of 'home cinema'; before one ever arrives in America, it has already presented itself through cinema, taking its place in our own spaces. This is as true for Americans as it is for Europeans or Algerians: The image of America precedes itself, and through that image the idea of America installs itself in a phantomatic relation to the psychic terrain of culture. American global influence does not require boots on the ground in the form of liberating G.I.s; it reaches much further and more effectively through the cinematic image—an image that is associated with pleasure and with eroticism, where childish fantasy is preoccupied not by troop movements but by images of Tom Sawyer and Becky Thatcher in peril.

These impossible stories are always love stories, like Cary Grant and Eva Marie Saint on the train from New York to Chicago heading west in *North by Northwest*. Derrida's letter is also an impossible love letter, 'I would have liked to tell you of my love for Laguna'. The recent death of Lyotard turns this love into melancholy and the work of writing into a work of mourning: mourning America, as well as his friend. Perhaps, this is what happens during the preoccupation of the global cultural imagination by American cinema. The image of America that presents itself is one that has already gone, gone before us and departed, but also one that never truly existed, or disappears in its presentation. The work of the image and of receiving the image is the work of mourning for what is gone but which must by 'neither courage nor masochism but another law' be incorporated into the psychic terrain. We have no choice because the image of America presents itself before we have even begun to choose between receiving or not. It is an originary loss, a re-presentation that has always already disappeared, initiating a mourning that precedes all work and desire. In the beginning was America and I will never get over it, to paraphrase the Derrida of *La Carte Postale*. To which we might add, America, if there is such a thing, given that America in this sense is an image of an idea that is already lost before it is presented.

Cinema is not uniquely American but Southern California is a uniquely American site of cinema, the place of projection for all the fantasies and phantoms of American film and everything that falls out from it, which includes U.S. cultural and economic imperialism, but also the erotic initiation of a young Jackie Derrida. In this letter, cinema is *eros* to the *thanatos* of the academic conference. Two different types of performance, one that takes the form of a pleasure that cannot be spoken of, the other that takes the form of a duty that cannot be explained. One is a life-affirming escape; the other is a passivity that requires subordination. But that escape has always failed in advance, the image is not true, Las Vegas or Hollywood Boulevard is not a place to stay, the traveller must always return. America, in this sense, the image and idea of America, is a melancholy pleasure. It is a terminus, the end of the line, the last stop on the rail track, where one goes to end a story, not to initiate new ones. This is the idea of America that Walter Benjamin knows so well in his text 'Central Park':[4] if America lies in your future, it is only death that awaits you. Equally, the passive subordination to duty that compels the professor to attend the academic event leads to writing: the need to write and the fear of turning up at the event without having written. The university conference gives rise to philosophy and to performances that can be avowed (like Derrida's trip to UC, Davis), while cinema is something that must happen in the dark, both in the darkest of screening rooms and under the cover of darkness on the night train. The trip to Death Valley escapes writing ('there will not be time or place'). Perhaps, one pays the debt for such moments of pleasure by the crushing sense of duty to work during the day, in an economic exchange that runs by its own circuit of desire.

The setup here is too neat, though. The Derrida who says he should not admit to his train ride to the Grand Canyon is like the Freud of 'A Disturbance of Memory on the Acropolis',[5] who goes on holiday to Greece only to be wracked by guilt that he is not worthy of his vacation because he has not worked hard enough to deserve it. In this sense, the trip for pleasure becomes just one more occasion for work as an instance of self-analysis and the topic for another essay. Equally, Derrida folds his own line of flight back into a writing that constitutes a contribution to an academic publication and once again the other law of academic duty reasserts itself as the recuperation of pleasure into the work of the university. This work knows no boundary, especially when it comes to cinema. How often does the pleasure afforded by watching the much-loved film transform itself into the duty to produce academic writing? When one is a humanities academic, one cannot watch cinema as if one were not an academic, any more than the philosopher can read philosophy as if a philosophical ingénue. However, one can always read or view, as if for the first time; this would be an inaugural, singular and unique reading or viewing familiar to Derrida. It is not without its own economy of debt and duty, pleasure and desire, that anchors it to the context of the technical and the university, and the ludicrously 'professorial', but it also gives the text or the film a chance, a fighting chance to surprise—just as this letter from Derrida makes an intervention in the professorial text of Malabou, bringing surprise and pleasure as a strategy of interruption and disorientation, directing the law of the university against itself to save itself from its own desires. Here we might note, without further elaboration, that if the professorial law of duty wants to be saved from itself, then what the university wants is cinema.

When asked, Derrida would say that he did not have a favourite film but that he was fond of The Godfather, 'I have watched The Godfather ten times. I must watch it whenever it is on'.[6] One can only speculate as to why Jacques Derrida, a charismatic and influential man who sat at the centre of an extensive network of friends, associates, clients and supporters, some of whom offered protection, some of whom sought favours, faced with external competing interests that would have happily seen him wiped out, would find Francis Ford Coppola's 1972 film so compelling. In the past, I have used the term 'the Family' to refer to the worldwide affiliation of scholars who were close to Derrida.[7] In particular, I use the term in relation to a certain omertà of deconstruction, which was often in operation in order not to bring disrespect onto the Family. In the time since Derrida's death I have used the term 'the Family' to refer to those who were particularly close to Derrida and who have made such efforts to open up a future for the legacy of Derrida through ongoing translations and publication, even if such a project carries within it the risk of another form of interment. In particular, and to be precise, I have used the term 'the Family' to distinguish one form of fidelity to a Derridean future from that of others who mobilize and incorporate deconstruction according to other horizons and logics. The idea of the Family raises the questions of legitimacy and inheritance: Who is the true heir, who are the legitimate ones, shall the sons or the daughters inherit, who are the adopted ones, and who are the disavowed bastards? Derrida himself is of course 'the purest of bastards leaving bastards everywhere'. However, I have never used the phrase 'the deconstructive Mafia'; this would surely be pushing a metaphor too far. We also might recall that from childhood Derrida would go to the cinema precisely to have time away from his family. To which we should add, Family, if there is such a thing.

Coppola's film might be characterized as *Two Weddings and a Funeral, and a Baptism*. The film is punctuated by a series of set-piece displays of the sacramental that binds the Corleone family to the authority of the church and state, which it corrupts and erodes in turn. The idea of the Family, as we inherit it from, say, a Rousseau or a Hegel, takes its authority from the state as the proper configuration for the inheritance of property; the Corleones use the idea of Family as a way to establish a border between the legitimacy of the state and their own form of criminality. The Family in this sense poses a challenge to the state by questioning the state's monopoly on violence that gives it legitimacy. In order to maintain the status quo, and the fiction of the state's legitimacy, deals must be done, contracts set and payments must be made that seemingly separate the criminal Family from the legitimacy of the state but in fact ties one closely to the other through the corruption and bribery of public officials as a mafia state within a state.

In *Specters of Marx*, Derrida describes the mafia as a 'super-efficient and properly capitalist phantom-State'.[8] The idea of the Family in the western political tradition upholds the state as its minimal founding unit, while the Corleone family puts the state at risk by compromising its ability to act with sovereign impunity. In two key scenes, the one echoing the other, two successive Godfathers, first Vito and then Michael stress the importance of preserving the unity and self-sufficiency of the Family. When Sonny speaks out of turn at a meeting with a rival Mafioso, his father upbraids him, saying, 'Never tell anyone outside of the family what you are thinking again'. When Fredo questions his brother Michael's plans to buy out a casino in Las Vegas, he is put in his place: 'Don't ever take sides with anyone against the family ever again'. Don Vito stresses that a man should spend time with his family, and he who does not cannot be truly a man, while Sonny beats his brother-in-law to a pulp for assaulting his sister, but keeps a mistress in the Bronx. The same brother-in-law, Carlo, betrays Sonny to a rival family who gun him down on the Long Island Causeway. In turn, Michael brings Carlo into the family business only in order to have him garroted in the film's closing scenes for his part in the betrayal of Sonny, leaving his own sister a widow, having just taken on the role of baptismal godfather to her child. As Tolstoy dryly observes, all happy families are alike, each unhappy family is unhappy in its own way.

The fault lines in the Corleone family appear whenever there is an attempt to uphold a rigorous distinction between the Family and 'business'. The Family is family and Business is business, as the logic would run, but the Corleone empire is a Family Business; it both is run by members of the family (genetic members and adopted members) and concerns the business of the Family. The 'Dutch Irish' consigliere Tom Hagen tells Sonny that he is as much a son to Don Vito as Sonny ever was. The action of the second half of the film revolves around a feud and subsequent truce between the five families of the New York Mafia. On Don Vito's retirement and Michael's ascension to head of the Family, members of the Family, Tessio and Clemenza, wish to establish their own 'families'. Michael has at least two families of his own in the film: through his marriage to Apollonia in Sicily and to Kay Adams in New York. The Mafia Family presents itself as closed, sealed by armed guards at the gates of their mansion, but the film proliferates families and family ties, making and unmaking them, affirming them and betraying them, opening the Family up to the risk of its own undoing.

The economy that runs between business and the Family predicates the matrix out of which all the structures and thetics of the film run. Sonny silences Carlo when he tells him over a family dinner, 'We don't discuss business at the table'. But commerce is what provides for the occasion of the family dinner; the story of Michael as one of the eponymous godfathers is the narrative of one who should not have been involved in the family business but who makes it his business to run the family. The feud between the five families revolves around a dispute over the regulation of an emerging narcotics economy in New York and Don Vito's refusal to allow his state contacts in public office to offer protection to the new trade. 'The Turk', Sollozzo, who attempts to assassinate Don Vito, repeatedly notes that he has no disrespect for the Corleone family; 'It's just business'. Tom Hagen cautions Sonny not to take the shooting of Don Vito personally, 'It's just business'. One should respect the Family, but equally one should respect business; the boundary between them is paramount, just as the outcome of the business of business is the assassination of family members, which bleeds into the domestic and all its relations and affiliations. In the climactic scenes after his father's funeral, Michael declares, 'Today I settle all family business'. This includes the murder of Sal Tessio, a family member, who has betrayed Michael to a rival don, Barzini. As Sal is driven away to be executed, he tells Tom Hagen, 'Tell Michael it was only business, I always liked him'.

The effect of the film, and Mario Puzo's novel, is to undo the fiction of strict divisions between the power of the state, the family structure, and an economy of capital that runs through increasingly indistinguishable legitimate and illegitimate routes, from cartel to cartel. In New York, as in Sicily, wherever the mafia takes hold, states and para-states accommodate this circuitry of blood and capital to the point where the functioning of the nation-state or the state of New York becomes dependent upon the parasite, which both drains it and feeds it. As the dons frequently comment, this is a question of 'respect', of showing respect and of receiving respect for the respective values of family, business, the church and state.

As Derrida points out in an interview with Bernard Stiegler, respect is an anagram of both spectre and scepter.[9] Respect concerns both sovereign authority and a phantomatic relation to that authority, insofar as any relation as a relation is not a thing of essence but an experience of difference. The sceptre of the sovereign is to the finger of the ruler as the phallus is to the penis, a phantomatic fetishistic structure that defines a set of imaginary relations. The state and the para-state, the police and the mafia, business and the family are all installed one in the other in a set of spectral relations, the one haunting the other. When it comes to the business of ghosts, there is no exorcism that does not result in an immediate conjuration, a coming back of ghosts that defines the future rather than the past. There can be no settling of accounts with ghosts. Michael's ruthless settling of family business, taking revenge for the death of his brother and the shooting of his father, crosses the line between what is 'just business' and what is 'proper to his family'. Like Hamlet, he seeks to avenge his father's ghost, only to give rise to further apparitions that draw him inexorably into the vice of the family and its business. The godfather is a ghostfather, a phantomatic sovereign who presides over a kingdom of ghosts, in which learning to live is so closely related to learning how to take life. The power of the film and its ongoing cinematic influence lies in this ambiguity that puts the criminal family and the criminality of the family at the centre of the screen, suggesting that life (and death) is a complicated business.

The film concludes with Michael literally taking on the role of godfather to Connie and Carlo's son; Vito had previously been baptismal godfather to the singer Johnny Fontane, whose career he assists by leaving a horse's head in the bed of a Hollywood producer. The godfather is the one who names and anoints, giving responses on behalf of the child and taking responsibility for that child. For Vito and Michael to take on the role of godfather to an infant is a serious responsibility, one that Michael gives long consideration to before agreeing, as a way of squaring the circle of the murder of Carlo. Michael substitutes himself for the child's blood father, the name of 'God' here standing as an exchange and surrogate, adopting the child as his own as one more iteration of kinship and kingship in a chain of affiliations that is also haunted by a sequence of betrayals. In this ghostly economy, responsibility on the part of the godfather always takes the form of an offer that cannot be refused: an exchange without reserve. This is a contract that cannot be refused, a gift that cannot be returned, and an obligation that must be repaid in full. Such an offer usually involves a threat to life, there is always the option to refuse, but the result of such a refusal is not just the severed head of a horse under the bedclothes in Southern California but the threat that worse is yet to come. Ultimately, the Hollywood producer gives Johnny Fontane the role in his movie that he had previously refused.

The offer cannot be refused because of the consequences that determine not the present but the future. It is a promise without the possibility of prolepsis; that is to say, a promise that threatens to fulfill itself without risk of failure. As Paul de Man comments in his reading of the Lawgiver in Rousseau's 'The Social Contract', only a god could make such a promise.[10] For mere mortals, a promise is only a promise insofar as it contains within itself the necessary possibility of its noncompletion. The promise that auto-completes is no promise at all, merely the enactment of an inevitable calculus. This is the sort of promise and contract that a Godfather purports to offer, one that cannot be refused. This is a promise that is underwritten by the threat of a future violence if the contract is not honoured. However, this is not necessarily an aberrant form of promising; it is, after all, not personal, it is only business.

The Godfather threatens violence if a contract is not upheld, while the state and Business, and the state as Business, has its own rule of law that is equally underwritten by a violent monopoly, more or less visible than that commanded by the sceptre of Don Corleone. However, despite threats and appearances, the Godfather's promise must remain as phantomatic as any other promise, insofar as it is a promise, or contract, and not another calculation that operates under the displaced name of a promise; it must still be necessarily possible that the threat is not carried out or the debt not collected. However, the force of the law of the Godfather is such that one dare not accept that wager: Death remains the most likely outcome for those who break their side of the bargain. Death lies at the end of the circuit of a promise that auto-completes. Business is business and depends upon the rule of law that upholds the contract, even when it is the business of death at the hands of the Family. This is the super-efficiency of a properly capitalist phantom state.

For some, reading Derrida is an offer that they cannot understand: an impossible failing gift, like the stories of the personal American cinema that Derrida views from the train window. Today, Derrida is the ghostfather who returns to the stage to make us an offer that cannot be refused. Imagining Derrida, we must take responsibility for him, to tell his story aright, whatever route that story might take and however 'right' or legitimate its telling might be. The ghostfather watches us behind his visor; there is always a question to be answered in that phantomatic relation, as we are inspected by the law of the spectre who looks back at us, like the reflection in the glass on the night train. In Derrida this question of the ghost has always been related to cinema.

The question of the ghost in Derrida receives its first fully concentrated consideration in the 1981 film made with Ken McMullen, Ghost Dance, in which Derrida plays himself, opposite Pascale Ogier as an anthropology student named Pascale. The film is justly famous within a certain philosophical community for the onscreen appearance of Derrida in two sequences, one shot in the Le Select restaurant in Paris, lasting around a minute, and a longer sequence filmed at Derrida's office at the Ecole Normale Supérieure in which he is in conversation with Ogier.[11] The two moments, however, constitute only a fraction of the film, which is notable for an early-career performance by Robbie Coltrane as a drummer who improvizes rhythms to accompany the Shipping Forecast on BBC Radio. Other significant moments in the film include an appearance by Dominique Pinon as a tour guide at the Mur de Communards in Père Lachaise Cemetery in Paris. The film explicitly places the question of the ghost in conjunction with the task of reading Marx some twelve years before Derrida's lectures that constitute *Specters de Marx* first given at the University of California, Riverside, during one of his sojourns at Laguna Beach. The sequence that immediately follows the interview between Derrida and Ogier is a cut to Marianne, played by Leonie Mellinger, who appears to be reclining naked and postcoital on the tomb of Karl Marx in Highgate Cemetery. As the camera pans out, we become aware that the image of Marx is in fact a reproduction, a poster on the wall of Marianne's flat, placing Marx in a double phantomatic relation to us, first as his own gravestone and second as a copy of his own image. Marx is another ghostfather in this film, who slips from a godlike sovereignty into the complicated playback loop of the cinematic image—in this case, one that passes through what Benoît Peeters termed earlier, 'a certain erotic initiation'.

The setup for the scene in the café Le Select is familiar to watchers of philosophers on film. Here we have the male master and the female student; Pascale being passed on to the character Derrida by a colleague who calls her 'my problem student'. The introduction occurs because Pascale has lied to her tutor about having previously been in correspondence with Derrida as an explanation for persistent absenteeism. On the face of it, the scene in the restaurant represents a classic frieze of gender relations within the institutional setting of university philosophy. A scene that echoes the episode 'Nana fait de la philosophie sans le savoir' from Godard's *Vivre Sa Vie* from 1962, in which Anna Karina plays a prostitute who attempts to pick up, in a café, the philosopher of language Brice Parain, playing himself. As part of her routine Nana asks the philosopher, 'What do you think about love?', but rather than sweet nothings, she receives an improvised lecture on contingency in Leibnitz. An entire essay could be given over to Karina's eye-line, as it moves between Parain and the camera, roaming between distraction and incomprehension, looking out into the cinema audience as if for confirmation or assistance. She makes philosophy without knowing it in a performance that simultaneously presents the epistemological and the cinematic image; the response of one to the other finds its place in the lines of sight opened up by the direction of Karina's eyes looking out into the dark of cinematic space. It is a scenario that is repeated in McMullen's later film, An Organisation of Dreams, in 2009, when Gabriella Wright, playing the journalist Nagra, interviews Bernard Stiegler in the Arènes de Lutèce on the topic of American cinema and cultural imperialism: 'Trade follows films', quotes Stiegler. While this setup is visually important to McMullen's representation of philosophy on screen, the narrative that follows in both Ghost Dance and An Organisation of Dreams cannot be read so simply as another reinscription of sexual difference within philosophy as an experience of inequality.

In Ghost Dance, the two women, Pascale and Marianne, are the protagonists of a philosophical adventure. Pascale is completing a thesis on cargo cults of the Far East, including the myth of a giant bird which divides into two women who, when together, have magical powers. The agency of the Pascale and Marianne, as screen magicians, combining performance with proposition, the phantomatic with the technological, leads the film into a deep consideration of the Paris Commune, capitalism and gender.

Aestheticization, femininity and agency are considerable stakes in the cinema of Ken McMullen, as they are in the history of art, to which McMullen's painterly films properly belong. It is no accident that Leonie Mellinger's character is named after the revolutionary figure of France, her appearance in front of the tomb of Karl Marx referencing Delacroix's Liberty Leading the People of 1830. But this is a curious kind of figuration, not a goddess advancing with revolutionary standard and musket, but a flat-share in Kentish Town in the early years of the Thatcher government. The peeling interiors, decorated with communard posters, seem at a remove from the heroic panorama of Delacroix. The walls in the flat with their revolutionary iconography reflect the scenes in Père Lachaise when Dominique Pinon informs a group of American tourists that this is the site where 147 fédérés of the Paris Commune were rounded up, shot and thrown into an open trench at the foot of the wall. The flaked and flaky surfaces of the walls in London and Paris are the ground to the figure and figuration of Marianne and Pascale. As in the case of the tomb of Marx, the relation between figure and ground is not straightforward. There is artifice at work here:

The tomb is not a tomb, and the walls are not mere background; they work more in the manner of a screen. In Le Select café we also see Derrida sitting in front of a poster for an exhibition by Titus Carmel, which he in fact contributed to and discusses in La Vérité en peinture. The art direction here was by accident rather than design, but the directorial technique of McMullen relies on such designed accidents, in the collapse and reworking of figure and ground, art history and cinema. In this film, Liberty is compromised by Thatcherism, the Commune is replaced by the economic necessity of the flat-share or even the squat at a time when there is no such thing as society. This film, like Derrida's later book on Marx, is not only a sustained imagining of the hauntology of telecommunications but is also a work of mourning for a revolutionary inheritance now out of joint in the age of the global economy. Marianne is a haunted and haunting figure, every bit as spectral as the late Pascale Ogier (of whom we shall speak in a moment).

The women in the film are ghosts; they move through scenes and scenarios as phantoms are said to walk through walls, whether that wall is in a Kentish Town flat or a Parisian cemetery, or even on the screen of a cinema. However, it is not clear whether the women should, like myths and radio waves in aboriginal cultures, be accorded supernatural origins. The unscripted and improvised nature of the film is every bit as technical as any other film in the cinematic canon: The magic of the movies is neither natural nor supernatural; it is, like all magic, technical. It is not a coincidence that the Magic Castle of the Academy of Magical Arts of America now sits in Hollywood, Southern California, or that many of the early European cinematographers were stage magicians who recognized the potential of the new medium as a tool for conjuration. Magic in this sense is the conjuration of ghosts by technical means: making appearance appear in its disappearance, making 'seem' the origin of show, or 'be finale of seem' as Wallace Stevens might have put it.[12] A conjuring trick is the combination of faith (or credulity) with the rhetoric of a proposition leading through technical legerdemain to the prestige (the seeming magical outcome). It is the seeming making possible of the impossible that defies the ontological certainty of the sensible and the intelligible. Cinema, magic and psychoanalysis are closely related in, if not what Derrida calls, improvising in this film, 'the science of ghosts', then in a craft or art (a techne) of ghosts, whose origins and returns are stagings of disruption, not as an ontological aberration but as the turning inside-out of the inner working of the visible and what presents itself as presence. Magic and cinema are every bit as technical and spectral as metaphysics. One might even say, not just that magic is metaphysical, but that metaphysics, in the sense that Derrida means it, is a form of magic. Equally, it is not that cinema relies on a metaphysics of presence but that metaphysics is in its own way cinematic. It has its screens and its walls that its own ghosts walk through.

While the scenes between Ogier and Derrida offer us an iteration of an anchoring point in the history of philosophy and cinema, they are not the end of Derrida's involvement in the film. As Pascale and Marianne stand on the banks of the Thames looking out onto a postindustrial London, they notice a large letter *D* written on the side of a factory. They comment in turn, 'D for . . . drugs, dole, depression . . .' and 'D for Derrida', but also 'D for desire', repeated twice over an exchange of knowing looks. During a previous conversation, Marianne asks Pascale, 'In France, is it easier to sleep?' She replies, 'It depends upon how much rage you can get rid of in your lovemaking. How much you are cared for and how much you care'. This may be revolutionary rage, it may be the rage of youthful rebellion, it may be the rage of the indignant woman in patriarchy, or it may be the rage of one passing through mourning from denial to anger. The question is, how much do you care and who or what do you care for? What makes you angry is what drives a revolution, even if it is only a revolution of the self. How one accommodates ghosts within that revolution defines how much you care. Pascale tells Marianne that she gave up on her studies in Paris: 'I used to love my teacher'. It is not clear if this is a reference to Derrida or the tutor who accompanies them to the café Le Select, or another as yet unseen teacher. 'One day I caught him staring at photographs in a book called *The Sex Lives of the Primitives*. He gave me bad marks as well'. This circuitry of desire between Pascale and her teacher, the teacher and the anthropological image, sexual difference and the university, is quickly dissolved into a fiction. 'I made that bit up', Pascale tells Marianne, 'One day I'll tell you what really happened when I've learned to trust you'. Magic requires trust as much as faith. In the flat in London, Pascale comments, 'I studied with Jacques Derrida once. He couldn't teach me everything, there are some things a man can't teach a woman'. The relation is always split, ruined from the beginning by difference. Even in the sisterhood of the two women there remains a gap, a relation without relation, a fiction and magic, difference at the heart of a singularity. Ghosts install themselves in a dance to the end of love, as Leonard Cohen might call it. It depends how much you are cared for and how much you care.

Care of ghosts is one of the stakes of this film and perhaps of film in general. How shall we attend to them? How shall we respect our ghosts, and can our ghosts ever care for us? Each of us lives with his or her ghosts; there is no history and no future without a care for those ghosts, but learning to live with ghosts is also a learning to live among the living. Respect for the ghost, for what has been lost and yet returns, requires us to respect the living as well. To learn to live is to accept that the work of mourning is incomplete until we can accommodate the living within our own castle of ghosts. The choice for the mourner, to have a future or not, is the choice to engage once more with the living, with those who live on, out of respect for the ghost. This is not a forgetting of the ghost or an incorporation of it within a successful and closed work of mourning, but the acceptance of another duty without courage or masochism, the duty to the other, which is another heading of militant melancholy without end.[13] It is the duty to accept the failing and impossible of life; without this step, there is no future for the living beyond imprisonment with ghosts. It is a risky step, one that we make as an act of faith rather than in the certainty of a known outcome. We might call it a 'wager'. Pascale, as a character, takes her name from the philosopher who makes a wager with God. He concludes that belief in God is the best hedge for an unknown outcome. In this film, Pascale makes a wager with the Godfather, or the Ghostfather, in which belief in the necessity of the living with all their faults is the best way to respect the spectre. The promise of the Godfather is to guarantee a known outcome; the promise of the Ghostfather knows no such certainty, but in order to live, we must accept that bet, to double down on the living and the ghosts they live with rather than sticking with the ghosts that haunt us. Pascale leaves her city of ghosts to make a new life in London. Her future lies with the living; even if she as a character resides in magic, a figure of cinema, forever flat against the surface of a

The Godfather ~ 179

screen. Cinema then produces figures that are melancholy without end, one dimensional but alive through the magic tricks of perspective and a metaphysics of sight. Liberty and the wager on life (a faith in people) are companions in this film, failing and impossible of course, but when they are together they possess magical powers: powers of revolutionary agency beyond simple allegory or image, as another heading of affiliation and solidarity beyond the Commune. One that troubles the *comme une* [as one] because it respects the otherness that haunts that contracting relation; it is a commune beyond communism, more like the collective endeavor of filmmaking; both agency and allegory, scepter and spectre, Godfather and Ghostfather, Sisterhood and Liberty. If Walter Benjamin imagined a revolutionary potential for cinema beyond the fashions set by Hollywood capital, McMullen's cinema of ideas offers us a curious kind of revolutionary merit. It is on the side of Liberty and Life but if it were confronted with the injunction of 'Let them eat cake', it would hedge its bets and first ask, 'What kind of cake is it?'

In the interview on *Ghost Dance* with Bernard Stiegler in *Echographies of Television*, Derrida comments:

> I would like to tell you what happened with this film, *Ghostdance*. Having invented the scene with Pascale Ogier, who was sitting across from me, in my office, and who had taught me, in the intervals between shots, what in cinematic terms is called the eye-line, that is to say, the fact of looking eye to eye (we spent long minutes, if not hours, at the request of the filmmaker, looking into one another's eyes, which is an experience of strange and unreal intensity: you can imagine what this experience of the eye-line can be when it is prolonged and passionately repeated between two actors, even if it is only fictional and 'professional'), and after she had taught me that . . . I had to ask her: 'And what about you, do you believe in ghosts?' This is the only thing the filmmaker dictated to me . . . And repeating it over and over, at least thirty times, at the request of the filmmaker, she says this little sentence: 'Yes, now I do, yes' ['*absolument, bien sûr, certainment*']. And so already during shooting, she repeated this sentence at least thirty times.[14]

Derrida finds the repetition a little spectral, outside of itself, and out of joint. The experience of filming and of playing oneself as another, performing oneself as an originary fiction or reproduction, haunts the cinematic response to philosophy that once more takes its location in the eye-line between actors and philosophers, seeing and not-seeing, responding with absolute responsibility, a sight that sees sight. Derrida goes on to then recount the experience of watching *Ghost Dance* three years later in a cinema in Texas after the untimely death of Pascale Ogier. Sitting in the dark of the cinema, Derrida has the uncanny experience of once more catching the eye-line of Pascale Ogier, who his own performing other self asks on screen, 'And what about you? Do you believe in ghosts?' The ghost of Pascale Ogier speaks back from another place, according to another law, watching Derrida across from her on set and simultaneously out in the audience, with a gaze 'di-symmetrical, exchanged beyond all possible exchange, eye-line without eye-line, the eye-line of a gaze that fixes and looks for the other, its other, its counterpart, the other gaze met, in an infinite night'.[15] It is the visor effect of the ghost who retains the rights of absolute inspection, making an offer that cannot be refused.

The Godfather Part II

Who cares for the Godfather? This is the question presented by the closing image of *The Godfather Part II* (1974) as Michael Corleone sits alone, wrapped up against the cold, looking out of the screen towards another audience. The second part of Coppola's cinematic saga begins with the Family under pressure, having relocated its activities from New York to Nevada. The Corleones are becoming more American, just as America is becoming more like a mafia family: the assimilation works both ways. Michael tells the corrupt Nevada senator that 'we are both part of the same hypocrisy', the integration of political institutions, business and criminality. 'But', Michael tells the senator, 'don't think it applies to my family'. He wishes to make a distinction between the Family as a business and the family as a domestic unit; the slow disintegration of the family over the course of the film is the result of the pressure brought to bear upon that unit by the integration of the Family as a business into American civil society.

The Godfather is the one who takes care of everyone. He takes care of everything and takes care of business. 'I'll take care of it', is one of the most repeated phrases across both films. Taking care is an ambiguous thing in *The Godfather*. The Padrino can offer to take care of anything, but it always comes at a price, with a debt to be settled later. Taking care of someone can mean death, like Don Fanucci, the Black Hand extortionist whom a young Vito kills to establish his credentials: He tells Tessio and Clemenza, 'I'll take care of everything, just remember I did you a favour'. The care of the Godfather, to be taken care of by the Godfather, contains within it the very ruin of care. This is the case when advantages in business are preserved through assassination, but also in the domestic family as well. Michael takes care of the family, but it is diminished since the deaths of Vito, Sonny and Carlo. As Fredo argues with his drunken wife, Deanna, at a family party, he receives the message from Michael's bodyguard: 'Freddie, Mike says take care of it, or I have to'. Deanna is summarily bundled away. The conflict between Michael and Fredo comes to a head when the Godfather says, 'I've always taken care of you', leading to an outburst from Fredo:

> Taken care of me. Mike you're my kid brother, and you take care of me. Did you ever think of that? Ever once? Send Fredo off to do this, send Fredo to take care of that . . . take care of some little unimportant night club here and there; pick somebody up at the airport. Mike, I'm your older brother; I was stepped over!

The care of the Godfather is stifling. Fredo is resentful of Michael and conspires with business partners of the Family to take care of his brother, perhaps imagining himself as a substitute Godfather. There is an assassination attempt on Michael at the Nevada compound, facilitated by a traitor in the family. Michael suspects both Corleone caporegime Frank Pentangeli and his own business partner Hyman Roth; he later learns it was Fredo. In turn, after the death of their mother, Michael has Fredo taken care of, shot while out fishing at the Tahoe compound. This is after his sister has pleaded with Michael to forgive Fredo. After failed relationships and reckless behaviour, on the death of her mother, Connie wishes to be reintegrated into the family:

> I hated you for so long, Michael; for so many years. I think I did things to myself, to hurt myself, so that you would know—and you would be hurt too. But I understand you now; I think I do. You were being strong for all of us, like Papa was. And I forgive you, and want to be close to you

now. Can't you forgive Fredo; he's so sweet and helpless without you. You need me Michael. I want to take care of you now.

Having the attention of the Godfather is one thing, but Connie says she now 'understands' what it means to be head of the family. She returns to the family to take up the matriarchal role vacated by both her dead mother and Michael's wife, now expelled from the family for having terminated the pregnancy of their son:

> It was an abortion; an abortion, like our marriage is an abortion, something unholy and evil. I don't want your son; I wouldn't bring another of your sons into this world . . . it was a son, and I had it killed, because all this must end!

The care of the Godfather does not extend to forgiveness. Kay had the abortion in order to end the family, she tells him 'I knew there would be no way you could ever forgive me'. Despite his sister's intervention, Fredo is not forgiven, either, while Michael never forgives or forgets a slight to his person, family, or business. The Godfather does not forgive, the unforgiveable being the only thing worthy of forgiving for forgiveness to be true; rather, he takes care of people, one by one. Care in this sense is its opposite, a form of brutal revenge without the possibility of forgiveness. This care cannot account for individuals; rather, it is a machine, a code of honour that must treat everyone the same. Every relationship, fraternal or spousal, must die in one way or another; they must all be taken care of. As *The Godfather* ended with climactic scenes of Michael taking care of all family business, the second film is the slow accumulation of an inexorable terror in which the family turns in on itself, with its members caught within the machinic code of death. Michael tells Tom Hagen, 'If there's anything certain; certain in life; if history has taught us anything, it's that you can kill anybody'. This is what it means to be taken care of by the Godfather. Members figuratively then literally have the life squeezed out of them by the family in a care towards death. Frank Pentangeli commits suicide in his bath, in an echo of David's painting of 'The Death of Marat', following the code of traitors to their emperor, having first confirmed with Tom Hagen that his family will be taken care of.

Care is the English translation for what Heidegger calls '*sorge*' as a fundamental basis for our being-in-the-world. However, this form of care, care for business and care for traitors, is the means by which the Godfather grows through the film orienting being-towards-death. The film concludes with Michael sitting alone by the lake, surrounded by so much death, having taken care of everyone and having taken such care to be careful about everything, following his father's advice: 'I spent my whole life trying not to be careless'. Who then cares for the Godfather?—Michael, who started along the path to become the Godfather when he promised to take care of his father when recovering from bullet wounds in hospital, and who returns from Sicily to ask Kay to marry him with the words 'I care for you'. Having been so careful not to be careless, he is left care less; he has taken care of his family but his family has been taken care of, taken away by his form of care. If care for the other is the ruin of the self, the care of the Godfather is precisely the death of the other because it is really a care borne of self-interest. Could one care less about Michael Corleone? The image of Al Pacino at the lakeside is haunting: If the flashback sequences of the life of Vito tell of his becoming the Godfather, then the main narrative sections are the story of Michael becoming the Ghostfather, locked in his castle surrounded by the ghosts of his family. The care that the film takes with its characters and story over four hours means that we still care about Michael even after all that has happened, at this point more than ever.

'It depends how much you are cared for and how much you care', Pascale tells Marianne in *Ghost Dance*. The Godfather's care is a care that cares too much, one that wipes out the family. Michael has individuals wiped out; he also wants to wipe out his business rivals. Tom Hagen asks him, 'Is it worth it? Do you want to wipe everyone out?' But it is the family that is at risk. Michael asks his mother whether it is possible to lose the family entirely. A senate committee hearing threatens to wipe out the Corleones. Here witnesses testify that the criminal business and the Family are one and the same, and the proposed testimony of Pentangeli risks a charge of perjury against the Godfather. The committee has a duty of care to investigate mafia activity, and Michael, accompanied by Hagen, has to be careful in what he says. However, he takes care of the witnesses and the threat of the committee and later Pentangeli. Democratic oversight fails to wipe out the criminal affiliations that have worked their way into public institutions. The only serious reverse that this 'super-efficient and properly capitalist phantom-State' experiences are at the hands of the Cuban revolutionaries who seize their assets. Batista's corrupt regime is described as 'the kind of government that knows how to help business' and the investment in Cuban hotels is referred to as 'partnership with a friendly government'. Hyman Roth tells Michael, 'We are bigger than US Steel'. The revolution wipes out mafia interests in Cuba, if only to replace one phantom state with another, demonstrating the reliance of the capitalist state on mafia practices. The care of the capitalist state is not necessarily any different from the care of Don Corleone.

'Wipe out' is also an editing technique in film much loved by Akira Kurosawa as a means of transitioning between narratives. The stories of the Godfather and the Ghostfather are a cinematic 'wipe out' that catches us out and causes us to lose balance, leading to a fall as if we were skiing or surfing. We fall into caring for the Godfather; we fall into caring for cinema and for ghosts. At the end of the film, Michael is wiped out, exhausted, drained and haunted. At the end of seven hours of watching the first two parts of this saga, even the most devoted cinema audience is wiped out. *The Godfather* always wipes me out.

Notes

1. Jacques Derrida and Catherine Malabou, *Counterpath: Travelling with Jacques Derrida*, trans. David Wills (Stanford: Stanford University Press, 2004), p. 278.

2. Ibid. p. 278.

3. Benoît Peeters, *Jacques Derrida: A biography*, trans. Andrew Brown (Cambridge: Polity Press, 2012) p. 22.

4. Walter Benjamin, 'Central Park', trans. Lloyd Spencer and Mark Harrington, *New German Critique*, No. 34 (Winter 1985), pp. 32–58.

5. Sigmund Freud, 'A Disturbance of Memory on the Acropolis', in *The Standard Edition of the Complete Psychological Works of Sigmund Freud*, vol. 5, trans. James Strachey (London: Hogarth Press, 1971).

6. Reported *Time Magazine*, Monday November 18 2002, 'Life with the Father of Deconstruction', Joel Stein.

7. See Martin McQuillan, *Deconstruction without Derrida* (London: Bloomsbury, 2013).

8. Jacques Derrida, *Specters of Marx: The State of the Debt, the Work of Mourning and the New International*, trans. Peggy Kamuf (London and New York: Routledge, 1994), p. 83.

9. Jacques Derrida and Bernard Stiegler, *Echographies of Television: Filmed Interviews*, trans. Jennifer Bajorek (Cambridge: Polity Press, 2002).

10. Paul de Man, *Allegories of Reading: Figurative Language in Rousseau, Nietzsche, Rilke and Proust* (New Haven: Yale University Press, 1982).

11. Some of the outtake material from this latter interview appears in *Love in the Post: From Plato to Derrida*, directed Joanna Callaghan, Heraclitus Pictures 2014, screenplay and commentary published by Rowman & Littlefield International 2014.

12. Wallace Stevens, 'The Emperor of Ice Cream', *The Collected Poems of Wallace Stevens* (London: Faber & Faber, 1982).

13. See Geoffrey Bennington, *Not Half No End: Militantly Melancholic Essays in Memory of Jacques Derrida* (Edinburgh: Edinburgh University Press, 2011).

14. Jacques Derrida and Bernard Stiegler, *Echographies: On Television*, p. 119.

15. Ibid., p. 120.

INTERVIEWS

Interview I: Étienne Balibar

'Thinking things through differently: in fact the right way 'round'

Paris, Rue de Seine, June 11, 2013

Martin McQuillan: I wonder if we could begin by discussing your recent philosophical interventions in the Greek crisis and your longer history with Greece and its intellectuals.

Étienne Balibar: I went to Greece for the first time when I was fifteen, on an organized trip to visit the archeological sites, because at that time I dreamed of becoming an archeologist and work on the excavations of the sites in Greece. Obviously that's part of my boyhood romantic memories, but I did see Greece at that time, and then I went back much later, because in the meantime there was a period when it was absolutely out of the question to go to Greece: It was the dictatorship period.

By the way I think that if you try to understand the current problem of what's facing Greece and the rest of Europe—the rest of the world—but the rest of Europe on a cultural, moral and political level, you absolutely have to take into account the importance of the dictatorship period, which I don't see mentioned very often in the discussions about Greece. Or else we refer to antiquity, or we refer to the Romantics and the role played by the Greeks in the Romantic imagination of Europe: the Greek fight for independence against the Turks, Byron, etc., etc. Or we evoke more recent circumstances, which refer to post Greece's entry into the European Union and the Euro, but we mostly block out the dictatorship period. So, the period of dictatorship and my relationship with Greece are very important; on the one hand because obviously it was part of a set of problems that already, in my view, at the time concerned the whole of Europe. It was the problem of authoritarian regimes, fascists, anti-Communist dictatorships in Southern Europe, Spain and Portugal obviously, but also Greece and Italy ... as has since been confirmed, was a country in which there was also a sort of rampant coup d'état and all that was naturally linked to the Cold War and the strategy of imperialist America in Europe.

If you like, for us, the coup d'état in Greece was closer to home; it was just as important, if not even more important than the coup d'état in Chile, or other examples of the same. One of the consequences of this coup d'état was the fact that a great number, as you know, of Greek artists, intellectuals, political militants were obliged to leave the country. Most of them were Communist, but in varying degrees. And they came to France and England for the most part, and some to Germany as well. Some of them, I'm thinking more particularly about some who were about the same age as me, that's to say that at that time were thirty years old, who because of that played a very central part in intellectual circles, politics and the arts in our countries.

Some names are very famous: Nicos Poulantzas in political philosophy, Costa-Gavras in cinema, Mikis Theodorakis in music. All those people knew each other, all those people were very militant, all those people were full of imagination. So, if you like, I think that to talk about my relationship with Greece, I have to go back at least as far as that period when I couldn't go to Greece but that Greece came to me or, at least, she came to us in a certain way. That created very strong bonds and we shared of course, according to circumstances, in between fun moments, joint responsibility, total agreement and those of differences and at times conflicts.

It was also a time, and I insist on that (I know you'll cut all this because it's all too long. But I think it was also a time that's imprinted very strongly in my mind and in that of a lot of my friends and colleagues, not the idea that there was a European culture, that's obvious, it's a commonplace, but the idea that there was a European policy and that European politics was obviously the domain of pseudo-Federal institutions gradually put in place by Brussels, but Greece wasn't a part of that at that time. She was integrated later for strategic reasons after the fall of the dictatorship, but it really was a political space, partly in a virtual sense, but already occupied by real people and by conversations of real value, which were also the affair of the peoples, youth and intellectuals and artists.

Obviously the fact that I myself was a militant Communist at the time—or one of the variants of militant Communists—and that these Greek immigrants were also Communists or Communist sympathizers, which was the reason that they'd obviously been persecuted, tortured, imprisoned, and whatever else happened in Greece—played a very important part in all of that. It created a sort of joint responsibility at the beginning. It was multinationalism in the general sense of the term, a sort of common ideological font. But I think rightly that at that time we started to transform classical internationalism into something else. I won't go into the history of Euro communism and all that, it's not the subject. So, moving on, I'll continue my confession. I hadn't prepared it, so I can't make it short.

So obviously Greece was then liberated from the Communist hold. I was on the one hand a militant intellectual, but on the other hand after all I was a teacher, a university philosopher. As it happens in Greece those people who closely followed what was happening in France, fundamentally had the same 'masters' for the most part, the influence of Althusser was very great for a number of Greek philosophers, Derrida too: Derrida and Lacan arrived on the scene later. But it was very important. So I continued to exchange signals in any case. The strongest signal and the most important for me was the fact that some of my friends who taught philosophy in Greece, who were about my age or a bit younger, for example Gerassimos Vokos at Thessaloniki who had created a sort of independent school of philosophy (nowadays we'd call it 'French Theory') sent their best students here to France to study for their doctorate. If I had to name all those that came, I can think of a dozen names off the top of my head. A dozen or so young men and young women, mostly young men, but there were also some young women, who were coming to the 'source' in France, or what they considered the 'source', to work on Spinoza, Marx, psychoanalysis, the theory of 'ethics', etc. Obviously those whom I taught or were taught by some of my friends like Pierre Macherey, or others that I saw a lot of, became very close friends of mine. There's a little bit of the paternalistic in this affair; I should say paternal rather than paternalist, but luckily they're no longer children and haven't been for quite a while.

So, I'm cutting off brutally, but with all these different contexts, if you like, I occasionally went, but not very often, to Greece. I have to say it was more that they came to France. All these things explain that when the Greek financial crisis exploded in 2010, as the first dramatic development on the European side of the economic crisis that had started in the U.S., I immediately had the feeling, not only that this affair concerned us directly, and that it would have long consequences for the situation in the whole of Europe, but that we had to be more than jointly responsible. We had to go there to understand what was happening, not only from the point of view of the effects of the crisis and the disastrous and devastating treatment that the European monetary system inflicted upon them, but also of course from the point of view of the Greeks themselves and their initiatives.

That's why I published in *The Guardian* and also on a French website in May 2010 an article that was widely spread and that I don't refute today (I did have some doubts afterwards, but I finally realized that I wasn't wrong) which I entitled 'Europe Final Crisis?' with an important question mark. Is this the start of the final crisis in the construction of Europe, in its current form? I said, of course: if we do nothing to stop it. The article was obviously translated into Greek, and in other countries. At the same time other European friends, mostly in London, more than in Paris at the time, Costas Douzinas and others had launched initiatives for discussion and joint responsibility. Quite naturally, my former students and other friends in Greece told us they would like to organize a general debate with Greeks and thinkers from other European countries in order to understand and discuss what all this meant. It was before the elections and the change of government in Greece, I think, if I remember rightly, it was in June 2010 or around that time that I went back there, that we had a great debate at the Pantheon University that has since been published. Since then I've been back about twice a year, the last time in the month of December. But obviously I'm not the only one to have gone to Greece. But I did try as hard as I could to think of the problem as a European citizen and not as a French or British citizen, nor as a Greek citizen. It's an important point, because in discussions as to the question of whether the Greek crisis should bring the left-wing intellectuals like us to try to prepare the refoundation of Europe, even if it's very improbable, there are those who think the opposite, that it's now or never to liquidate the European construction, because it's a construction that's inevitably reactionary and whose people are the victims. I'm on the first side, if you like we can talk about it, but I realize that it's a very difficult question, and the data changes all the time. Which means that it's vital to discuss via exchanges, online for example, and they do take place, not enough to my mind, but they do take place. Lately there have been a lot of interesting contributions to this debate, a lot of which have come from Germany, which is very important for me. But it's just as vital to go there and it's vital that the Greeks—they don't all agree on it—should have a voice—I wouldn't say preponderant, but an audible and sonorous voice, actively important in this debate.

I did say at the end of my intervention at the Pantheon in 2010, which obviously tried to avoid any useless pathos, but that was after all a little emotional—it was inevitable—I said, and I still believe it more than ever, that on the one hand it's my conception of European citizenship to think that we all have a sort of right to observe what's happening in the political space of the others. That means I have no scruples when it comes to judging what's happening in English politics, German politics, Spanish politics or Greek politics. And naturally I expect in return that the English, the German and the Greeks judge just as seriously, even very severely, what's going on in French politics. Only that's a general idea. Then we must add that we can never know better than the people who are living it themselves and obviously, if we don't go to Greece, we can't know what the Greeks are living.

MMcQ: If the Greek crisis signals the possible end of a certain Europe does it also signal the end of a certain capitalism?

ÉB: Those are two very different things, *very* different things. You must understand that I don't think that the current situation in Europe is independent from the evolutions of capitalism and the phase in which capitalism finds itself today. I use the word 'end', 'final crisis', etc., at a certain moment concerning not Europe as a historic and cultural space, but the European political construction in the form that she's acquired it historically. But I don't use the word 'end' when talking about capitalism. I'm very mistrustful of apocalyptic speeches concerning the final crisis of capitalism. Some of my closest friends, some Marxist in particular and post-Marxist theoreticians with whom I've worked or discussed throughout the course of my life, have recently adopted, obviously with very important nuances, a new variation of the old classic speech of the Marxist tradition, which concerns the final crisis of capitalism.

My reaction is that everything is worthy of discussion. Even the word 'crisis' is a 'polysemic' word, but let's not play on words. I totally agree with the idea that capitalism or the global capitalist system is in a critical phase. That is to say a radical transformation that could have brutal aspects and that could even violently affect the alternatives of construction and destruction. Plus, depending on one's point of view, destruction and construction are not the same. The collapse of the international financial system, which is probable, which is possible, but not certain, would obviously have consequences for capitalists themselves, even if others end up paying the price. I try to keep informed of current debates and I'm prepared to discuss the capitalist crisis, but I'm extraordinarily mistrustful of the idea that capitalism is on the brink of collapse, on the brink of mutation, that's what Marx thought back in 1848. He announced it at the end of *The Communist Manifesto*, and Marxists have often believed it and repeated it at various times, only to find, each time, not that capitalism is immortal, but that capitalism finds in its own crises the way to reorganize itself on other bases. Which ones? Well, it all depends on relationships of power, which are not fixed, and cannot be fixed ahead of time.

So, I think that the crisis of the construction of Europe has in the background radical and brutal transformations of capitalism, especially the transformations that completely modify the place of Europe in the world, in the process of globalization, and which probably destroy from within some of the implicit and explicit presuppositions that were inherent in the construction of Europe. But I don't think we're living the end of capitalism. On the other hand, yet again we must understand in 2010 I voluntarily used that expression with a question mark, 'Final Crisis?' because I wanted to inject, to introduce into the discussion—amongst others, I wasn't the only one—the idea of what the start of European construction signaled—we weren't quite yet at the Euro crisis at the time, because speculation about the debt of the sovereign States hadn't yet begun—we were only at the collapse of the Greek finances and Europe's difficulties in putting in place a joint responsibility policy with Greece. I wanted to say that this was not one of the numerous jolts marked by tension or political divergence, economic conflicts of interest among the different countries. It is not only the countries but let's call it the different components of European construction, which have regularly marked the history of the European Union in the last fifty years, but that it was in a certain way an existential crisis in which the nature and perhaps the survival of the institutional system were at stake. What interested me in this diagnosis was to deduce a certain number of consequences, especially to explain why, or rather ask the question as to why, left-wing Europe—which I consider I myself to belong—in its different components was just so very blind and unarmed against this situation.

Since then three years have passed—we won't go into the ups and downs—periodically we have been told that the crisis is over. I read in this morning's paper that the French president has just informed Japan that the crisis is behind us. It's only the tenth or fifteenth time that one of the leading members of the European Union has made such a declaration. I don't believe it any more than the other times, because I think there are structural causes. On the other hand, obviously the word 'end' is a dangerous word, because it looks like the announcement of a prophecy, even a short-term prophecy, or something like that. In one sense that's not what I mean. My proposition was in the conditional tense, it was more 'it's the end of the European system IF a certain number of radical transformations aren't undertaken'. Finally this idea has become a banal idea and is sometimes even the object of a sort of insistence, or is knocked down by the media, which makes me think that it's also useful as an instrument of blackmail. They tell the European people that the political and economic construction has become the frame—well England is a part, the English still think that they can leave because they've never completely entered, so the situation is a bit different—but there are also those people who explain to us that the Greeks should never have been allowed in, and consequently they can leave. We hear all of that. But for the 'core countries', the countries at the centre, let's say at the core of the construction of Europe, the idea of abolition or going back to the start is fundamentally a surrealist one.

So the problem posed today is an alternative between the different ways of refounding Europe. I think that's taken as read, at least by the more intelligent, that we can't just get by with a bit of patching up (as we say in French), repairing bit by bit, even if that's what we do on a daily basis. We have to *refound*. Obviously, the refoundation is demanding; I shan't even go into the legal questions. When I say we have to refound, I think we should start by writing new treaties. But before new treaties can be written, we need a new political project. It's not in that sense obvious. It's on this point that the divergences are radical. They're even more radical, as there are many different ways of taking advantage of Europe, I'd say for the dominant European classes. Some are simply instrumental, others, on the contrary, consist of a sort of hegemonic project for the European space. To be provocative, we could use Carl Schmidt's language 'ein gross Frau' (a fat European woman). It's not at all the same thing, but in any case there are radical alternatives. Some philosophers, Habermas and others, Ulrich Beck in Germany, have stated their position. In France it's incited a lot of discussion, in England people like Timothy Gorton Ash and others, longtime specialists in European affairs, have also spoken of it.

So, it's easy to see that there are several directions. There's an authoritarian direction, which could finally be accompanied by the idea that Europe lacks democratic legitimacy, but in the end what's first is the idea that we need to reinforce the structures that allow Europe to create a sufficiently stable currency and to make the European economy work in a time of neoliberal globalization. But on the opposite side there are those for whom the fundamental question isn't legitimacy, but rather democracy. In any case, we can't resolve the problem if we treat things in that order, but by asking the question as to what is democracy? The new forms of expression, public opinion, you see flourish at certain times, at demonstrations in Greece that call for the expression of a new policy, a 'New European Deal' or a new European policy. So, in reality, there is clearly not one strategy, there are several, some of the extreme ones are radically contradictory with each other. And I can't see in the near future any power capable of enforcing one. There's a certain imbalance of power at the moment—Europe is trying to reconstruct itself in the crisis, but it is a certain Europe that's not just capitalist but neoliberal.

On the other side, on the contrary, the perspective of a, let's say, socialist Europe, I don't see why we should avoid the word. To my mind, it's absolutely inevitable. It's extremely fragile and goes against the flow of current globalization, but I don't think like Zygmunt Bauman who I think was the first one to use this category that comes from Gramsci, a famous passage from the work of Gramsci, that the current situation is a situation of inter regnum. Gramsci invented this term, in his prison diaries, when he tried to elaborate this sort of category to rectify the fundamental classical revolutionary definitions. I have friends who think that we're in a revolutionary situation. In Greece certain leaders of Syriza are prudent, but some of their admirers, of whom I am one, by the way, think that through their intervention we can see the outlines of a revolutionary situation in Europe. As we know, Lenin's definition, that Gramsci tried to correct, is that the revolutionary situation is the situation in which the dominant classes can no longer govern as they used to and where the dominated no longer want to be governed as before. It's very difficult to apply this kind of formula to the current situation. So, I think we ought to prefer Gramsci's formula, which is obviously more pessimistic, when he says that certain forms of politics and thus certain speeches about the nature of the construction of Europe are dead. We can repeat them as often as we like, but it doesn't mean they're not dead. And new ones that could replace them haven't yet been born. In any case they are not viable, obviously not viable.

Obviously Gramsci was writing in the early '30's and we shouldn't forget that, I'm very wary of simple comparisons, just as earlier for the end of capitalism, between the situation of Europe in the '30's and Europe's situation today. But finally there are two elements of similarity, which are worrying and that the development of the situation in Greece over the last two or three years has illustrated. On the one hand, the enormous rate of unemployment among the young generation and, on the other hand, the decay of the political system (the loss of representation and efficiency of the political system). That produces what we call great internal confusion, the rise of populism in its different forms amongst the European countries. I'm also wary of this because it's used for propaganda purposes to explain that the extreme left and the extreme right are the same thing. But it does have the advantage of drawing our attention to the potentially destructive character of mass reactions to the crisis in the construction of Europe, if there is no political perspective to, I don't want to say to channel them, that's not the right term, but to mobilize them, to offer them a future.

MMcQ: Which text from the traditions of Greek literature and thought might help us to think through the crisis?

ÉB: Thucydides, *The History of the Peloponnesian War*, and for a precise reason. Firstly because I think that Thucydides is one of the greatest political thinkers in western tradition. I think, like others like Arendt, etc., that there is a tradition of political thinking in which coexists, and that's what is all the more remarkable about it, the conscience of one's own permanent tragic dimension and the will to be realistic and absolutely lucid. It starts with Thucydides and has come through the centuries to us, through Machiavelli, Max Weber and others. And by the way they are always people who are politically engaged, they're people who know that we can't read politics from a synoptic point of view: As Plato used to say, people who are situated outside the maul or out of the caves. But that doesn't mean that we can simply take sides blindly, we have to take sides without being blind. But there's another reason, I read it in the commentators of Thucydides and I elaborated on it in my own way. Thucydides thought the great war, the thirty years war that devastated Greek cities and of which he was both instigator and witness, represented a form of intermediary conflict between civil war and foreign wars, or to be more precise, there was a mix of both. That's why he tried to understand and analyse the situation in which the great Greek cities—via fluctuating alliances—made war on each other, Athens vs. Sparta, vs. Thebes, etc., until a foreign imperialist stepped in, or at least half foreign, and brought order to the situation. And then on the other hand, there is the conflict that existed within each Greek city, between the two great parties, the democratic party and the oligarchic party. Because each party looked for help—or had alliances with foreign cities—both types of conflict ended up fusing together in an extremely violent form. But what's extremely interesting is that Thucydides had, according to certain commentators at least, and I agree with them—he had a Pan Hellenic perspective. Ultimately, he sketched out the idea of Greece considered as a whole. The Greece of his time was not yet one state, one single political place. You couldn't call it a nation at that time, even if there were hereditary enemies, the Persians, etc., but it was made up of places that could try to build their common community, in a common place. A commune, as some of our contemporary philosophical friends would say, founded through the resolution of its own internal civil war.

I really think this idea is very contemporary. Yes, there's violence—not quite the same sort of violence, rather social destruction, just as we see in a greater part of Southern Europe where there's a great deal of violence. I think that the Greeks who think that Mrs Merkel is the new Hitler who's coming to occupy Greece are wrong. It's not the right comparison, but it is true that the latent hostility towards the construction of Europe that has burst through right now has both aspects of what we've just evoked; i.e., it's a conflict between European nations and it's a conflict within each of the European nations. It's important to understand how both aspects fuse and determine each other and it's important to pose the question, even though we don't have a healthy answer. To know how to, in a certain way, transform this conflict, to take sides and find a solution which could allow us to reinvent a new Europe. Ultimately, we realize that the construction of Europe was undertaken upside down, or the wrong way round. I mean we imagined a beautiful European unity based on certain cultural values but which over the years have become essentially financial concerns, which create difficulty. And we thought that all the components that went hand in hand, not without difficulty, with 'pulling apart' as we say in French, would take their place under this general idea, which is a Platonism in a certain way, you know the European Platonism. Well, I think that Thucydides is an extraordinary source of inspiration for thinking things through differently: in fact the right way 'round.

Translated from French by Suzy Foster

Interview II: Hélène Cixous

'To out Ajax Ajax'

Paris, June 11, 2013

Martin McQuillan: Perhaps if we begin by discussing how this moment of crisis is playing out in France.

Hélène Cixous: What is happening in France, or the misfortune of France, is a very small misfortune if we compare it to the misfortune of our neighbours. What I mean is, if we imagine that what's currently happening in Europe is a Greek tragedy, as in Greek tragedy there are great misfortunes, average misfortunes and small misfortunes and vice-versa. What's happening in Greece, what's frightening, is what's already happened elsewhere. I remember a few years ago, Argentina was in the same state as Greece, which meant that it was suddenly thrown out of the global economy. In France we're still independent. There is still a normal life, we have not yet got that feeling of mad war, intestinal war, such as there is in other countries like Spain or Greece. I think that needs to be said. And I'd like to say that if I compare it with England, what my English friends and colleagues are living through right now, I mean the destruction of access to universities, which signifies that we're actually closing the door to knowledge, progress, success, on the young. We're currently preparing tomorrow's misfortune in England. We're not there yet, France is not thus far catastrophic, and I think that difference needs to be made.

Now, the question of solidarity is primordial, for me. I think the misfortune of Europe is not being Europe, being anti-Europe, being in a permanent state of malfunction, and being 'out of joint' all the time. And that's a huge problem. What with the tension, rejection, phobias between the countries, the antipathy and disdain of some European countries towards certain others, that's a huge problem, which is the soul of Europe's future. That also begs the question of culture: When I hear 'Greece', for me Greece is me. It's our grandmother, our grandparents. Unfortunately, the different cultures in the various countries of Europe are falling apart. I think that for most people now, Greece is just a bad manager that's gone bankrupt. For me, Greece is our past and our future. It's the cradle of a great part of our thinking, our political orientation. I think it is extraordinary that Europe forgets that we owe Greece half of our political vocabulary. I mean, we can't even think in terms of democratic power without being Greek. But we forget. And the cultural catastrophe is primordial for me. It really starts at school and then in research, at university and we're free-falling. In France we're currently losing everything intellectually. So ethically speaking, I'm not saying morally but ethically, and not just economically, and that's very dangerous, for me, we are not paying our debt. We are not paying our debt; we should be paying our debt. We owe Greece; it is not just economic, of course, and we're not paying it.

MMcQ: I believe that *Antigone* is not a play that you feel particularly close to.

HC: I don't have a particular affinity with the play, nor with the character of Antigone, even though I have great admiration for Sophocles. Obviously it needs to be justified. Let's say that what I admire about Antigone is not what is usually considered to be the core of the play. For example, as a playwright, which I am too, I am much more interested in, much more fascinated by, the violence of the secondary tragedies within the principal tragedy, for example, the extremely subtle tragedy that occurs between Creon and Haemon. I think that is very strong, and obviously to bring that out, you have to work on all the tragic models of the struggle between father and son, the son who is the father of the father, because Haemon becomes his father's father, and also the other cases of antagonism between father and son, of which there is an abundance in the Greek world. That is what interests me, and it interests me because it is not obvious. I also find the character of the guard passionately interesting; I think he is marvelous. He is the one I remember as crossing the centuries, as very life-like, and he walks on stage, just as Sganarelle walks on stage, or as Falstaff walks on stage. He is a very complex character like the Messengers in *Antony and Cleopatra*. That is a character who, for me, is a *man*, a little man sure, as you also find in Brecht, etc. So Antigone bores me. I have to say it; I have always thought it. When I was young, there was a series of Antigones, because Antigone is very popular in France. I always wondered why. I mean, she has already worked it out; there's no conflict, there's no twist in the tale, there's no surprise. All she can do is hike up the hardship. For me, she is uninteresting, but we can discuss it, of course, but that is my feeling.

In France we have a character, a very strong dramatic character who also chose a sort of glorification of a theme, which would be the theme of honour, or the respect of a superior law. In France it exists, it is Joan of Arc. Joan of Arc is someone who, in the face of death, trembled, who did an about-face, who repudiated herself. She was also a young girl, eighteen or sixteeen, and at the same time as she obeys a superior law, in which she believes, she is ready to disobey because she is scared, whereas Antigone does not. So I just say that she is not someone who interests me, personally. Yet again, as a playwright, I can't do anything with Antigone, except repeat something that could be interesting poetically. I mean she could say magnificent things poetically. But trying to find what takes the audience's breath away, what makes them cry and get angry, no. I think she leaves us cold. That is why Antigone is not the character that interests me, and it's always been that way.

There are some things, in the detail for example, but it's always coded, for example, the way she presents herself as an object to be looked at. She is the first of what we nowadays call an icon. She is an icon and it's always 'look at me', 'can you see?', 'are you looking at me?' from start to finish. And I find that it is a character that does not make me want to look at her. I've already seen it. However, she does gain a little bit of dramatic force by the coupling of the antagonists who share something with her. In the couple she forms with Creon, there's something interesting, because they are both stubborn. Both of them are 'obdurate'. In that mirroring, one being the mirror of the other, there is something which comes out, who will be the most stubborn, who'll go the furthest down the path that has been traced out towards the loss of life. There is a sort of fight that is not without interest. And then, of course, why is she so successful? She appears to be—and it's not what I think at all—the first feminist in literature. But a hard feminist like that doesn't interest me at all. She has no relationships, for example. She has a relationship with her dead brother; she is the dead brother. Her fiancé, who by the way is united with her in an arranged marriage, is a very complex character. But she has no respect for him, she is the brother; that is it for her, she is her brother. She is not a sister but a brother. For me the real sister is Ismene, a very interesting character, but I think there's a sort of reading cliché of Antigone that's been repeated and we have ended up with a sort of ready-made character who doesn't interest me much. However, the Greeks themselves were more astute than us. There are many different versions of the end to *Antigone*, and they are very Antagonic, very different: she survives, she marries Haemon, they have children, and then, there would be a follow-up, a real soap opera. We've inherited the rigid Antigone.

MMcQ: We might indeed regard the play as Creon's tragedy rather than that of Antigone.

HC: I think in fact that if anyone is tragic it is Creon, and that is what is manifest in the theme of tragedy up until today. Every work of tragedy from time immemorial is animated by, or has that terrible feeling of the question of 'contretemps', which means it is too late. That is what comes out of tragedy, because it is always too late. It's not just saying: 'Oh, I've got here too late, it's too late' as in Romeo and Juliet, etc. It is that no human being—and that is tragic—can flee the 'contretemps', because we never know the first minute of when 'it's too late'. What is the last minute that everything can still be spared? That is what interests us. It is when death becomes inescapable, but—as Edgar Allan Poe says—it also depends, mysteriously, on part of our own will. We give in to death, only by a fault in our own will, according to Poe, and that is what is staged with Creon. At one point he ends up only hearing—and it is all very beautiful—with Creon we have all the complicated and paradoxal themes of blindness. Blindness is always that paradox, which means that it is the blind that can see. It is Tiresias the blind man who is clairvoyant, and those who think they can see, do not see. That is something in all literature that I find moving, for example in *Samson Agonistes* because in a certain way it is really our problem: we don't understand anything. We humans don't, we don't see. It is there, but I just did not see it. So we are subject to mistakes, we make mistakes. Thus, and what makes it beautiful, a mistake is only fatal if, in the race against it, we are not quick enough. I mean, and that is marvelous, that we can catch up with and counter the mistake. That is when the 'contretemps' occurs, which means there is a countdown, the stopwatch *chronos* is organized by thousands of determining factors and we have the chance, *a chance*: a chance and then it's too late. Then we no longer have it. And it is out of our hands. And that is where the tragedy is; we do not know when the last minute is up. The last minute is hanging in the air. It is an extraordinary character, 'the last minute'. And that's Creon.

MMcQ: It is also, in terms of time, Tiresias's play.

HC: In fact he is a character in a piece of my writing 'The name of Oedipus, or the forbidden body'. It was the libretto for an opera that was played in Avignon in which I slightly shifted the accent from the story of Oedipus to Jocasta, and Tiresias is a key figure. I think Tiresias is everywhere, in the Greek Imaginary, and he is a great character. I sometimes think the Greeks have left us Oedipus, and we only talk about Oedipus, but they have also left us the 'other' blind man Tiresias. There is the blind man who has not noticed that he is blind. That is the model that will become Samson. And then there is Tiresias, the marvelous Tiresias—but he is not the only one—there are also the other prophets who cannot see in order to see better. They are blind in order to see better.

We all know the myth, which I also think is extremely potent, because Tiresias has been blinded, punished by Hera for having answered an enigma. First, we have to say that Tiresias is the first transsexual. He was for nine or seven years, I don't remember, a woman, and nine years a man, and that is marvelous. He is a character for us who is very modern. He has sexual experiences, bisexual, he is transgender, etc., and in the quarrel between the great gods to know who has the most orgasms, is it the man or the woman, they say, well, let's ask Tiresias because he has experienced both. He is unique. He has this trait, which is that he always tells the truth. He says that if he has to do a statistical calculation, man has one orgasm to the woman's nine. Woman has nine more orgasms than men. They do not like the answer, neither one nor the other, because you should not reveal secrets. It is the story of sexuality, if I might say, orgasms, and because he is witness to those sort of things, he is punished with what? By sight, sight which is purely organic, but analytical sight is preserved. He remains the one that can see ahead, the clairvoyant, he always knows what's going to happen. So he's a very interesting character.

One thing I do like about *Antigone*, the play by Sophocles, is, and again this is the playwright speaking, the arrival of Tiresias because he enters the play, unannounced, and suddenly he is there. That is very strong. For me that is a lesson, because as a playwright, one says that if a character is going to enter in the next act, he should be announced. Someone comes in and says, 'we are waiting for', or 'we have summoned', etc. . . . but no, in Sophocles, he is there, and that is very strong.

MMcQ: What other resources are there within the classic tradition to help us understand this present moment?

HC: I should like to start with Homer, *The Iliad*, *The Odyssey*; they are our stories. I should probably mention the Bible, but as we are in Greece, let's stay in Greece. Everything has been written and played in the western world, by Homer and his tragic descendants, and the Bible. That is everything.

All the stories about Kings in the Bible and all the stories about Kings in Greek literature are our stories. There is no difference; there is just a time shift. I always say that what changes is the furniture and the means of transport. For example, in 1994 when I wrote *The Perjured City*, which was about contaminated blood, a global question: it was the start of the global scandals, the big financial scandals. For economic reasons we had sold poisoned blood to thousands of sick people across the world, and that is exactly what is happening now. The master of life and death throughout the world is profit, in a way that is absolutely unregulated. Governments are trying to fight it, but they are already poisoned by profit. So that is a huge problem. When I wrote *The Perjured City*, I had just translated *The Eumenides* and I thought it was the same story: what's the power of law, rights and justice in a context where profit has all the power and uses all its violence. So I brought on today's stage the old Eumenides, who are poor old women who still cry out that we should punish wrongdoers, that the victim has rights, all the things that are ignored today. So I brought them back to life and they said that nothing had changed in three thousand years, except that we now have the telephone. Now we could say that there is the Internet, so there is an acceleration in terms of communication of bad things and catastrophes. That is the difference between the Greeks, the Bible and us, an acceleration.

The character that interests me in Greek tragedy, the one who moves me, the one with whom I have the most sympathy—to use yet another Greek word—with whom I suffer, is Ajax. Firstly because he is someone in-between, he is between the gods. He is a man who has almost superhuman powers, but he is a man who is treated badly, tortured—both by man's injustice—their stupidity, their lack of respect and their small-time calculations, and he has also got against him those strange Greek characters, the gods (those mysterious allies of man). To put it quickly, there are two heroes in *The Iliad*. The uncontested hero is Achilles, the hero of all heroes, and who is a character that is extraordinarily pure, beautiful and powerful, and who is, in the end, the beholder of passions that, in some ways, we bridle, of anger. Because literature starts with anger, literature always starts in anger. And then, in a secondary role, there is Ajax, who is also an angry character—but they all are to a certain extent—and in the hierarchy of power, I would say inequalities, produced by the conjuncture of nature and divine desires, he is the second behind Achilles. He is the second strongest after Achilles, and everyone recognizes that. That is marvelous. It is a bit like, for example, all the heroes who form a couple, for example, Gilgamesh and Enkidu, there is the strongest and then just behind him there is the one who permits the strongest to be the strongest, because there always has to be a comparison.

Ajax, who has always accepted Achilles's superiority, and who protected the Greeks in their defeats, who helped them out and who was always loyal, who never schemed, always said yes. Ajax was always sent for and told we have come for you to go to war on behalf of those bastards Agamemnon and Menelaus, and he says yes, because he always replies 'present'. He is responsible. Then, when Achilles dies they distribute, they share out his inheritance: Achilles's magic weapons. They ought to go to—according to epic law—Ajax who is the strongest and, by the way, the only one able to lift them. But there is traffic; comparable to the trafficking we have today in government, in parliament (it is corruption). Through corruption and also by a lack of solidarity and political ingratitude, which is the lot of power—there is never any recognition in politics—there are discussions as to who should inherit. The Trojan prisoners are asked, as are that horrid, horrid couple (and that's very interesting) Agamemnon and Menelaus, who are supposed to rule all the Greeks, and it is decided that Ulysses will receive the inheritance. That makes Ajax mad. That makes him very angry, very angry, because he is really a victim of injustice.

You cannot say that, for example, in *Antigone*, there is injustice. There are different justices, different rights, and different powers. You can debate it. With Ajax, we are confronted with pure injustice, and that comes across very strongly. There is no reason—except the twisted Odyssean take—and we know that Ulysses and Polyphemus always play around, that is a Greek invention. Ajax cannot bear the injustice, because in some ways he is thrown out of the world. He always thought there were supposed to be forms of retribution. The injustice makes him mad. In the very long plot that I won't go into here he is pushed to the edge. He is just pushed beyond his own image, in the end, as Shakespeare says to actors 'to out Herod Herod', so he 'out Ajaxs Ajax'. It is an unexplained malediction; he commits mad acts, he massacres. To avenge himself, he massacres all the Greeks, he massacres Agamemnon, Menelaus, Ulysses, etc., except that, when he snaps out of it, he realizes that what he has massacred are not his enemies at all, but animals. He has massacred cows, sheep, etc., which is wonderful. He is sent to the depths, he has a blind crisis, he had lost his sight, but he gets it back, and he gets it back in order to suffer all the more, for him to suffer all the more.

Ajax is someone, even more so than Creon (who after all is just a poor guy) who is pure, who is inflicted with a succession, an accumulation of suffering, one after the other. The only way out is death. When I say death, Ajax has a loving relationship with death, because he has a beautiful death, an unpleasant death, because there are different ways of dying. He manages to seek death in the most elaborate manner. He does not commit suicide. He arranges it that death becomes him by sword, the great sword that belongs to Hector. During a fight with Hector, which is a noble fight, the two heroes take each other on and in the end it is a draw. It is a draw, they agree, night falls and they hug—that is a scene worthy of Eisenstein, straight from Eisenstein—and they both say: 'OK, I realize you're just as strong as I am,' and they exchange gifts. Hector gives Ajax his sword. Ajax gives Hector his very powerful belt. So Ajax has Hector's sword. It is as if he has Hector's soul, it is very archaic, but it is marvelous. It is Hector's sword that will kill him. He will die by Hector's sword. There is another beautiful thing in that Ajax has to hide to kill himself. He has to hide to seek the death that has been refused him, because everyone has refused it, yet it is his deliverance. He puts the sword down thus, he sticks it in the ground, so it is like an enormous tree of life and death and, secretly, without any witnesses, he is going to throw himself on the sword. It is a scene of immense beauty. And that is the end of the first part of Ajax, because there is a second part.

The second part is where his burial is forbidden. It is a sublime problem. The Greeks arrive, the enemy and in particular that bastard Agamemnon, who has done his worst, as usual, and Ajax's burial will be refused. It is like a second tragedy that I will not recount now, but the finality is a great dialogue that has often been reused by the Greeks, it appears in Ovid, etc., which is the dispute over life in death: death is not death. That is what the Greeks teach us. They say that after death, there is life in death, and the dead man has a history. He has a life, suffering, another tragedy, as we see when Ulysses goes down to

Hades. Ulysses who is alive goes down to Hades and all the dead who are, of course, led by Tiresias, rush towards him and Ulysses gives the dead news of the living and the dead give Ulysses news of their death. They explain how they died. It is absolutely wonderful. Of course only the dead can discuss death. Ajax is the origin of literature; it is with him that great literature starts. Great literature is there in order to give the dead their chance to talk and to return. The dead have something to tell us and we, as readers, are on the edge, with Ulysses, on the edge of Hades. That is the origin of literature, with Ajax.

MMcQ: And perhaps with the question of the Sphinx?

HC: The Sphinx is traditionally, in what's been left to us, the figure of what we do not understand. It is incomprehensible. When Oedipus answers the Sphinx, it is only a way, an artifice to enable us to continue along a faltering path from one misunderstanding to another. It has to be said that our impulse, our need, our desire, the spirit of research within us needs to proceed in steps. We need to understand, but understanding is only one step to enable us to advance to another stage of incomprehension. That is what happens in all sciences, and of course in all analysis of the subject. In science, for example, we are always the Sphinx. In astrophysics, or in biology, we arrive at a certain stage and yet again we do not understand, and that is life. It is not understanding. The Sphinx is the figure of that. What Oedipus says—and it is very banal—is only, I would say, the invention of yet another small microscope, yet another small piece of equipment to enable us to further—for worse or for better—what we do not know. After all, the figure of Oedipus replies to the Sphinx, and then does not answer anything after that.

Translated from French by Suzy Foster

Interview III: Antonio Negri

'An example of a very bad example'

Paris, June 10, 2013

Ken McMullen: What do you think of the situation in Greece today?

Antonio Negri: It's just an unfortunate country, that's the least we can say. I think that today Greece is being used as the scapegoat, as the example of the neoliberal or totalitarian restructuration of Europe. Europe was a grand idea. It was born as an idea, as the first form of association of great countries at the end of the Second World War, which was fundamentally the destruction of the memory of nation states. It came about after both wars, or after what we could call the thirty years' war, from 1914 to 1945, after the mutual destruction between France and Germany, but above all between the working classes, who'd been sent to the trenches. Every family had their share of death at home; it was really a regime of terror, with fascism in the middle, between one war and another. The idea of Europe was born that way. And there were great powers, a great capacity to develop new experiences, and above all new imaginations.

I remember after the war, I was then a young boy and for me Europe had been an ideal since my youth. And I learnt to travel, I learnt languages, I learnt to study in different universities, a bit like Erasmus today. But we started doing that in the '50's. We hitchhiked in Europe and between people, we really felt like comrades, friends and all that. Europe wasn't only one thing—the end of the war. It was also the Welfare State, it was development, and so on. Then came the great crisis, the crisis that came from the US and moved to Europe and the new European institutions were incapable of expressing the popular spirit and desire, major freedom, because it was built from and by many people. That's when the tragedy started, the tragedy of Europe. And above all this tragedy hit the Greeks the hardest. But the Greeks are a great people, with their great traditions that go back to before Jesus Christ. They are the basis of our civilization. It produced the great philosophers, like Sophocles who is present in our lives, in our form of thinking. It even produced the first example of our vices, of our capacities to be surprised and to surprise life. It invented literature, poetry; it invented the Parthenon, classical art and so on. It even invented the richest forms of language, because they're the intellectual forms in which we always express primary ideas of our civilization: our fundamental ideas.

That is all well and good, but apart from that the Greek people have always been a people in crisis, always. Oppressed by the Romans, by the Venetians, by the Turks, by the Pope, and priests, by a bourgeoisie or an old aristocracy which was an extremely egotistical aristocracy and self-contained. But the Greeks have also always had the capacity to be a migrant people, who went everywhere, to all corners of the Mediterranean. There are places that the Greeks set up themselves. Greek cooking is very good from that point of view. And we have all learnt from spending summers in the Greek islands that they are a paradise. Once we've said all that, perhaps because of this 'aboriginal' exemplarity, that fundamental principle, Greece could be a good example of a scapegoat: an example of a very bad example.

It is said these are people who have spent everything, these are people with a lot of corruption, these are people who don't have the capacity to make the great rich of their country pay their taxes—the big entrepreneurial families, the maritime entrepreneurs. They have a country in which there's a lot of mafia. The mafia isn't the bad mafia, like the Italian or Mexican mafia, but they are mafia, little mafia, small corporations, it's a strange country from that point of view. So we should make them 'stand out'. We should show what could be done for all the other European countries, if they don't accept a certain policy, and that is the policy of liberal reorganization, essentially economic and political, and European. It's a policy in which the order of financial capital is absolutely fundamental, central. It's an order that starts from the top and descends by determining the division of labour, according to certain rules that are simply financial regulations. It's the form in which Europe ought to be transformed, by which manufacturing and industrial countries are turned into a service country, totally linked to the financial capital. But because a service Europe is a Europe that produces less, because it is inserted in the world order, they had to choose which sectors were to be excluded from development.

The Greeks, perhaps to some measure the Portuguese too, perhaps to some measure the Spanish, perhaps to some measure Italy, will be excluded from this development, from this new organization of development, which rightly sees financial capital in the centre. This financial capital isn't just in the centre of Europe; it's a capital that's coordinated with all the rest of the world, through all the rest of the global market. We have to be careful, because when we say 'market', we're not saying a place, where merchandise circulates, we mean a place that's regulated by money, a capacity to produce money which determines the differences, which determines the organization of the world. That is the new form in which we are trying to learn what money is, which is no longer simply a tool for work, the capacity to work, but it's also the accumulation, a tool for exploitation. It is a saw for the extraction of social value. In this case Greece, yet again the first, yet again the example, yet again an unfortunate example.

KMcM: What are the dangers for the Greek people at this time?

AN: The danger is always in impotence. It is in impotence that there is danger. Normally democratic states live in a struggle, an antagonism, an 'agonism'. There cannot be democracy without 'agonism'. You just have to think about the great industrial nations, there are the poor and the rich, there are lots and lots of examples, several differences and these differences are always defined by antagonism. Antagonism is thus confrontation. Democracy can recognize the rich and the poor, but there has to be confrontation. There has to be the hope of changing things. When there is no more confrontation and there is only impotence, then you have a reaction that is deaf: deaf, bleak, and desperate. This deaf, bleak, desperate reaction is often a reaction that is capable of building strong organizations that organize the future. There are other times when these situations, these misfortunes withdraw into themselves and became fascist. They became fascist and that's one of the most terrible things we find in Greece today. Golden Dawn is an extreme right-wing organization that is organized according to classical forms with a very hard hatred for the immigrant or all those who are not of Greek origin, which greatly plays on the mystification of misery. They present themselves as the defender of the 'miserable' and that's something that's very dangerous. It is very dangerous even in this case, for example because we see the right very ferociously, dangerously permeating throughout the whole of Europe.

That is one of the results, and this time we start to wonder if it isn't in the project of the Troika (that is to say of all of them, the European Central Bank, the European Commission, the IMF) to make this project that we used to call Greece the scapegoat. If these projects show that in some countries there is no further possibility of governing, then the governing should be transferred elsewhere. I think that those are perhaps the unpredictable consequences and today, yet again, I say 'poor Greece, unfortunate country', but I don't know. You see, in my life I was a bit, how can I put it, 'exuberant', when I was young and I was 'condemned' for having done things you were not supposed to do. One of those things was to pass weapons to the people who were fighting the Greek Colonels, and I sent a lorry full of weapons and explosives. I hope I won't have to do that again.

KMcM: Do you think there may be something in the Greek identity or the European identity, or in the idea of identity, that might help save Greece in some way?

AN: It's a complex question. We would obviously have to talk about it for a long time. I don't think identity is something positive, we could start by saying that. I rather think that our civilization, our philosophical language, and other ideologies are linked to a fundamental idea of identity: the identity of a nation, the identity of a people, individual identity, etc., etc. I think that all of these individualities might have some reason to exist, as a functional product to different, we say philosophically, '*epistēmē*', and we could say there have been reasonable reasons in some forms of thought, forms of life. But I think that today in reality and above and beyond that, postmodernism from this point of view is something that is extremely positive. It teaches us that we are above all singularities and that means not individuals, but intellectual, moral and, above all, corporeal forms that suppose a rapport with others. Our existence is in our relationship with others.

Identity becomes a more and more vague concept, often empty, quite simply because we live as a rapport, a relation, a network.

Production is a fundamental element of our life because it is the thing that allows us to reproduce, to put us into circulation, to know a lot of things. Production is the production we do, we no longer do it alone, but always together. We invent things all together. Being together is not an outcome; it is something that comes first. We are singularities who become, who get together in the multitude. It is the multitude of things that exists and which exists as a productive phenomenon, but above all as a linguistic phenomenon. Imagine, for example, an identity without language, language demands, so to speak, the end of identities because it is through language that people form the world.

I have a conception of identity that is rather negative. It is something that I would rather put to one side. I think that when we use identity to talk about nations, classes and power in general, or races, we often arrive at terrible results that are disastrous. Just think of signification of the identity of being German or French for centuries. They cut each other's throats in the trenches. What was that identity? It is horrible, isn't it? If you think of identity of black [Americans], being a slave for centuries, it is only by overturning this identity, by recognizing that we are cosmopolitan, that we are different, that we are singular, that we have a richness in ourselves because others recognize it, because we are together, because we love each other. That's it, that's the real phenomenon. It is always horrible to talk about love, no? When we talk about those things, because we are thought of as being religious or talking about of Eros. No, no, it's not that. It is joint responsibility, it is moral rapport, it is just ethics, which is born from love . . . self love [*amour propre*].

KMcM: If you were to choose one piece of Greek literature or philosophy, from the classics, to help understand the present crisis, what would it be?

AN: The character from Greek tragedy I like the most is Dionysius, who appears in the Bacchantes. It is Dionysius who represents himself as the avenger of the town against the Tyrant, the one who animates the women who run on the mountain looking for the bull in search of wisdom and love and who rightly denounces the King, the tyrant who doesn't want women to be liberated. It is Dionysius who reveals that freedom is the most beautiful thing in the world, the most beautiful in life. Also, which should be defended, even killing family identity. It is the mother who kills the King, a mother destructor who destroys the closest form of identity, which is that of mother and child, that is what's sacred in life, no?

Translated from French by Suzy Foster

Interview IV: Manolis Glezos

'I don't need Tiresias. I just need my comrades . . .'

Athens, May 15, 2013

Martin McQuillan: You have a long personal history of resisting powers of occupation and tyranny in Greece; perhaps we could begin by talking about some of those experiences.

Manolis Glezos: I am of course full of experiences from the Occupation era. I can say that I still experience intensely all that period. I cannot escape from it. I am now preparing a book, which is about to be published, is called 'Nekye Ode', inspired by Homer's *Odyssey*, by a rhapsody devoted totally to Nekyomandeia, I use this as a point of inspiration and I call all my comrades with whom we lived together, to discuss that era. In the ancient times, as described by Homer, there was a ritual in Greece to call Tiresias, the blind oracle, to ask about what was to happen in the future. So, I call my comrades, whom I knew closely, whom I held in my arms, and who were lost in battles, in demonstrations, in executions. I call them all to discuss what the future holds for our country. The book consists of over seventy poems, each of them written about a comrade I knew and who was lost, or for many together, and I invite them to come and discuss with me the future of this country. These are not lamenting songs, we are not crying. We are not lamenting, they are songs of conversation about what the future of this country will be and they are written in a very sharp spirit, a critical spirit, about everything we have suffered, both from our opponents and from our own mistakes.

MMcQ: What do the other texts of Greek culture have to tell us about this critical moment?

MG: In my opinion, they have predicted it already, both the Greek philosophers and ancient Greek poetry. Menandros, 2,300 years ago, has stated clearly and categorically that loans turn people to slaves. He has already made clear that on no occasion can we find a solution through loans. He said we do not want to turn into slaves. Do we need to discuss it again? Do we need to say it again? Sophocles has said it in *Antigone*. Other Greeks have said it, Plutarch also; many have talked about this issue. Loans are no solution.

Therefore, on top of that, the ancient Greeks have also said something else. They have developed the ideology of resistance. 'Medizein', that is, submission to *Medes*, to foreigners, was the greatest indignity in ancient Greece. The same was true during the 1821 revolution, was said in different words by Kolokotronis: 'Fire and axe to those who surrender to the Turks'. Therefore, we have the ideology of resistance, to the coming enemy but also to the tyrant, to the governor who wants to dominate the country, as it is clearly shown in Sophocles's *Antigone*, with the conflict between Creon and Antigone.

But in the case of contemporary Greece, we have something new, which is even worse, and this is that modern Germany breaks the laws that it has established itself: a tragedy even greater than the one described in ancient Greece. Allow me to explain. In 1946 the nineteen allies met and talked about what Germany should pay for the destruction it caused in each country's economy. Germany paid each country back, all but Greece. Here we have a violation of its own laws, like I said before, on Germany's part. Then it was decided by the Ally committee that Italy and Bulgaria, who also came as conquerors to our country when the Wehrmacht invaded us, should also pay for the destruction they caused. Both Italy and Bulgaria paid what the Ally committee charged them with. Why does Germany exempt itself?

MMcQ: With resistance comes sacrifice.

MG: I did what all the other Greeks also did. I am not an exception. I don't consider myself an exception. And it is a mistake to say that Apostolos Sandas, my friend, and myself are pioneers of the resistance in Europe. This is wrong. I will give two examples. On the 2nd of May 1941, a convoy of tanks progressed from Pylos to Tripoli to occupy it. And suddenly, a young man steps out in the middle of the road and says, 'Stop! You will not enslave us. Right now I am alone, but the whole of the Greek people follow behind me.' The German commander stopped the convoy. He asked his interpreter what is this boy saying? The interpreter explained. The commander took out his gun and shot the boy. But he doesn't stop there, he orders his soldiers to take a big rock and smash the head of the dead boy. Let us analyze this. What did the boy say? 'Stop!' They stopped. 'You will not enslave us', meaning that you may have beaten us by tanks, but you will not enslave our souls. And if right now I am alone, here is a message. You should learn, German, that behind me the whole of the Greek people follow, and the Greek people (I did my sacrifice) follow my example. Of course the German commander executed him in accordance with the Nazi mentality that such heads producing such ideas should be destroyed. Mathios Potagas was the name of the boy. He was seventeen years old. And he was executed on the 2nd of May 1941 before the Germans occupied the whole of the Peloponnese. This is the first act of resistance in Greece, but we have a second one from France. In 1963 I was invited by the former French resistance fighters to be introduced to some of them. We went high up in the Alps, at Vercors where the paratroopers massacred thousands of hostages with airplanes. We went down to Grenoble and then we reached the French–Italian borders. There the French told me 'you boast of being the first resistance fighters, we were the first!' I asked them what they had done. 'We came here, at the French–Italian border and put up a banner facing towards Italy, and on it we had written, by the time you were fighting in Albania, "Greeks, careful, don't go any further, France starts here!"' It is the French sense of humor, in this joke we drive the Italians into the sea, we disembarked in Italy, we swept through it, got to the borders and the French tell us don't go any further, France starts from here. It is very clever and it shows how much our epic fight in 1940–1941 gave hope to the peoples of Europe.

It is of course very funny, but let me also show you something, in what spirit young boys in Greece were going to their execution. What was their spirit, how they faced death.

Here we have a letter, let's look at it first from its emotional side. What does it say? 'Dear mother, I kiss you. Greetings'. And it says, 'Today I am going to my execution'. It doesn't say they are taking me, it says I am going, I offer myself. You can see the spirit, the qualitative difference. It doesn't say they are taking me, it says I am going, I offer myself. And it explains for what reason 'Falling for the Greek people'. You see how it is written, though, the word '*Laos*' people, is written with a capital L, it could also refer to the German people, to the English people, any people. This is my brother's letter. He was three years younger than me, and a first-year student at the Teacher's Academy. He was only nineteen. And see, just in these few lines, he says everything. I publish more letters in this book; they are all in the same spirit. I mention my brother because his story is compressed in a very succinct way.

And the question that now arises is this: Why is Germany following this policy against Greece? We are talking about the German governments. Why are they doing this? Are they taking revenge against Greece because it was the first country that demolished the myth of the invincibility of the Axis? Remember, the Axis was winning at all fronts until then: in Asia, Africa and Europe. The first who demolished the myth of the invincibility of the Axis were the Greeks; I am not a nationalist, but how can I erase History? So I wonder, are the German governments taking revenge because of that? I go further, Germany sets off from the other end of Europe to attack Greece, why? Had we taken any colonies of theirs? Had we taken any financial space of theirs? Did we share any borders and we had conflicts in these borders? No, but they came from the other end of Europe and this amazing one month fight took place until they beat us. How long did France last? How long did Poland last? How long the other European countries until then? Greece lasted for one month. And with the battle of Crete, where for the first time in World History, people fought against a state army and it upset all of Hitler's plans: all of them.

MMcQ: Perhaps you might tell us about your act of resistance on the Acropolis?

MG: I don't like to talk about this. Because everyone thinks that I am only this. But, not to disappoint you, I will tell you. When the battle of Crete was over, Hitler came out of the Reichstag and gave a speech, a terrible speech. 'Europe is free today' were his words, he meant continental Europe. 'There is no enemy of ours in continental Europe and we are victorious'. And me and Lakis said to ourselves, 'You think so? Now we'll show you, now the fight begins'. That same night we took down the Nazi flag, the swastika, from the Acropolis, and replaced it with the Greek one. This is our contribution. I think this is enough to say about it.

MMcQ: We are making a film based on the *Antigone* of Sophocles. What resources of resistance can we find in this play?

MG: In my opinion, it is the moment when Antigone says to Creon that above your law are the customs of our city. We cannot abandon the customs and leave the dead unburied, to be eaten by vultures, no matter who they are. Antigone expresses what I have referred to as this ideology of resistance in Greece both against the invader and the tyrant. And it is characteristic that democracy, which was born here in Greece, not representative democracy, but real democracy, people's democracy, the city's democracy, has a special significance. The city was the basic core of the existence of democracy. When the citizens of the city exercised policy, the result was civilization. There is a sequence in terms of meaning, polis (city), politis (citizen), politiki (politics), politismos (civilization). When Solon was called by the Athenians to apply the law, he said that whoever is a-polis, who does not take part in the affairs of the city, will be exiled. If you don't want to participate in the common affairs of the city, go to another city. So we also have apolis (without a city), polis, politis, politiki, and politismos. These were all adopted by the culture of power in the West, in Western Europe, who studied them carefully and said, we also want to add something to these but without moving away from the root—pol. And what did they give us? Police! The organ for the repression of people's will. This is what the West gave us. I am not a nationalist, but I am proud of this sequence—pol, polis, apolis, politiki, politismos.

This is why I left the Greek Parliament back in 1986 when I realized that nothing could come out of it. And I returned to my village and I applied direct democracy, real democracy, where people decide about everything. They may be wrong, but one must respect even the wrong decisions of the people. Let me give you an example. Inside the village there is a cemetery. The rainwater went through the buried bodies and contaminated the springs. In our first meeting I told them we must move the cemetery to another place. A woman stood up and said, 'I want to be able to see my husband'. So I said to her, 'What about the other woman, who lives in the other side of the village and she can't see her husband?' Her answer was that she should come nearer to her own house so the woman could visit him. A vote took place and I got only 4 votes. So the village waited to see what I would do. I had the right by law, as President of the Community, to move the cemetery elsewhere but I didn't do it. At that point the village changed and became in favor of direct democracy. Many years went by and the decision was later taken to move the cemetery to another place. In the beginning we built a new cemetery and eventually the whole of the cemetery will be moved there. This is direct democracy, real democracy, people making decisions. It is difficult, unquestionably, very difficult. I experienced it for twelve years. And because they were saying that all the things that happened in the village, many things, were the work of Manolis, I resigned from my position as President of the Community before the end of my term, after two-and-a-half years and I remained just a member of the community. And for the following eight years I was nothing, I was not a member of the Council. We have in Greece a great history regarding real democracy—a very long history.

It is wrong to believe that democracy was born in classical Greece. In Homer's years democracy was better. In ancient Ithaca, Telemachus learns about the arrival of the last king, Nestor, the king of Pylos, and he wants to know what happened to his father. Straightaway he calls a meeting, '*agorein*'. The next day all the citizens of Ithaca are gathered and the most senior of them asks 'who called us and why?' Today I would ask, could we call a meeting of a city? Can each citizen by himself call a meeting? Because it is a clear question: who called us and why? Since Ulysses left, many years went by without a meeting being called and I wonder, what was the issue, Penelope or power? What were the suitors after, Penelope or the power, what was the cause of all the struggle? This is hypothetical of course, but no one can doubt the words uttered by the most senior of the Ithaca citizens, 'who called us here', amazing words. This is why I believe that the biggest problem of humanity today is this: Who will have the power, the people or the shrewd guys? This is the problem. Even if we ignore ancient Greece and say nothing existed so far. There is a need for people to be in power, we must bring them into power.

MMcQ: What would Tiresias tell us now about the future of Greece?

MG: I don't need Tiresias. I just need my comrades to talk with, the ones I lost. Allow me to explain what I mean. On the eve of every demonstration, on the eve of every battle, on the eve of every execution, we used to get together and we would say to one other, Manolis, Kostas, Pavlos, if you live, if 'the good bullet' misses you, don't forget me. And they would tell of their dreams for Greece, about the world, but also other, more personal ones: 'I haven't drunk wine so far, I want to drink, you will drink for me. I have never walked in the forest to hear the rustling of the wind; you will hear it for me. I have never walked by the sea to hear the waves lapping on the beach; you will hear them for me. And when you meet people on the street and you say good morning, you will say it for me also.' So I am not alone in this moment, as we talk I am also the voice of all these comrades, of their dreams and their visions.

I am going to recite you a poem dedicated to my friend Kostas Kouloufakos, poet, writer, publisher and chemist. The title is 'Unbowed', the word is not mine, it is his. It comes from a text of his:

> You thundered out, Kostas, in Macronesi
> On the 20th of December 1949
> And your voice chiseled it on the Tables of History

'And if death is to come
Let him come as I choose
Unbowed
So that my life is as I command it'
You cried it in your ringing voice
And your actions attest to it
Unbowed
To all the enemies who tried to control your beliefs
To all the friends who tried to manipulate you
Who tried to wall you in Party mechanisms
You participated actively in every collective effort
You patiently remained silent, listening to your interlocutors
You abolished, like a sarcophagus, your personality
And you moved on, through the depths of thought
Even more than when you strode with your long legs
across Makronesi, Yaros, Leros
Unbowed
Always and always
I remember when we got together
Stathis Dromazos, Anastos Papapetrou,
Elli Pappa, Potis Paraskevopoulos, Yorgis Spanos
And the two of us
And we decided to put the blazing iron
Deep inside, and find the causes of the defeat
And map out our route
You kept the minutes of our meeting
And in out next meeting you announced
'I could never imagine that the lancet of thought
Would go so deep'
Despite all our deep thoughts
What did we achieve?
We are still struggling to find the way to vindication.
You heard it clearly.

This poem is dedicated to my friend Kostas Kouloufakos, his profession was chemistry, but he never exercised it; he was a poet and a publisher. I dedicate to him the poem 'Unbowed', the title is his own, because he has used the word in one of his poems 'Days in Macronesi'.

Translated from Greek by Katerina Iordanoglou

Interview V:
Theodoros Terzopoulos

'Today God does not exist.
In God's place we see the bank'

Athens, May 14, 2013

Ken McMullen: What interests you in tragedy?

Theodoros Terzopoulos: I started approximately thirty years ago with Euripides's *Bacchae* because I consider it a very important tragedy. It embodies a very big and important subject, which is fundamental for ancient tragedy, the conflict between instinct and logic. This beginning, the conflict between instinct and logic, helped me a lot in making the next tragedies, in the sense that the tragic person always has this internal conflict. We can say, in a nutshell, that the tragic person is conflictual. The tragic hero is in conflict, aiming to be like God, trying to look God in the eyes. He is in conflict with God, with himself, with the world. What can we call this? It is creation; the tragic hero is creative. What is happening today is that people are not conflictual, they are passive, and this raises a big issue.

In the old times, in classical Greece, classical civilization was the emancipation of the ancient Greek myths. That was the great classical civilization. But there was also another very important principle, beyond conflict, namely the unity between the city, nature and man, something that does not exist today. We might think of Aeschylus, where this unity existed, and I think harmoniously so, while in Sophocles we already have the destruction of the city, and eventually the absence of God. Whereas in Euripides we have man at the center, and slowly what we call character begins to make its appearance, but very shyly, in a psychological way. Today God does not exist. In God's place we see the bank. In the place of the city, what do we see? Ruins, not just architectural ones, but human ruins. Because what is the city without man?

And, of course, nature is absent, as it functioned and still functions in ancient tragedy. Nature is constantly destroyed. So, what do we have? We have really the dissolution, in essence the destruction, of this relationship between the city, God and nature. What happens with the staging of ancient tragedies? In the staging of tragedies in ancient Greece, God was always opposite: Dionysus. The performance had a religious character, it was ceremonial, and it was a ritual. It was dedicated to God, the god Dionysus. The actor was looking through the spectators. That is why in Epidaurus he was speaking from the middle and above, both in order to be heard, it was technique, and in order to meet the eye of Dionysus, through the spectators. Now God does not exist. To which God can you talk? This is why tragedies are staged as dramas, as psychological dramas, where in the place of God we have the bank or the Mayor or the mother-in-law or family members. So we can see the differences between tragedy and drama. In tragedy God is present. In drama God is absent. In tragedy the tragic hero is in conflict and dialogue with God, with what transcends him. In drama this is absent, because in its place is the Mayor, the bank, another family member, with whom you are in conversation, not in conflict (in drama this basic conflict we talked about does not exist).

We now live in our present time; I live here in Athens. We say that we are living through a tragedy; is it a tragedy or a drama? I don't think we are living through a tragedy, because we use the word tragedy too easily. We are living through a drama. Why? Why don't we live through a tragedy? Because God is absent and nature is destroyed, and because modern man is not conflictual, he is passive. He is an obedient instrument of various situations, economic, political, ideological, and he lacks the power, the energy, and most of all the conflictual mood that is creativity. He is not creative anymore; he is passive. He is the receiver of many terrible things, many bad messages. He is a passive receiver of bad political discourse, of bad television programmes, of soaps and serials about this life, which really have sank to a very low level.

To take it even further, I would dare to say that our times are post-dramatic, not even dramatic, because even the elements of drama, of a family drama or a political drama, all these pieces have come apart. They have disintegrated, and we are trying to recompose them to create an image, and what we are actually creating is a post-dramatic image.

KMcM: Do you think that the current crisis in Greece could give rise to a creative synthesis through a dialectical moment?

TT: A creative synthesis, never. If we see it as a stage event, we would see in the place of the father a computer, in the place of a child five numbers, in the place of neighbors various serials or TV programmes or trash, really. Let me point to the epitome of post-dramatic art; men work without knowing anymore why they work. They produce products, they eat them, consume them, they defecate them. Man is his waste after all, his garbage; the two become identical and this is really harsh.

I live here in Athens with my theatre group ATTIS, and we tour around the world. I think that things are not better in other places, I mean I go to countries in Asia where there is significant production, high growth rates, and I see man literally nonexistent, living in pollution, ruined cities, destroyed nature, alienated, and I always think of ancient tragedy and I cannot find the equivalent, it doesn't exist. And when I try to do the lamentation of the Trojan women, inevitably I have to dig very deeply into the human body to find the root of lamentation, or the root of laughter or the root of doubt or the root of mourning. Today men, as they have degenerated, have no sources of memory; no sources of energy, and you have to invent a system in order to find all these elements that have been repressed, to literally unearth them in order to do an ancient tragedy. But by unearthing those, you do some excellent work with the actors themselves, who regain their health.

Modern man is in a very bad state: he is bodiless. In his everyday life, he is spending so many hours in front of a computer that the body becomes malformed, the axes are destroyed, he has no spine, no triangle, no diaphragm, he doesn't breathe properly. I mean we are talking about a humanoid, a passive creature, through all this corrosive, alienating situation and we, in order to stage the tragedies, must dig deeply, to find the deep sources of sound, the deep sources of memory, the deep sources of energy. It is not easy, but it is comforting and produces good results. I would say that the body today could really be, in a way, a political response, and a tool. The body can be the bearer of energy, of memory, of anger, of laughter, of all these situations, which have been repressed, and one can be a creative and active, not a passive, body. And an active body is really dangerous for today's capitalism.

KMcM: Perhaps you could tell us about your experiences of staging *Antigone* and other parts of Sophocles.

TT: I first staged *Antigone* twenty years ago at the Teatro Olympico of Paladio in Vincenza, where there still exists on stage the set from the first staging around 1520. It was with Italian actors, because it was a coproduction between Piccolo Teatro, Teatro Olimpico and ATTIS, at that time a small theatre company, and it was in two languages, Italian and Greek. There I really had to fight with Italian classicism, and things were not simple. The Italian language has too many vowels and is musical, and the consonants were not firm enough to restrain the vowels, and I had the sense that the language had no columns, they were singing. I did some work supporting the consonants so that the language would not sound oblique but upright.

I went through a big artistic crisis, since we are talking about crisis, before I found the way. Because, Antigone, who takes these terrible decisions and in her conflict with Creon we see her coming out triumphant; Antigone, who is often portrayed as a heroine, I portrayed her as a fundamentalist, as a maniac. Antigone does not accept dialogue. Literally the tragic person, the confusedly tragic person, really confused, is Creon, not Antigone. I didn't accept this view that was dominant in social realism and in Latin America too, that Antigone is the ultimate heroine. I saw her negative side, her refusal to understand, and her insistence in her positions.

In all the versions, even in China where I staged it in Beijing, I followed again this concept. I illuminated and I worked on her negative side. This doesn't mean that I portrayed Creon positively, no, but I portrayed Creon without a tragic way out, in a tragic dead end. Whereas Antigone, even in prison and walking to her death, has a solution, a way out. The short-circuited person, the tragically enclosed person is Creon. We should entitle the tragedy *Creon* and not *Antigone*.

I directed *Oedipus Rex* in Russia; the title there was *Oedipe Czar*, at the Alexandrinsky Theatre, which is the oldest academic theatre of Russia, where Meyerhold achieved great things with great Russian actors, on a very big stage, and with a very big chorus. I based the staging very much on the chorus, because without the chorus we cannot talk about tragedy but about drama, when the chorus is absent from the stage. We know the story very well and it has offered amazing material to psychoanalysis, because of the Oedipus complex of course. Really, the structure of the play is very geometrical, very particular and very simple. I didn't really want to focus on the Oedipus–Jocasta relationship, the family affair; rather to a certain extent, I put a lot of emphasis on Tiresias's presence, but I saw the whole thing as a deep hallucination, a nightmare.

It was a wild projection of a dark material of the subconscious; this was my interpretation. Because the interpretation of Oedipus can create a big sentimental reaction, not what tragedy should create, which is fear and pity: this shock, this global emotion, this is what interests me in tragedy. When I say global emotion, I come once more to the body, to a perfectly energized body, which can be still and yet have a very strong internal vertigo: a great speed, exactly like a spinning top, which at the moment of its greatest speed, is still. This is the energy of the tragedy and this is the stillness of the tragedy, the faces in tragedy, especially in Aeschylus, look still, but internally they have a great speed, a dizzying speed, which creates stillness, like a spinning top.

If you see an ancient Greek statue, like Myron's *Discobolus* or any of the works of the great sculptors of ancient Greece, by the positioning you are instantly aware of the internal movement. If you see a Roman statue, you will see that it is the total of its outer limits. It lacks internal vertigo, internal movement. And this is the big difference between the classical and the classicist; the classical has internal vertigo, which shapes the body, the idea, and the thought of the tragedy. The classicist is external.

KMcM: Which tragic playwright would help us most to think about politics today?

TT: It is Aeschylus, because Aeschylus is very close to the archetypes. In Aeschylus we can still talk about 'pre-tragedies' because the personae are not yet emancipated. We see in *Prometheus*, especially in *Prometheus* since it is one of the oldest plays, something like Ocean in human form, or we see various elements of nature, like the Oceanids. Being close to the archetypes means being close to God, and in this sense I like both his rhythm and his language, especially in the chorus parts, which have many Doric, prearchaic elements. They have an excellent rhythm and allow you to create a ritualistic style. This is great, and I am closer to this, it is closer to God and nature and quite a lot to the city.

In Sophocles, we see the city; the city prevails, even when it is destroyed. We see in Euripides the prevalence of man. Euripides doubts God. Whereas in Aeschylus we have God, and this gives him a greater weight and an openness to cosmos. Aeschylus is more cosmic. What I mean is that with Aeschylus you take a very long journey, because he is beyond the horizon. He has a great range, and he goes to the perpetual. Becket admires him for that reason. But Beckett, in this journey to cosmos, or even to Hades, stays in the grey zone before Hades, in this grey zone a little after life, towards the end of life and before Hades. Beckett stays in this grey zone, which exists very much in Aeschylus, less in Sophocles and is present, at a psychological level, in Euripides.

From *Antigone* I could choose the remarkable goodbye scene, when she bids farewell to the citizens of Thebes and she sings 'farewell my friends, farewell my compatriots, farewell Thebans, I am leaving now, I am leaving', but in all this there is an element that she leaves for a journey that will never end. It will not end in the grave; she leaves for the perpetual, for infinity. It's what she says and the way she says it, it's not like I am leaving and that's the end; there is no end, there is 'infinitivo', and this for me is remarkable. Not only because she says I am going to meet my brothers, I am going to meet my mother, I am going to meet my relatives, no. It is because this entire farewell, the lamentation of Antigone, is a stage for death, it is a step. We might say that in ancient Greece, in all great ancient civilizations, all of life was a preparation for the other life, the afterlife, and this created exceptional pieces of art, because preparation means ritual, it means festivals, events and these events were songs, laments, works of art and this gave beauty to life, as one bid farewell to it through stages for Hades, that made life more beautiful.

I staged *Oedipus Rex* three times, and there are major scenes, remarkable scenes, like Jocasta's monologue, Jocasta's entrance, but for me the most beautiful scene is the narration of the messenger. This is the one. Both messengers. How Oedipus left, how he stabbed his eyes out and how Jocasta died. These narrations are truly top scenes, both of them. If you have a good actor, and I always had a good actor performing both monologues, you can really do great work. The narration was talking about the evil we didn't see, because usually we see the bad things on stage, and there's quite an art to that. This scene, however, is connected with the troubadour, with the narrator, with the storyteller who narrates a story from the old times. And this contains also the idea of the *Verfremdungseffekt*, the Brechtian distancing effect, because I never wanted this messenger to be sentimental. He should certainly have a lot of energy but at the same time he should have a critical stance. He shouldn't identify with the event, which takes on great value through his critical stance and we never see it but we hear it. We never see the terrible events in Greek tragedy; we never see a murder, a suicide. When you enter the area of tragedy, you also become a fundamentalist. You can't get out. You enter a very creative space and at the same time a prison from which you can't escape.

KMcM: What insights are to be found today in *The Frogs* by Aristophanes?

TT: The value of Aristophanes, and of this particular play, is certainly great. In *The Frogs* he demystifies the tragic poets and he gives us really a lesson in democracy, that you can demystify these icons and these monumental plays. This is how it was in ancient Greece and this is democracy.

KMcM: Could you imagine a way to stage a tragedy around the events of today?

TT: I don't think so; it has nothing to do with tragedy. In tragedy, as I mentioned before, there are certain terms, very important terms, we need. Let's say, the city being destroyed, like Thebes, where a civil war took place and the city was ruined, but still a power was present and active, let's call it God. I wouldn't say that this could happen today; we have no Che Guevara here. I am saying something is different now. There really isn't any such great, catalytic figure, to take a position in a dialogue and take part in a conflict. We have mediocrities on one side and mediocrities on the other side, who clash and are minced by this reality, out of which nothing comes. There is no conclusion. There is no catharsis. In tragedy all conflicts really happened for the catharsis. But to reach the catharsis, certain terms have to be in operation, terms of the tragic or the social, the definition of people, whom we can see as the chorus in ancient tragedy: in ancient democracy, this was the role the chorus played. Here we often have to do with a crowd, a mob rule, which cannot have consciousness under the current circumstances, you understand? There is no person, no figure, if not God, who could be Achilles, or Prometheus today, there is no nature. Here we are talking about a totally deconstructed situation, at all levels, which does not constitute tragedy but a postmodern drama. What was always required of the chorus was a sense of consciousness, of origin, of identity, always trying to create a big idea. These things are absent today.

Translated from Greek by Katerina Iordanogbu.

Interview VI: Kostas Vaxevanis

'Europe is neither the dream of
Mrs. Merkel, nor the dream of the Bundesbank'

Athens, May 15, 2013

Martin McQuillan: I wonder if we could begin by discussing your decision to publish the so-called Lagarde list.

Kostas Vaxevanis: I think it is evident now that Greece is in a very bad situation; in the last two–three years there have been people eating from garbage bins, and at the same time three governments, two ministers were keeping in their drawers the names of about 2,500 people who should be checked for their Swiss bank accounts. The names of these people who should have been checked for tax evasion were never given to the Greek people, they created a very bad, very sick situation. Some people were eating from garbage bins and others could evade taxation, until we were obliged, for reasons not just moral or journalistic but also political, to publicize these names, demanding an investigation to be launched.

So, several lists appeared, fake lists, incriminating people. The political scene was in a sick situation, because everyone blamed everyone and they were all concealing things. When this list came out, whilst everyone should have been happy that it existed and the names were real, a very violent process started against me. A special police force within very few hours, even before the magazine was out for sale in kiosks, arrested me and took me by force to court, announced that I was wanted, as if I was a big criminal. After the court tried me and acquitted me, the Public Prosecutor intervened and asked for the trial to be repeated, because it was not held properly. It has become evident that the list was a great piece of evidence; if one reads the list and sees the people on it, one is faced with all the system of corruption in Greece—politicians, journalists, publishers, businessmen—all of them are the political system of Greece, and this is exactly what they were hiding.

To start with, when we publicized it, we said this very simple thing, that it is a list of people who have money in a Swiss bank, and which was leaked by Falciani. There are still dozens of such lists, regarding deposits of Greeks abroad. We do not know if this money is illegal or legal; what we do know however is that this money should be checked as to whether it is illegal or legal, and at some point Greece should sort out the corruption issue. It is obvious that the majority of the people in the list, as on other lists (in other banks, in Lichtenstein, in Britain, in the Virgin Islands), it is obvious that this money is the product of corruption, of money laundering. It is not possible for a housewife to have five million Euros in deposits, nor is it possible for a minister to have offshore companies.

As someone, a very serious person, once said, the point of journalism is to reveal what someone powerful wants to hide. Anything else is public relations. Right now Greece is on the edge. The corrupt system is still in power and every day makes laws that legalize corruption, every day. Those who say they will save Greece make laws that legalize corruption, and there are dozens of examples. Unfortunately journalism for years has not played its role. Journalism is a fourth estate but it is a power that should be opposite all the others and close to the people, not close to those other powers. Therefore we have lost our role. To find our role again and tell the truth to help Greece save itself is the job of every journalist. Unfortunately, because what should be self-evident is not so in Greece, in our profession too, to rediscover the journalistic profession will have a cost, and if this cost for me personally is to be convicted, because this is what they want, and go to prison, I will do it to prove that there is an issue of the freedom of press in Greece.

I am talking about freedom of press. Many will say, what is Vaxevanis talking about, right now he is speaking freely to a British film crew, but freedom of press is not to be able to write something at one given moment; it is not a momentary freedom, it is the climate in which journalism must operate, this is freedom. It is not I being able to say something freely at a certain moment but for journalists to operate freely. If you open Greek newspapers right now you will not see a single column, not a hundred words about the dirty role banks play in Greece, about how much money they have stolen, and they were recapitalized with money from the Greek people, not one column. The reason is that the official sponsors of all media in Greece are the bankers; either by loans or with the advertisements they place. Therefore, journalism is not free in Greece; it needs to become free again.

A year ago we had issued a copy of the magazine in which we were describing how the Greek banks, without a single euro, were falsely increased their share capital, to show that they had money. They were lending one another through offshores, money that didn't really exist moving around in circles. We also discovered some other things regarding the banks. As a result, the day the magazine came out I saw a document publicized in which I appeared to be working for the Greek secret services. This document was obviously fake, and it was dealt with. It was made to create a situation against me. When we continued to write things on September the 9th, four people appeared at the crack of dawn in the garden of my house: of course, they were not gardeners . . . A month ago we revealed this extermination plan against us. That is, we revealed, through the testimony of a woman who took part in this plan, how a part of the secret services which was used privately, by bankers, was employed to exterminate us physically. We had photographs, documents and graphology tests. We gave them to the police seven months ago, we publicized them, and not a single Greek newspaper wrote, not even a hundred words, about the fact that a journalist at least claims that he is in danger.

MMcQ: How has austerity affected Greece?

KV: I think what is happening in Greece after three years is exactly what many people thought would happen. Greece is in a continuous fall. They came to a country which was facing certain problems, they imposed austerity measures, the austerity measures in essence diminished the real economy, people were laid off, the economy came to a halt, money stopped circulating, so what happened was the opposite of what they claimed would happen: recession and unemployment. Every time these measures don't yield any results they introduce new austerity measures. Nowhere in the world has austerity yielded results. For economies to work, growth is needed. For growth to exist, people are needed to create it. For people to create growth, a healthy environment is required within which they can operate. As it is now, the whole country operates in a sick environment. And they are giving an aspirin to a country that suffers from cancer, not only because of its own choices.

Right now there is a serious problem, not just in Greece but also in the whole of the European South. It is presented as a Greek problem, that Greeks are corrupt, that they drink ouzo on the beach or looking at the Acropolis. This is not true. There are quite a lot of parasitical phenomena in Greece, but the crisis in Greece as in the whole of Europe is basically due to one thing, that we have a European Union which fancies itself as a united country, as a union, whereas the only thing that unites it is the common currency, it has no united economy, no united policies. So, today the South is poor, the South which, for ten–fifteen years had been taking loans to buy German cars, German weapons, German and French technology, German submarines, like Akis Tsochatzopoulos; all this was bought by loans. Now Greece is called to deal with all this in a different way, it cannot devalue its currency, because it is a common currency, therefore it cannot cope with the demands of the crisis. As a result, it is sinking deeper and deeper into the crisis while Germany becomes richer and richer.

America is also a Union, like the European Union. However when a country, an area of the United States has a surplus, financial surplus, like Florida, this money will go to another state, such as Alaska, to create a balance in the economy. This is not the case in the European

Union. Germany's surplus, from goods the whole of Europe buys from Germany, does not return to European countries, which, for various reasons have a deficit. Therefore we cannot talk for balance or for a united Europe.

The debt in Greece is a very big hole into which money is constantly thrown. It was never regulated; there was never a balance in the debt. When the time came for the European aid, with regard to the debt, Europe acted as a very big loan shark. For example, let's assume that the debt was 300 billion; let's assume this number. In the free market this debt at that time could be bought for 50 per cent of the price, meaning Europe could go to the free market and buy the Greek debt for 150 billion and then Greece could repay it. This didn't happen. They didn't buy the debt from the free market at a reduced price. They accepted the debt as it was and were lending Greece, which had to repay back the whole of the debt, not at the value of the market at the time. Instead of telling Greece, take 150 billion to pay for the debt and then you pay us back in installments, they gave Greece money in order to pay for a debt of 300 billion, and as a result Greece now pays only interest and the debt is not viable and cannot be dealt with. Therefore we have a big hole, the size of Greece, which someone is trying to fill with a bucket.

MMcQ: What is the state of the debt in Greece today?

KV: How was the debt created? The history of the Greek debt starts in the very distant past, after Greece's war of liberation from the Ottoman Empire in 1821, when the English gave the first money to Greece to help it. This money never reached Greece, we never found out how much money there was, and, because of the compound interest, Greece does not have to pay just one debt but one more on top of that. In our times, the times of the European Union, Greece's production was disrupted, and the country stopped producing. This disruption of production had nothing to do with some laziness on the part of the Greeks; the European Union was subsidizing particular cultivations, not quality of cultivation. It was not subsidizing the best quality cultivations; it was subsidizing specific cultivations, unconditionally. So, the Greeks turned to these types and every other cultivation was destroyed. Specific types of cultivations appeared in Greece with a single aim, to get the subsidies. So it was easier for someone to cultivate bad quality products in order to get the subsidy than sell good products. Greece became addicted, a parasitical mentality was developed, that one is not obliged to produce but can still make money. Next, the German banks, the European banks, opened their funds to give loans, which created a sense of euphoria to people; in essence these loans were educating the whole of Greece for what was to come, that is, its exploitation.

In previous years in Greece one could get a loan for holidays, for weddings, for studies, for how to deal with dandruff, for everything. This was all part of a policy to weaken and make dependent all the countries of Europe. I would say that Europe is not what the Bundesbank and Merkel want, nor what is planned in London's City. Europe is a whole culture, a whole economy; it is the culture of the English, the civilization of the French, what the Spanish people bring in their history. It is the philosophy of the Greeks; it is the philosophy and poetry of the Germans. All of this is Europe; it is not only the choices of Mrs Merkel.

Greece was systematically deprived of its production; it lost its production and its relationship with the real economy, systematically. The European Union was subsidizing cultivations that had nothing to do with Greece, traditional cultivations, such as tobacco, disappeared, some years ago. They were subsidizing the uprooting of olive groves; they were subsidizing the cutting of Greek boats fishing in the Aegean. A number of different productive activities that existed in the country stopped, on the pretext of a central planning in Europe. The result was the creation of several parasitical phenomena, without any control; people were directed to cultivate various useless things, only to get the subsidy, and often to cheat, since there was no control. It was more profitable to cultivate inferior tomatoes, then throw them away and get the subsidy, for example, or cotton, than to cultivate quality tomatoes for people to eat here or in England or in Germany. In the years that followed, also systematically, the 'taps' opened, funding from the banks opened, and people were driven to a false sense of euphoria, taking loans for everything. Mr Papademos, the head of the Bank of Greece at the time, who gave the order to the Bank to open its funds and lend without limits, and without collateral, without guarantees, is the same man who some years later, as a Prime Minister, said that the loans, taken thoughtlessly by the Greeks, were to blame, the very man who gave these loans.

MMcQ: What in your opinion does the future hold for Greece?

KV: So today they come and say that we must comply with the markets. Who are the markets? What are these markets? The markets are the ones who, back in 2008, managed to cause the whole of the planet's real economy to collapse. Are these the markets that now promote the rescue? Europe is neither the dream of Mrs Merkel nor the dream of the Bundesbank. Europe is not the skyscrapers of the City in London; it is the people of England and their culture. It is the philosophy of the Greeks, it is the poetry of the French, it is the culture of the Italians; this is what Europe and European Union is, it is not plans around a table about how some will get richer. The other day there was an article in *The Guardian*, in which one of the well-known bankers was saying that all this process, all this greed was the result even of cocaine use by those people who got addicted to power and money. I don't know if this is true, but this is exactly how these people are behaving, like people addicted to money, who see no importance in human beings, in their functions and needs.

The bad thing is that this story that has been going on for so long has changed people; it has also changed poets and philosophers. Some days ago we had in Greece the example of a very well-known female poet, who, talking at an event in the center of Athens, expressed positions which were considered racist. Philosophers, poets, artists, thinkers have lost their pace, lured by the sirens of the markets. We must rediscover human values, we must rediscover collectivity, we must rediscover how people exist, close to one another, not in a way where one builds a swimming pool next to his neighbor's house and the neighbor is envious. I think that Greece has all the potential to rediscover the values that thousands of years ago were first established here. We exchanged those values; we exchanged them with a political amorality, with an economic amorality, with a Party Machiavellianism. All of these values have been exchanged; we must rediscover them. I think

Greece has the potential, but in order to make use of this potential, it must rid itself of the political system that governs it. It must throw away the corrupt system that in Europe and the rest of the world appears as a system for salvation. I don't know which political power will do it but it can't be done by those who brought Greece to the point it is today.

Translated from Greek by Katerina Iordanoglov.

Whatever Still Remains

Richard Wilson

What do we owe the dead? Three hundred and forty-one billion euros, according to Greek prime minister Alexis Tsipras. That was the sum he demanded Berlin should pay in reparation for German atrocities perpetrated in Greece during the First and Second World Wars, in a parliamentary speech on 10 March 2015. The figure, which eclipsed the 241 billion bailout to Greece by the European Central Bank, was calculated by the Greek Finance Ministry on expert advice in December 2014 and consisted of 9 billion for the First and 322 billion for the Second World War, plus 10 billion that the Central Bank of Greece had been forced to loan the Reichsbank in 1942. The demand also included the return of 8,500 antiquities and artworks looted by the occupiers yet still held in Germany. But it chiefly related to compensation for war crimes, in particular the massacre of 218 civilians, including women and children, by the SS in the Boeotian town of Distomo on 10 June 1944. 'We owe it our history, we owe it to the fighters of the National Resistance', Tsipras solemnly affirmed, when he announced that his government would 'wholeheartedly back the initiative to reestablish the Reparation Committee in order to seek what Germany owes Greece'.[1]

The leader of the radical left Syriza coalition liked to recite the poetry of Cavafy during debates, by casting the German chancellor Angela Merkel and her European Union satraps as the Hunnish horde of 'Waiting for the Barbarians', where the senate is paralyzed in its delusion that 'the barbarians, when they come, will do the legislating', and by challenging the 'worthy orators' to cease 'sitting there without legislating' and start to realize a future 'without barbarians'. Conservative leader Antonis Samaris would duly quote back that they could then 'say good-bye to the Alexandria you are losing'.[2] But Tsipras's exhumation of the historic debt owed by Germany to Greece's hungry ghosts invoked nothing so much as the *agôn* of *Antigone*, Sophocles's tragedy of entombment:

> TIRESIAS: It is you—
>   your high resolve that sets this plague on Thebes . . .
>   No birds cry out an omen clear and true—
>   they're gorged with the murdered victim's blood and fat.
>   Take these things to heart, my son, I warn you . . .
>   Stubbornness brands you for stupidity—pride is a crime.
>   No, yield to the dead!
>   Never stab the fighter when he's down.
>   What's the glory, killing the dead twice over? (*Antigone*, 1122–40)[3]

In Sophocles, the seer's judgment that Creon should honor the slain Polynices is instantly trashed by the tyrant as a sophistic scam to extract more cash: 'Old man, your ilk has tried to sell me short for years', he indignantly retorts: 'Well, / drive your bargains, traffic as you like / in the gold of India, silver of Sardis. You'll never bury that body in the grave, / not even if Zeus's eagles rip the corpse' (1145–51). Creon's refusal to look beyond what he is owed blinds him to his own indebtedness and betrays his inhuman mercenary priorities. Likewise, the spokesman for the German finance ministry reacted with incredulity to Tsipras's accusation that 'after German reunification, the legal and political conditions were created for this issue to be resolved, but since then German governments chose silence, legal tricks and delay'.[4]

The German tabloid *Bild* conceded this point, when it protested that although his claims were 'bizarre, presumptuous and impertinent', Tsipras 'positions the lever where Germany is most vulnerable—the crimes committed by Germany. It's moral blackmail'.[5] Speaking with the true voice of Creon, therefore, Martin Jaeger lectured reporters in Berlin: 'We should look forward together. Making these emotional backward-looking allegations doesn't help in the context of the work we need to tackle together with the Greeks'. As many as 13 per cent of Greece's population perished between 1941 and 1944 as victims of the Axis forces; but in response to Tsipras's reminder that 'Germany has never properly paid reparations for the deaths and destruction in Greece under the Nazi occupation', Jaeger impatiently reiterated: 'We won't be conducting any talks or negotiations with the Greek side about Second World War compensation'.[6] This banker-speak about authority and order might have been lifted straight out of *Antigone*:

> CREON: Show me the man that rules his household well,
>   I'll show you someone fit to rule the state . . .
>   But whoever steps out of line, violates the laws
>   or presumes to hand out orders to his superiors,
>   he'll win no praise from me . . .
>   Anarchy—
>   Show me a greater crime in all the earth!
>   She, she destroys cities, rips up houses,
>   Breaks the ranks of spearmen into headlong rout.
>   But the ones who last it out, the great mass of them
>   Owe their lives to discipline. (739–56)

The tradition of reading Sophocles's play as an allegory of Nazi occupation dates from the war itself, when Jean Anouilh produced his *Antigone* in February 1944 to reflect the ambivalence of French attitudes towards the Resistance, personified in the anti-heroine who brings disaster on her family by burying the body of her brother in defiance of her uncle's order. Thus the German cultural commandant of Paris, Otto Abetz, sponsored Anouilh's production, because this Antigone appeared to expose the selfish futility of resistance when her act of sabotage put Creon in the 'tragic dilemma' of a 'practical man whose desire to rule firmly but fairly' compelled him to exact reprisals in response to the irrational disobedience of a fanatic: 'exactly the terms in which the German military authorities would have described their position in occupied France'. In the event, 'the first performance was greeted with applause by French and Germans alike', because Anouilh's *Antigone* spoke to the logics of both confrontation *and* collaboration.

After the war, Bertolt Brecht would present a communist reworking of Hölderlin's translation, as his fantasy of the people's uprising against Hitler's dictatorship, 'a resistance that never came to birth'.[7] But in Paris in 1944, a wave of modern makeovers of the Greek tragedies, often by deeply compromised figures like Jean Cocteau and Jean Giraudoux, said something far more disturbing about Europe's collusion with fascism, and the taint of conniving complicity which Jean-Paul Sartre exposed in *The Flies*, his rewriting of Aeschylus's *Orestes*, where 'the real drama I wanted to write was that of the terrorist who by ambushing Germans becomes the instrument for the execution of fifty hostages'.[8] The ancient Greeks were everywhere in Paris during the last days of the occupation, because in these claustrophobic tragedies they seem to have anticipated the impasses of both resistance and reprisal, and foretold how history's debts and indemnities never cut one way.

Suddenly 'Britain's theatres can't get enough of the Greeks', an editorial in *The Guardian* noticed the day after the German officials rejected the Greek demand with such cool contempt: 'There are two productions of *Antigone* in circulation—one starring Juliette Binoche, another reworked by Roy Williams into a contemporary gang-culture setting'. Remarking how 'not one but two *Oresteias* will be staged this year in London', Greek culture and language are 'part of our democratic inheritance', the editorial proclaimed.[9] But if so, this was an inheritance that needed to be handled with circumspection in the capitals of capitalism, as a simultaneous editorial in *The Independent* revealed when it dismissed Greek myths about what was owed the dead as a mere 'distraction'. Greece was a 'Compensation Nation' obsessed by past wrongs, the editorial stated. So, instead of fighting a 'war of words' about how 'Germany should atone for war crimes', this bankrupt country should 'face up to the reality' that it 'remains a fundamentally uncompetitive economy', which 'fails to pay its way in the world'.

Coming from a fundamentally uncompetitive newspaper that survives as the toy of a Russian oligarch, this sounded rich. But *The Independent* line, that 'now is the not the time' for talk 'about "reparations" from an unwilling Germany', when 'the international community needs to stay calm and patient as the world works through these problems', could again have been spoken by Creon. And the message—'don't mention the war'—was clearly not lost on the 'creative team' behind the Binoche *Antigone* then playing at the Barbican Center in the City of London. For there the shrieking performance was connected by the director Ivo van Hove to 'the unanswered question' about the rotting bodies from the Malaysian airliner shot down over the Ukraine, while not a single word was said in the copious marketing material about the relevance of this 'dark modern and mythical' drama to unanswered questions of Greek debts, let alone of Germany's wars.[10]

The silence about the Greek crisis at the bankers' arts center was hardly surprising, given that this official *Antigone* was a high-gloss filmic concoction funded by European governments that had just premiered in the mecca for tax evasion, at the Théâtres de la Ville de Luxembourg. Yet it was this very repression that made the Greek play look so timely in these plush surrounds. The Barbican *Antigone* thus inadvertently complemented the interpretation of the one adaptation of the text that confronted the balance of German and Greek debt, Ken McMullen's film *OXI*. For if van Hove's deluxe *Antigone* decanted classical theatre into the emptiness of modern cinema, McMullen's filled that cinema with the intoxication of the ancient stage. *OXI* thereby performed its own theme, as a sustained reflection not on what Greece owes Europe, but on what Europe owes Greece.

OXI's act of restitution was possible because, while a Teutonic European Union was suppressing the fraught memory of its violent totalitarian love–hate relationship with Hellas, of Hitler, Heidegger and Hölderlin, the disaggregating United Kingdom in which McMullen was working had never been more conscious of its elective affinity with that other disputatious archipelago at the opposite end of the continent, nor of what *The Guardian* called Britain's democratic Hellenic inheritance, its long and 'radical history of thinking with the Greeks'. The former *Manchester Guardian* was harking back to its own nineteenth-century origins in classics-trained Gladstonian Liberalism. But its 14 March editorial explained that it was also determined that contemporary Labour politicians would not be allowed to forget 'how classicist Karl Marx's ideas on historical materialism had their roots in the ancient atomist Democritus' he studied in the Reading Room behind the Doric columns of the British Museum:

> How George Grote, in the 1820s, forged his campaigning stance on universal suffrage in the crucible of his thinking on ancient Greece. How the Suffragettes recited the great speech from Euripides's *Medea*:

"I would rather die in battle three times than give birth once!" And how much appetite there is for thinking with, and thinking about, the ancient Greeks in the wider culture. There is a deep cultural need to test and frame our own times by reference with the strange, and sometimes strangely familiar, world of the Greeks.[11]

This statement reads like the work of the popular classicist Mary Beard. But whoever was responsible for *The Guardian*'s philhellenic manifesto could not have written a more charged rebuke to the Creons in Brussels and Berlin, nor a more loaded backup to *OXI*'s socialist take on *Antigone*. They were evoking an Anglo–Hellenic romance that, if it did not go back to Pytheas's fabled discovery of the 'Tin Islands', embraced Shakespeare's argumentative 'Merrygreeks', the Athenian influence on Milton's Puritan Revolution, Byron's paean to 'The Isles of Greece', and Shelley's heroic 'Hellas'. That love affair would be severely tested by Victoria's 'protectorate' over the Ionian Islands, by Churchill's brutal barging into the Civil War, and by the debacle of Cyprus. But the myth of 'British democracy hand in hand with Greek democracy', when the citizens of these two piratical marine confederations together 'dreamed that Greece might still be free', is a legend that was also underwritten by the Anglophile Greek poets on whom McMullen draws.[12]

As though pitching optimism of the will against pessimism of the intellect, *OXI* opens up Sophocles's stifling cryptomaniac tragedy to the counter-drift of the Homeric voyage, ventilating the incestuous horror of landlocked Thebes through choric sequences which glorify the rowing of the Argonauts, 'the companions' George Seferis saluted in his epic poem 'Mythical Story': those 'good lads' who 'sweated at the oar with lowered eyes / breathing in rhythm' as they sailed west, and 'passed many capes many islands the sea / leading to the other sea, gulls and seals'.[13] Himself the postwar ambassador to London, Seferis haunts *OXI* as an unspoken witness to 'the hope deep down' he shared with his bonded Atlantic oarsmen, that 'Though much is taken', what *abides* is the democratic comradeship of 'Souls that have toil'd, and wrought, and thought with me':[14]

> Their souls became one with the oars and the rowlocks
> with the solemn face of the prow

with the channel made by the rudder
with the water that shattered the image.
The companions with lowered eyes
died one by one. Their oars

mark the place where they sleep by the shore.[15]

The director of *OXI* has taken account of modern scholars, who point out that the archaic Thebes of *Antigone* would have been viewed with deep suspicion by the seafaring audiences of maritime Athens, as an autocratic anachronism, and that the agoraphobic protagonist's 'defense of blood relationships' strikes at the heart of 'the egalitarianism of Athenian institutions'.[16] Thus, McMullen emphasizes that the fratricidal House of Oedipus does not own the whole of Greece, by transporting the action of the play from the mountain shadows to the blazing sun of an Aegean island, and by counterpointing Antigone's aristocratic mourning to modern Greek poetry, with its demotic uplift that 'When you set out for Ithaka, / ask that the way be long, / Full of adventure'.

Shots of rosy dawn fingering the ocean therefore illustrate lines from Cavafy's 'Ithaka' in *OXI*, to suggest a diasporic counter-path to the nihilism of the girl condemned to be buried alive in lonely intransigence, as we are urged 'to enter ports—with what gratitude, what joy—to stop at Phoenician trading centers . . . to visit many Egyptian cities', but to 'Have Ithaka always in mind', because 'Your arrival there is what you are destined for'. The polyglot Alexandrian poet thereby lends authority to Ismene's farewell to her sister: 'You are truly dear to the ones who love you' (116). And the very poverty of Cavafy's destined isle of Ithaka becomes, in this telling, the guarantee of what *abides*, when all the bling, the trashy 'merchandise, / mother of pearl and coral, amber and ebony, / and sensuous perfumes of every kind', is taken away.[17]

In Seferis's epic, 'no one remembers' the comrades who died beside each other, 'one by one'. But at the end they raise a one-word cry: 'Justice'.[18] This is the 'Greek Style' of poetic justice to which Seferis appealed when he called the poet 'a legislator and better guide politically than any number of public speakers'.[19] No wonder German officials were thrown when Syriza's finance minister Yanis Varoufakis marked the party's victory by tweeting Dylan Thomas: 'Greek democracy chose to stop going gently into the night. Greek democracy resolved to rage against the dying of the light'.[20] In Berlin, no one had deferred to poetry as a higher realm since Stefan George, let alone set poetry against profit. But in Athens, Shelley's notion of the bards of Hellas as 'imperial spirits', who 'rule the present from the past', was alive in the language of Syriza.[21]

OXI foretells this poetic turn, when economists, philosophers and politicians are invited to apply the plot of *Antigone* to the debt standoff. Thus, the most affecting scene comes near the end of the film, when the leonine ninety-four-year-old Resistance hero and Syriza MEP Manilos Glezos orates what drives him to fight for a 'Europe of democracy and equality where money is not the ruler that decides': 'Before every battle, every protest, we told each other: "If you live, do this for me". I am paying a debt to those I lost during those terrible years'. Clearly, what Merkel's bailiffs had not grasped was that in this 'compensation nation', with its 'white courtyards where the south wind blows', poetry and politics were fused into a 'mad pomegranate tree that combats the cloudy skies of the world'.[22] By this measure, Athens remained Europe's *symbolic capital*, for here poetry was *itself* the reserve currency, when everything else had been squandered, stolen or debauched:

> Three rocks, a few burnt pines, an abandoned chapel . . .
> Here we moored the ship to splice the broken oars
> to drink water and to sleep.
> The sea which embittered us is deep and unexplored
> and unfolds a boundless calm.
> Here among the pebbles we found a coin
> and threw dice for it.
> The youngest won it and disappeared.
>
> We set out again with our broken oars.[23]

'We who had nothing will teach them peace': when Syriza's ministers set off around the European Union in their euphoric Spring of 2015, it was as if they were prompted by the closing words of Seferis's 'Mythical Story', and the interviews Varoufakis gave became symposia on material and symbolic forms of capital, with the lesson that there is neither gift nor debt that is not paid on both sides. Chancelleries had not heard such poetic thinking since Keynes outlined his 'Grand Scheme for the Rehabilitation of Europe' at the Versailles Conference. A world in which it was as if the economist never lived was no more inclined to take the Keynesian prescription of all-round debt cancellation from a charismatic professor now, however, than it had been in 1919.[24] So, it would be left to the poets, and a film like *OXI*, to bring home the message of the Greek diaspora, that if your 'heart is buried, like a dead body, in a tomb . . . You will not find new lands, nor find another sea', since for you there will be 'no ship, no road anywhere', and it will be as though by 'destroying your life here / in this small corner, in the whole world you've wrecked it everywhere'.

By projecting such lines from Cavafy against Antigone throughout *OXI*, McMullen cancels the unpaid debt and buried heart with the Keynesian commission to 'go to another land, go to another sea, / find some better town'.[25] The poet whom Keynes's friend E. M. Forster famously snapped in Alexandria, 'standing motionless in a straw hat at a slight angle to the universe', was perhaps a more qualified courier for this cosmopolitanism than even the Mancunian filmmaker appreciated, as before his family settled in Egypt, Cavafy had lived from the age nine to fifteen at the impeccably British address of 12 Balmoral Road, Elm Park, Fairfield, Liverpool.[26]

The revelation that the most famous Greek writer of modern times was a Lancashire lad, and that the earliest erotic encounters of this poet of glancing boys would have been on the streets of Liverpool, provided an uncanny pretext when the film in which he is cited so often was shown the day after Greece's debt claim was reported, on March 12, 2015, in Lancaster. For if anything illustrated Cavafy's Hellenism, it was the thought that someone so interested in history must have visited this rain-washed northern garrison town, in the steps of his favourite emperor Hadrian, and stood at the Storey Institute, where *OXI* was being screened, to muse on Lancaster Castle, and its Roman-wall soldiers, posted so far from their homes in Athens or Alexandria.

'Where are the Greeks?' the poet asks in 'Philhellene', and answers, 'in Syria, Parthia and Italy'.[27] But nineteenth-century Lancashire also contained a large Greek colony. So it was his family's shipping firm, Cavafy and Co., that brought the future poet to the land of the *Manchester Guardian* and Free Trade Liberalism, and it was there that the fabulist of the 'unreal city' read Shakespeare, Milton, Byron and Shelley and took to heart what Tennyson has Ulysses whisper to his companions, the mariners who 'Push off, and sitting well in order, smite / The sounding furrows': that 'I am a part of all that I have met'.[28] The young poet studied so hard 'to gather stores of knowledge from the learned'.[29] But what Cavafy must have learned from imports and exports in the Liverpool docks, and what McMullen incorporated into *OXI*, was above all a consciousness of shared inheritance, of debts owed both ways.

The Greek for 'no', *oxi*, has a laconic resonance in Greece, as the uncompromising answer given by Prime Minister Metaxas to Mussolini's ultimatum on 28 October 1940: a date with destiny annually celebrated on 'Oxi Day'. The ensuing rout of the Italian invaders, who had to be rescued by the Wehrmacht, became a founding myth of Greek Resistance, another Thermopylae that is ceaselessly invoked by Glezos and Syriza's leaders. When McMullen boldly gave his film this title he was therefore raising some truly famished ghosts, Aeschylean furies he further incited with a subtitle intended to provoke: 'An Act of Resistance'. But the director of *Ghost Dance*, the improvisation in which Jacques Derrida riffs on spectrality, and the 'ghosting' of every text and image, must have known what he was doing by inserting into his screenplay the words from Cavafy, Hölderlin, and other philhellenes that celebrate the living legacy of a more haunting Greece than that of the catastrophic girl who hangs herself.

A syllable charged with the promise of 'creation', is how George Steiner describes the resistant word 'no' at the conclusion of *The Poetry of Thought*, his musing on the heritage of Hellenism. For it was too easy to identify in Antigone an avatar of the *indignados* who had lately filled the plazas of Europe with their great refusal, when she has more in common with the Islamist suicide bomber. Similarly, literary critics were quick to point out that Varoufakis cannot have been serious about the Dylan Thomas lyric, 'since in that famous villanelle the poet is urging a dying father to accept the inevitable'.[30] Rather, both the finance minister and film director seem to have had in mind the poetic resistance that Cavafy extols in a poem that neither quoted but which expresses a stronger purpose than self-extinction, namely the will to endure that outlasts all dispossession:

In a Large Greek Colony, 200 BC

>That things in the Colony do not proceed as they should
>no one can doubt any longer,
>and although in spite of everything we do go forward,
>perhaps, as not a few are thinking, the time has come
>to introduce a Political Reformer.
>
>But the objection and the difficulty is
>that they make an enormous fuss
>about everything, these
>reformers. (It would be a blessing
>if they were never needed.) Whatever it is,
>even the smallest detail, they question and investigate,
>and at once radical reforms enter their heads
>demanding to be executed without delay.
>
>Also, they have a liking for sacrifice:
>RID YOURSELF OF THAT POSSESSION;
>YOUR OWNERSHIP OF THAT IS DANGEROUS:
>EXACTLY SUCH POSSESSIONS DAMAGE COLONIES.
>RID YOURSELF OF THAT INCOME,
>AND OF THE OTHER CONNECTED WITH IT,
>AND OF THIS THIRD, AS A NATURAL CONSEQUENCE;
>THEY ARE ESSENTIAL, BUT WHAT CAN ONE DO?
>THEY CREATE AN INJURIOUS EXPENDITURE FOR YOU.
>
>And as they extend their investigation
>they discover endless superfluities, and these they seek to remove:
>things which are however renounced with difficulty.
>
>And when, with luck, the business is completed,
>and every detail is defined and circumscribed,
>they retire, taking also the wages due to them,
>allowing us to see whatever still remains, after
>
>such effective surgery.[31]

'Tho' much is taken, much abides': by transferring Sophocles's tragedy to a windswept Aegean shore, Ken McMullen pays homage to the mythopoeic seascape of modern Greek poetry, and its perspective on what survives the subtractive calculus of expropriation, with 'White sails and sunlight and wet oars / struck by a rhythm of drums on stilled waves'.[32] This was the minimal prospectus of indestructible hope Seferis figured in his elegy 'Santorini', with its 'islands—rust and ashes—that are sinking', among which 'we found ourselves naked on the pumice-stone / watching the red islands go down / into their sleep'. There the poet obeyed an archaic compulsion to 'write on your last shell / the day, the name, the place, / and fling it into the sea so that it sinks'.

'In this land that is scattered, that cannot resist', with its 'altars destroyed / and friends forgotten', the atavistic gesture would seem the ultimate act of futility, were it not that with this oceanic arc of resistance the hands which fling the shell or throw the pebble 'go journeying / here on the curve of time with that ship / that has touched the horizon'. So 'Santorini' concludes with an unconquerable poetic injunction that could have been spoken by any of Syriza's economists and politicians. 'When looking around you see the feet harvested, / everywhere the hands dead, / everywhere the eyes darkened', Seferis avers, 'When you cannot even choose any longer / the death you would like to be yours . . . let your hands, if you can, go journeying' with the hurled rock, and so 'free yourself from the faithless time, / and sink / as sinks whoever raises the great stones'.[33]

For the Greek poet, the testament written on the stone carries a deeper meaning than even a letter in a bottle. And it is a message to which *OXI* subscribes, this demanding screen I.O.U. for what we owe the Greeks. It says that the 'ship that has touched the horizon' sails towards a different destiny, so that after every item has been audited and deducted, and the reformers have confiscated even the most basic human essentials, what will remain in such a bare life are the words of freedom. McMullen's reimagining of *Antigone* within the genre of modern Greek epic is therefore itself testimony that among many things Greece has given us, in its so-called debt crisis, is the opportunity Derrida held out towards his end, to set the European ark in a different direction, under the sign of another heading.[34]

The barbarians who lord over the European Union in this faithless time are, as always, correct: Greece is indeed the compensation nation. And its compensation is the poetry of what can never be counted in coin or measured by markets. Thus, 'The houses I had they took from me', Seferis recorded at the beginning of 'Thrush', his finest work, because 'the times / happened to be unpropitious: war, destruction, exile'. But 'Houses, you know, grow easily resentful when you strip them bare,' he also warned his dispossessors.[35] In this way, when all has been taken, 'Athens still remains', as Derrida humbly testified, when he pondered the city's immemorial epitaphs.[36] Inspired by the sea and stones of Greece, *OXI* is an incomparably eloquent reminder-notice of what we owe the dead, and must pay to propitiate their hungry ghosts. But it is also a film about whatever still remains.

Notes

1. 'Germany Rejects Fresh Greek Calls for World War Reparations', *The Independent*, 12 March 2015, 4.

2. C. P. Cavafy, 'Waiting for the Barbarians' and 'The God Abandons Antony', in *Four Greek Poets*, ed. and trans. Edmund Keeley and Philip Sherrard (Harmondsworth, UK: Penguin: 1966), pp. 11–12, 14; E. Stallings, 'Freelance: Letter from Athens', *Times Literary Supplement*, 27 February 2015, 16.

3. Sophocles, *Antigone*, 1022–33, in *The Three Theban Plays*, trans. Robert Fagles (London: Penguin, 1984), pp. 111–12.

4. 'Greeks Could Seek German Reparations', *The Guardian*, 12 March 2015, 21.

5. 'German Fury at Greek Cash Demand', *The Guardian*, 13 March 2015, 31. On March 17, Ralf Stegner, deputy leader of the German Social Democrats, commented, however, that 'I believe we should be leading the discussion about reparations'; Gesine Schwan, a senior Social Democrat stated that 'it is a matter of recognizing that we committed terrible crimes in Greece'; and Anton Hofreiter, leader of the Green Party, insisted that 'Germany cannot just sweep Greece's demand off the table. The chapter is not closed, neither from a moral nor legal standpoint', *The Independent*, 18 March 2015, 21.

6. Op. cit. (note 1).

7. Bernard Knox, 'Introduction', Sophocles, op. cit. (note 3), p. 36.

8. Jean-Paul Sartre, *Sartre on Theatre*, trans. Frank Jellinek (New York: Pantheon Books, 1976), p. 188.

9. 'Greek Is Part of Our Democratic Inheritance', *The Guardian*, 14 March 2015, 32.

10. Ivo van Hove, 'The Unanswered Question', *Antigone* (London: Barbican, 2015), pp. 4, 6.

11. Op. cit. (note 9).

12. Stanley Casson, *Greece and Britain* (London: Collins, 1944), p. 107; George Gordon Lord Byron, 'The Isles of Greece', quoted in Elizabeth Longford, *Byron's Greece* (New York: Harper Collins, 1976), p. 82.

13. George Seferis, 'Mythical Story: 4', and '5', in Keeley and Sherrard, op. cit. (note 2), pp. 45, 47.

14. Alfred Lord Tennyson, 'Ulysses', in *Tennyson's Verse*, ed. Lord David Cecil (London: Faber & Faber, 1971), p. 93.

15. George Seferis, 'Mythical Story: 4', in Keeley and Sherrard, op. cit. (note 2), p. 46.

16. Bernard Knox, 'Introduction', op. cit. (note 3), p. 39.

17. C. P. Cavafy, 'Ithaka', in Keeley and Sherrard, op. cit. (note 2), pp. 15–16.

18. George Seferis, 'Mythical Story: 4', ibid., p. 46.

19. George Seferis, *On the Greek Style*, trans. Rex Warner and T. D. Frangopoulis (London: The Bodley Head, 1967), pp. 194–96.

20. 'Greek Prime Minister Appoints Radical Economist', *The Guardian*, 27 January 2015, 1.

21. Percy Bysshe Shelley, 'Hellas', ll. 700–701, quoted in Terence Spencer, *Fair Greece Sad Relic* (London: Weidenfeld & Nicolson, 1954), p. 294.

22. Osysseus Elytis, 'The Mad Pomegranate Tree', in Keeley and Sherrard, op. cit. (note 2), p. 77.

23. George Seferis, 'Mythical Story: 12: Bottle in the Sea', ibid., p. 51.

24. Robert Skildelsky, *John Maynard Keynes: Hopes Betrayed, 1883–1920* (London: Macmillan, 1983), pp. 367–68.

25. C. P. Cavafy, 'The City', in Keeley and Sherrard, op. cit. (note 2), p. 13.

26. E. M. Forster, *Alexandria: A History and a Guide and Pharos and Pharillon* (London: André Deutsch, 2004), p. 245; Robert Liddell, *Cavafy: A Critical Biography* (London: Gerald Duckworth, 1974), p. 25.

27. C. P. Cavafy, 'Philhellene', in Keeley and Sherrard, op. cit. (note 2), p. 17.

28. Tennyson, op cit. (note 14), pp. 92–93.

29. C. P. Cavafy, 'Ithaka', in Keeley and Sherrard, op. cit. (note 2), p. 15.

30. George Steiner, *The Poetry of Thought: From Hellenism to Celan* (New York: New Directions, 2011), p. 103; Stallings, op. cit. (note 2).

31. C. P. Cavafy, 'In a Large Greek Colony, 200 BC', in Keeley and Sherrard, op. cit. (note 2), pp. 31–32.

32. Tennyson, op. cit. (note 14); George Seferis, 'Mythical Story: 13: Hydra', in *Complete Poems*, ed. and trans. Edmund Keeley and Philip Sherrard (London: Anvil, 1995), p. 17.

33. George Seferis, 'Santorini', in Keeley and Sherrard, op. cit. (note 2), pp. 55–56.

34. Jacques Derrida, *The Other Heading: Reflections on Today's Europe*, trans. Anne-Pascale Brault and Michael B. Naas (Bloomington: Indiana University Press, 1992).

35. George Seferis, 'Thrush', in Seferis, op. cit. (note 32), p. 161.

36. Jacques Derrida, *Athens, Still Remains*, trans. Anne-Pascale Brault and Michael B. Naas (New York: Fordham University Press, 2010).

Filmography

Ken McMullen—Filmography

International Feature Length Films		Running Time		Production Company
1976	**RESISTANCE** (UK/France)	16mm	100 min	British Film Institute
1978	**STORIES** (UK)	16mm	100 min	MCM Films London
1983	**GHOST DANCE** (UK/France)	16mm	100 min	C4/ZDF/Looseyard London
1985	**ZINA** (UK)	35mm	100 min	ZDF/C4/Hemdale USA/ PALAN Entertainment
1987	**PARTITION** (UK)	35mm	100 min	BANDUNG Productions/C4
1990	**'1871'** (UK/France/Portugal)	35mm	100 min	ARTE/C4/SVEN Sweden
1998	**GLIMPSES OF THE GHAZI** (UK/Turkey)	Beta	120 min	ARTE /History Channel
2004	**ART, POETRY AND PARTICLE PHYSICS** (UK/Switzerland)	Beta	70 min	Arts Council England

258 ～ Filmography

2009	AN ORGANISATION OF DREAMS *(UK/France)*	*35mm / Digital*	100 min	Augustine Films London
2014	OXI: AN ACT OF RESISTANCE *(UK/France/Greece)*	*35mm / Digital*	100 min	SCAPE LTD/ STUDIO C Production
2015	MUJICA *(Uruguay)*	*Digital*	In production	Kingston Research/ SCAPE

Documentaries

1971	ROOM TO MOVE	*16mm*	15 min	KBSC Los Angeles
1973	LOVELIES AND DOWDIES	*16mm*	30 min	Arts Council Scotland
1980	PORTRAITS	*Beta*	180 min	Media Associates London
1984	BEING AND DOING	*16mm*	60 min	Arts Council GB
1993	THERE WE ARE JOHN	*16mm*	60 min	British Council
1995	LUCKY MAN	*16mm*	30 min	British Council
1998	ART OF SWIMMING	*Beta*	60 min	Shaw London
2001	METZGER	*Beta*	40 min	Arts Council GB

Motion Picture Gallery Installations

1971	PIECES	*16mm*		
1972	DISCUSSION WITH A GUN	*16mm*	10 min loop	Slade Research with Joseph Beuys
1972	WORD WORK	*16mm*		
1974	BLACKNESS	*16mm*	120 min	with Joseph Beuys
1994	MOLLY'S MIRROR	*Beta*	10 min loop	with Joseph Beuys
2001	LUMIN DE LUMINE	*Beta*	10 min	ARTE BBC
2003	MANIFESTOES	*Beta*	8 min loop	CERN/MCM Film
2006	FEMTO CAMERA	*Beta*	20 min loop	with Gustav Metzger
2007	COLLIDING GALAXIES	*Beta*	8 min	with SLAC/CERN
2007	ARROWS OF TIME	*Digital*	8 min loop	SLAC California
2008	SHAMAN'S ARROW	*16mm*	120 digital timeline built from multi sources	
2008	UNDERWATER	*16mm*	5 min loop	Archive montage

Martin McQuillan—Filmography

2012
'I Melt the Glass with My Forehead': A Film about £9,000 Tuition Fees, How We Got Them, and What to Do about It, documentary 56 mins, co-director with Joanna Callaghan for Heraclitus Films, http://vimeo.com/35083565

2014
Love in the Post: From Plato to Derrida, feature 80 mins (screenplay and coproducer) director Joanna Callaghan for Heraclitus Films, http://loveinthepost.co.uk

2014
OXI: An Act of Resistance, feature 97 mins (executive producer and interviews), director Ken McMullen for Scape Films.

Also published by R&L International Ltd.:
Love in the Post: From Plato to Derrida, The Screenplay and Commentary, by Joanna Callaghan and Martin McQuillan, 2014.

Index

Achilles, 207–8, 232
Aeschylus, 226, 229–30, 244
Agamemnon, 129–30, 208–9
Ajax, 54, 201, 207–10
Althusser, Louis, 191
Antigone, xiii, 15, 16, 19, 25–9,
  41–46, 63, 74–5, 77–8, 83, 88, 96,
  117–19, 121–25, 139, 202–4, 206,
  218, 221, 228–31, 242–50, 252
Anoulih, Jean, 243
Argonauts, 102, 246
Aristophanes, xiii, 32, 49, 51, 53,
  60, 231
Aristotle, 139, 146
Auden, W. H., 2

Bacon, Francis, 111–12
Balibar, Etienne, xiii, 26, 37–8, 42,
  61, 89, 143, 189–98
Baltas, Aristides, 143
Bank of England, 13
Barthes, Roland, 154–5

Baudelaire, Charles, 151–2, 155, 158
Bauman, Zygmunt, 197
Bear Stearns, 147
Beck, Ulrich, 196
Beckett, Samuel, 94, 230
Benjamin, Walter, 114, 167, 179
Beuys, Joseph, 111, 256
Binoche, Juliet, 244
Brecht, Bertolt, 125, 203, 231, 243
Brisley, Stuart, 111
Brown, Gordon, 138
Browne, John (Lord of Madingley),
  137
Bulgakov, Mikhail, 109
Byron, Lord George Gordon, 190,
  246, 249

Cable, Vince, 135
Carmel, Titus, 176
Cavafy, C. P., xiii, 16, 48, 58, 65–6,
  103, 241, 247, 249–50
Christoulos, Dimitris, 100

Churchill, Winston, 246
Cixous, Hélène, xiii, 25, 29, 34, 37, 47, 68, 89, 108, 201–10
Clinton, Bill, 1
Clytemnestra, 129–30
Cocteau, Jean, 107, 244
Cohen, Leonard, 178
Coldstream, Sir William, 111
Coltrane, Robbie, 173
Coppola, Francis Ford, 168–9, 180
Cornelios, Nikos, 26, 72, 89
Costas–Gavras (Konstantinos Gavras), 190
Creon, 15, 25, 27–8, 39–41, 43–44, 56, 70, 74–5, 77–8, 81–3, 88, 96, 121, 123–5, 139, 203–5, 209, 218, 221, 228–9, 242–4, 246

Delacroix, Eugène, 175
Democratic Left (DIMAR), 6
Derrida, Jacques, 95, 98, 113, 116–19, 143, 145, 149–51, 153–7, 160n23, 164–5, 167–9, 171, 173–4, 176–7, 179–80, 191, 250, 252, 257
Dickens, Charles, 109, 120, 154–5, 157
Dionysius, 216
Douzinas, Costas, 192
Durkheim, Emile, 2

Eisenstein, Sergei, 209
Electra, 96
Engels, Friedrich, 111, 126
Errejón, Íñigo, 142
Euripides, 2, 15, 50, 226, 230, 245
European Central Bank, 1, 5, 13, 149, 241
European Union, 2–5, 8–9, 11–13, 63, 76, 134, 190, 195, 214, 236–9, 241, 245, 248, 252

Falciani, Hervé, 234
Faure, Julia, 25, 88
Federal Reserve (US), 13
Forster, E. M., 249
Foucault, Michel, 143
Franco, General Francisco, 142
Frangiadaki, Martha, 26, 76, 89, 130
Freud, Sigmund, 95, 98–100, 106–7, 114, 120, 131, 167
Fukuyama, Francis, 109–10

George, Stefan, 248
Gide, André, 153
Giraudoux, Jean, 244
Glezos, Manolis, xiii, 25, 28–9, 70–1, 73, 89, 104, 217–24, 248, 250
Godard, Jean-Luc, 174
Gogol, Nikolai, 109
Golden Dawn, 6, 214
Goldman Sachs, 3, 149
Gramsci, Antonio, 197
Grant, Cary, 166
Guevara, Che, 232

Haemon, 27–8, 96, 121–4, 203–4
HBOS (Halifax Bank of Scotland), 147
Hector, 209
Hegel, G. W. F., 97, 117, 161, 169
Heidegger, Martin, 183, 245
Hellenic Broadcasting Corporation, 6
Hölderlin, Friedrich, 40, 45, 74, 88, 244–5, 250
Homer, 206, 217, 222, 246
HSBC (Hong Kong and Shanghai Banking Corporation), 6–7

Iglesias, Pablo, 142,
International Monetary Fund, 1, 4–6, 9, 13, 134, 149, 214

Ismene, 25, 41–2, 44–5, 65–6, 74, 77–8, 83, 88, 122–3, 125, 204, 247

Jocasta, 25, 37, 40, 64, 80, 88, 106, 122, 205, 229, 231
Jospin, Lionel, 143
Juncker, Jean-Claude, 10

Kallia, Eleni, 25, 88
Kantor, Tadeusz, 111
Karakepelis, Christos, 26, 57, 89
Karina, Anna, 174–5
Keynes, John Maynard, 12, 248–9
Kolokotronis, Theodoros, 218
Koppel, Heinz, 111
Kott, Jan, 131
Kouloufakos, Kostas, 224
Kouvelakis, Stathis, 141

Lacan, Jacques, 108, 143, 191
Laclau, Ernesto, 143
Lapavitsas, Costas, 141
Legarde, Christine, 6–7, 233
Lehman Brothers, 147
Lenin, Vladimir Ilyich, 197, 258
Lyberaki, Antigone, xiii, 26, 46, 63, 89
Lyotard, Jean–François, 163–4, 166

Macherey, Pierre, 192
Machiavelli, Niccolò, 55, 198, 239
Malabou, Catherine, 163–5, 168
Marx, Karl, 61, 95, 109–110, 126–7, 145, 153, 169, 174–6, 192–194, 245
Mauss, Marcel, 153
Medea, 2, 15–16, 245
Mellinger, Leonie, 174–5
Menandros, 28, 218
Menelaus, 208

Merkel, Angela, 76, 199, 233, 238–9, 241, 248
Merril Lynch, 149
Miller, Arthur I, 26, 38, 68, 90
Milner, Marion, 111
Milton, John, 205, 246, 249
Mitterrand, François, 143
Morgan, J. P., 148, 153
Morsi, Mohamed, 141

NATO, 3, 11
Negri, Antonio, xiii, 26, 29, 58–9, 72–3, 89, 108, 211–16
Nestor, 222
New Democracy, 3, 5–7
Nietzsche, Friedrich, 154
Northern Rock, 147

Obama, Barak, 138, 141
Oborne, Peter, 7
Oedipus, xiii, 25, 32, 34–7, 45–7, 64, 69–70, 72, 74, 79–82, 88, 106, 113–19, 121–23, 125, 139, 205, 210, 229, 231, 247
Ogier, Pascale, 173–4, 176–7, 179–80
Orwell, George, 155
Ovid, 209

Pacino, Al, 183
Papaconstantinou, George, 7
Papademos, Lucas, 5, 62, 238
Papandreou, George, 4, 6
PASOK (Panhellenic Socialist Movement), 3–7
Peeters, Benoit, 165, 174
Pericles, 57
Perrin, Bruce, 174
Plato, 96, 157, 198–9, 257
Pinon, Dominique, xiii, 25, 88, 97, 174–5

Plutarch, 218
Podemos, 142–3
Poe, Edgar Allen, 205
Polus, 96–7
Polynices, 122, 125
Potagas, Mathios, 219
Poulantzas, Nicos, 190
Prometheus, 230, 232
Pushkin, Alexander, 109
Puzo, Mario, 171

QE (Quantitative Easing), 13–14, 135

Rolland, Romain, 98, 131
Rousseau, Jean–Jacques, 146, 169, 172
Royal Bank of Scotland, 146

Saba, Della, 25, 88
Saint, Eva Marie, 166
Sakaridis, Yannis, 65, 89
Samaras, Antonis, 6
Schliemann, Heinrich, 95, 120
Schmidt, Carl, 196
Sevastikoglou, Petros, 26, 71, 89
Shakespeare, William, 109, 111, 208, 246, 258
Shelley, Percy Bysshe, 246, 248–9
Shrapnel, Lex, 25, 88
Shrapnel, John, 25, 88
Sophocles, xiii–iv, 15, 27–8, 32, 39, 46–7, 96, 109, 113, 123, 202, 206, 212, 218, 221, 226, 228, 242–3, 246, 251
Sphinx, xiii–iv, 25, 32–5, 37–9, 46–7, 54, 57, 61, 67–9, 77, 82–3, 88, 210

Standard and Poor's, 5
Stiegler, Bernard, 108, 171, 175, 179
Syriza, xiv, 1, 6, 9, 11–16, 141–3, 197, 241, 247–8, 250, 252

Telemachus, 222
Tennyson, Alfred Lord, 249
Terzopulos, Theodoros, xiii, 26, 35, 52–3, 66–7, 80–1, 89, 225–32
Theodorakis, Mikis, 190
Thomas, Dylan, 247, 250
Thucydides, v, 27, 38, 64, 79, 84, 198–9
Tiresias, 25, 35–7, 64, 69–70, 72, 79–83, 88, 119, 125, 205–6, 210, 217, 223, 229, 242
Tolstoy, Leo, 170
Troika (of creditors), 1, 6, 9, 11–12, 15, 99, 101, 121, 131, 214
Tsipras, Alexis, 1, 241–3

Ulysses, 208–10, 223, 249

Varoufakis, Yanis, 9–10, 12, 141, 247–8, 250
Vaxevanis, Kostas, xiv, 7, 26, 55, 62, 76, 79, 89, 233–39
Venizelos, Evangelos, 7
Vichas, Giorgos, 26, 43, 75–6, 129–30

Weber, Max, 198
Welfare State, 14, 57, 155, 212
Wittgenstein, Ludwig, 143
Wright, Gabriella, xiii, 25, 88, 175

Zeus, 53, 102–4, 110, 127, 242
Žižek, Slavoj, 143

Notes on Contributors

Ken McMullen is a motion picture director, artist and Anniversary Chair of Film at Kingston University London. His films include *Resistance* (1976), *Ghost Dance* (1983), *Zina* (1985), *Partition* (1987), *1871* (1990) and *An Organisation of Dreams* (2009).

Martin McQuillan is Professor of Literary Theory and Cultural Analysis at The London Graduate School and Pro-Vice Chancellor of Research at Kingston University. He is author of *Deconstruction after 9/11* (2009) and *Deconstruction without Derrida* (2013). His film credits include *Love in the Post: From Plato to Derrida* (Heraclitus Pictures, 2014).

Étienne Balibar is Anniversary Chair of Philosophy at Kingston University London, Professor Emeritus at Université Paris VIII, and also teaches at Columbia University, New York. His recent publications in English include *Identity and Difference: John Locke and the Invention of Consciousness* (2013), *Equaliberty: Political Essays* (2014) and *Violence and Civility: On the Limits of Political Philosophy* (2015).

Hélène Cixous is a celebrated novelist and playwright and Emeritus Professor of Literature at the Université de Paris VIII. Her recent publications in English include *Insister of Jacques Derrida* (2007), *Manhattan*

(2008), *Hyperdream* (2009), *Volleys of Humanity* (2011), *Eve Escapes* (2012) and *Poetry in Painting* (2012).

Manolis Glezos is a Member of the European Parliament for Syriza. He joined the Greek Resistance during World War II and during a lifetime of political struggle was imprisoned by the Nazis, during the civil war and the Cold War, and by the Regime of the Colonels. He is a politician, engineer, journalist, and poet.

Antonio Negri taught at the Université de Paris VIII and at the Collège International de Philosophie. His recent publications in English include *Art and Multitude* (2011), *Spinoza for Our Time: Politics and Postmodernity* (2013) and *Factory of Strategy: 33 Lessons on Lenin* (2014).

Theodoros Terzopoulos is an acclaimed international theatre director whose Athens-based company, ATTIS, specializes in the production of ancient Greek tragedy. He is the author of several works on acting and directing method.

Kostas Vaxevanis is a journalist and the editor of HOT DOC news magazine. In 2012 he published a list of Greek customers of the Swiss branch of HSBC suggesting they could be tax evaders. He was subsequently prosecuted, tried, acquitted, retried, and re-acquitted. He won the Index on Censorship Journalism Award in 2013.

Richard Wilson is the Sir Peter Hall Chair of Shakespeare Studies at Kingston University London. He is author of *Secret Shakespeare: Studies in Theatre, Religion and Resistance* (2004), *Shakespeare in French Theory* (2006) and *Free Will: Art and Power on Shakespeare's Stage* (2013).

www.ingramcontent.com/pod-product-compliance
Lightning Source LLC
Chambersburg PA
CBHW021836220426
43663CB00005B/271